A1

THE LAW AND MANAGEMENT OF
WATER RESOURCES AND SUPPLY

The Law and Management of
WATER RESOURCES AND SUPPLY

by
A. S. Wisdom
and
J. L. G. Skeet

LONDON:
Printed and Published by
SHAW & SONS LTD.
Shaway House, SE26 5AE
1981

Published - - - November, 1981

ISBN 07219 0910 8

CONTENTS

PREFACE

The purpose of this book is to present a simple guide or introduction to the Law relating to Water Resources and Water Supply. There have been significant changes within the structures and the concepts of the Industry reflecting the changing demands of society since those great pillars of environmental law, the Water Acts 1945—48 and the Water Resources Acts 1963—71 were placed on the Statute Book.

Before his untimely death, Alan Wisdom had been persuaded by his many friends and colleagues to produce a guide that would highlight those changes and place them within the context of the general principles of the relevant Law. Alas; he was prevented from completing that task.

As one of his colleagues, and I trust a friend, I accepted with alacrity the request from the publishers to complete the book. If it is of benefit to those who are interested in an industry that directly affects the quality of our daily lives then I trust that it will be regarded as a simple, sincere tribute to a greatly respected colleague and friend.

The Law is as stated at 1 August 1981.

August 1981   J. L. G. Skeet

TABLE OF STATUTES

PAGE

TABLE OF STATUTORY INSTRUMENTS

TABLE OF CASES

C cont.

D

E

F

G

H

H cont.

I

K

L

M

N

O

P

R

R cont.

S

V

W

TABLE OF CASES

W cont.

Y

The Law and Management of
Water Resources
and Supply

Chapter 1

HISTORICAL BACKGROUND TO WATER SUPPLY

1.01 Early legislation

The historical growth of legislation relating to water supply is manifestly too wide a subject to be treated exhaustively in any book such as this. The 19th century saw a series of statutory provisions establishing companies with special parliamentary powers to acquire land, construct works and supply water; there were similar statutes empowering local authorities to supply water.

Water Companies were created either by Private Acts or were granted powers to supply water under provisional Orders, confirmed by Parliament, under the Gas and Waterworks Facilities Acts 1870-73.

Private Acts incorporating a Water Company normally adopted the provisions of the Waterworks Clauses Acts 1847-63 (relating to the supply of water), provisions of the Companies Clauses Consolidation Acts 1845-89 (regulating the conduct of the Company's affairs) and provisions of the Lands Clauses Acts 1845-83 (containing powers to acquire land). The Gas and Waterworks Facilities Acts 1870-73 enabled companies, but not local authorities, to obtain powers of supply by provisional orders incorporating the Waterworks Clauses Acts.

The Waterworks Clauses Acts 1847-1863 provided a code of powers and duties which could be applied to any undertaking.

The Public Health Act 1848 which, for water, superseded the Towns Improvement Clauses Act 1847, empowered the local authorities to supply their districts, under certain circumstances, with water. The Act permitted local authorities to contract from time to time with any person whomsoever, or purchase, take a lease of, hire, construct, lay down and.maintain such waterworks, and do and execute all such works, matters and things as might be necessary for the purpose of effecting a proper and sufficient supply of water. Those powers were supplemented by the Local Government Act of 1858, as amended by the Local Government Act, 1858, Amendment Act, 1861. The Sanitary

Acts of 1866 and 1874 extended the powers of water supply by extending to sewer authorities the powers given to local boards; such sewer authorities were authorised to purchase, either within or without their districts, any land covered with water, or any water, or right to take or convey water.

The Public Health Act 1875, amended by the Public Health Act 1878, repealed all the above statutes relating to Local Authorities and imposed a duty upon Local Authorities to ensure adequate supplies of domestic water. In consequence of this duty, where no statutory undertakers were already supplying water, the Act of 1875 conferred powers upon Local Authorities to supply water. The Act incorporated parts of the Code contained in the Waterworks Clauses Acts. The provisions of the 1875 legislation were repealed and substantially re-enacted in the Public Health Act 1936 (Part IV — General duties and powers of Local Authorities for Water Supply).

NOTE: Section 303 of the Public Health Act 1875, so far as it applied to any local enactment relating to water supply, was repealed by sect. 62 of and the Fifth Schedule to the Water Act 1945. The general powers of the former local authorities (prior to 1st April 1974) to supply their districts with water were contained in section 116 of the Public Health Act 1936; that section is now repealed.

1.02 The Water Act 1945

The Water Act 1945 repealed the Waterworks Clauses Acts and substituted the modern Code, *i.e.* the Third Schedule thereto, as subsequently amended by the Water Act 1948 and later by the Water Act 1973. The earlier code continues to apply to statutory water companies unless and until the Minister by Order substitutes the code contained in the Third Schedule (*Section* 32).

Section 33 of the 1945 Act. (as amended by Section 14 of the Water Act 1948) conferred powers upon the Secretary of State, on the application of any statutory water undertaker, (which expression includes a statutory water company) to repeal or amend, or to consolidate, with or without amendments, any local enactment relating to the supply of water by those undertakers. These powers are exercised by Order. The purpose of section 33, as amended, was, and is, to achieve a fairly uniform Code.

The Water Act 1945 for the first time placed on Government the specific duty of promoting the provision of adequate water supplies, the conservation of water resources and the effective execution by water undertakers, under Ministerial control and direction, of a National Water Policy.

For these purposes, Part I of the 1945 Act considerably extended the powers of the Minister. The Act made provision for a Central Advisory Water Committee to advise the Government on general questions relating to water and for local Joint Advisory Water Committees to be constituted by order of the Minister where he is satisfied that they are necessary for any area. Such Committees had the duty of planning to meet the future needs for their areas. Part II of the Act was subsequently repealed by the Water Act 1973, see para. **1-04** *post*.

Part II of the 1945 Act provided the statutory machinery for securing, if necessary by compulsion, the combination of water undertakers and the transfer of undertakings, the variation of limits of supply and the supply of water in bulk. The default powers of the Minister in relation to the various types of water undertakers were defined in section 13.

Part III of the Water Act 1945 is concerned with conservation and protection of water resources, and the prevention of waste.

Part IV of the 1945 Act enables, or provides machinery for enabling, statutory water undertakers to construct works, acquire land, obtain and to supply water and to deal with various other matters essential or incidental to the carrying on of their undertakings. Provision is made for compulsory acquisition of land and of water rights. Water undertakers are required in certain circumstances to supply water for industrial, agricultural and other non-domestic uses. The powers and duties of local authorities were further enlarged as regards securing the provision of piped water in houses. Provision is also made for the revision of water rates and charges, and for the incorporating orders made under the Act, and ultimate application to existing Acts and Orders, of the modern Waterworks Code (*i.e.* the Third Schedule to the Act).

The Water Act 1948 improved and tidied up a few points from the 1945 Act. The Water Act 1958 dealt with droughts; it was repealed by the Drought Act 1976. The Drought Act 1976 re-enacted the powers formerly contained in the Water Act 1958 but in addition conferred new and extensive powers to be exercised by water authorities or statutory water companies being so authorised by the Secretary of State by Order.

1.03 Safety of Reservoirs

The Waterworks Clauses Act 1863 (*Section* 3 *to* 10) provided that an interested person could complain to two Justices of the Peace that an undertakers' reservoir was in a dangerous state. The Justices were under a duty to make enquiry into the truth of the complaint, and if it was well founded the Justices had powers to secure the repair of the reservoir. In addition under the 1863 Act two Justices could make enquiry on their own initiative, without complaint by any interested person. The Reservoirs (Safety Provisions) Act 1930 prescribed certain statutory rules regarding the design and periodic inspection of "large reservoirs", *i.e.* reservoirs designed to hold, or capable of holding, more than five million gallons of water above the natural level of any part of the land adjacent to the reservoir. The 1930 Act further preserved the right of civil action against a statutory water undertaker when damage or injury is caused by the escape of water from a reservoir in respect of reservoirs constructed after 1 January 1931; in other words the effect of this particular statutory provision is to make a statutory undertaker liable for any escape of water which has been collected although there is no element of negligence.

The common law rule of *Rylands v Fletcher* (1868) is applied (*Section* 7); an undertaker cannot establish what would otherwise be a good defence, namely that the collection and keeping of water has been authorised by statute and that either the statute created a statutory means of redress or that the escape was not caused by negligence.

The Reservoirs (Safety Provisions) Act 1930 will be superseded, on a date or dates to be appointed by the Secretary of State, by the Reservoirs Act 1975. This statute whilst preserving the right of civil action against the statutory water undertaker also introduces the concept of criminal liability in respect of both the undertaker or of any employees of the undertaker.

1.04 National Policy for Water

The Water Resources Acts 1963-1971 extended the power and duties of Central Government in the formulation of a National Water Policy, so as to include measures for augmenting, re-distributing and transferring water resources and established River Authorities and the Water Resources Board. The 1963 Act implemented the Government's White Paper on "Water Conservation, England and Wales" dated April 1962 (*Cmd* 1693) which was itself based on the Final Report of the Sub-Committee on the Growing Demand for Water for the Central Advisory Water Committee (the *"Proudman Committee"*). The Water Resources Acts 1963-71 imposed statutory constraints on the exercise of certain common law rights and also created "protected rights."

The Water Act 1973 (*Section* 11) transferred the responsibility for public supply of water to regional water authorities covering the whole of England and Wales. It is the duty of a water authority to supply water within its area. Section 11(9) and the Ninth Schedule repealed the relevant provisions of the Public Health Act 1936. The functions of local authorities in respect of public water supply after 1 April 1974 relate to "monitoring" the sufficiency and wholesomeness of water supplies; enforcement of building regulations (*i.e.* a satisfactory provision for supply of wholesome water for domestic purposes); the enforcement of powers requiring occupied houses to be provided with an adequate supply of water for domestic purposes, and environmental health control over polluted water used for domestic purposes or in the preparation of food or drink for human consumption.

In respect of polluted water, the local authority has powers to apply to a Court of Summary Jurisdiction for an Order directing the source of supply to be permanently or temporarily closed or cut off, or the water therefrom to be used for certain purposes only, or such other Orders as appears to the Court to be necessary to prevent injury or danger to the health of persons using the water, or consuming food or drink prepared therewith or therefrom (*Public Health Act* 1936 s.140).

There is a right of appeal "by the person aggrieved" by the decision of the Magistrates; "a person aggrieved" is a person, or corporate body on whom, as a result of the Magistrates decision, a legal or financial burden has been placed — as opposed to frustration in the performance of a public duty; *Ealing Corporation v. Jones* (1959) and *R. v. Boldero and others, ex parte Bognor Regis Urban District Council* (1962). An appeal would lie to the Crown Court (*Crown Courts Act 1971*) or by way of case stated to the divisional court of the Queen's Bench Division (*Magistrates' Courts Act* 1952).

The Water Act 1973 did not establish any new code for the supply of water but the Act did provide that, subject to any provision to the contrary in any Instrument made under or by virtue of the Act, Parts VII and IX of the Third Schedule to the Water Act 1945 (*i.e.* supply of water for domestic purposes and duties as to constancy and supply of pressure) apply throughout the total area of a regional water authority whether or not so applied by or under any other enactment (*Section* 11(7)(b)). The Water Act 1973 (*Schedule* 6, *paragraph* 11) further provides that notwithstanding the transfer of functions and the abolition of bodies it affects, any local Acts and statutory provisions will continue to apply after 1 April 1974 to the same area as before; where, as a result of reorganisation arising from the Water Act 1973, a local statutory instrument, after the 1 April 1974, applies to two or more regional authorities, the Act provides for the Order to be construed as referring to the water authorities for the area in which the Instruments will be operated (*Schedule* 6, *paragraph* 13).

The Water Act 1973 further provides that the appropriate Minister or Ministers may by Order (such statutory instruments being subject to annulment in pursuance of a resolution by either House of Parliament) extend, repeal, revoke or amend any statutory provision so as to apply to any part of or the totality of the Water Authorities area.

Subject to any provision to the contrary contained in any instrument made under or by virtue of the Water Act 1973, Part XIII of the Third Schedule to the Water Act 1945 (which contains provisions for preventing waste of water, including the right of an authorised officer to enter premises supplied by water, to detect waste or misuse of water) except section 61 thereof, (*i.e.* power to test water fittings) are to apply throughout the area of every water authority except in the area within the limits of supply of a statutory water company.

The effect of the Water Act 1973 was to completely restructure the water industry; a new system of water management was introduced. Central government exercise powers of general supervision and it is the responsibility of the Secretary of State and the Minister of Agriculture, Fisheries and Food to promote jointly a national policy for water in England and Wales; the Regional Water Authorities are the principal executive bodies.

The Central Advisory Water Committee (established by section 2 of the Water Act 1945) was abolished. The responsibility for advising Ministers is that of the National Water Council, which is also responsible, inter alia, for the promotion of water research and the establishment throughout the United Kingdom of a scheme for testing and approving water fittings.

The 1973 Act also abolished joint water boards and committees except where the membership of such joint boards and committees included one or more statutory water companies.

The relationship between water authorities and statutory water companies are prescribed by section 12 of the 1973 Act; where the area of a Water Authority includes the whole or part of the limits of supply of the statutory water company, the Authority must discharge its duties with respect to the supply of water through the company.

1.05 Water Charges

The Water Charges Act 1976 was enacted to meet a specific deficiency in the 1973 Act; it prescribes the Water Authorities' rights to levy charges in respect of mains drainage (*Section* 14 *of the* 1973 *Act*) and for charges under section 30 (as amended by section 2 of the 1976 Act).

The Water Charges Equalisation Act 1977 empowers the Secretary of State, by order to direct a statutory water undertaker to pay to the National Water Council an equalisation levy. The role of the Council is that of banker and, in accordance with directions the council receives from the Secretary of State, it makes "equalisation payments" to such statutory water undertakers as are specified in the direction. The intention of the Act is the equalisation, to some degree, of the burden of the water charge in respect of those premises where the supply of water is on an unmeasured basis.

The Water Charges Equalisation Act was introduced by the Government of the day at a time when there was some concern, following the reorganisation of the water industry, about the increased level of charges facing some consumers. In a few parts of England, but to a much greater degree in Wales, water charges had been held down at an artificially low level by subsidies from the general rate, which in turn attracted the resources element of the rate support grant. Under the legislation that was in existence prior to the 1st April 1974, that form of subsidy was quite permissible; with the establishment of the Regional Water Authorities such form of subsidy came to an end. The result was that consumers, in many cases for the first time, were affected by the 'real cost' of providing them with mains water. To some extent, the effect of this was cushioned by the introduction of equalisation across the boundaries of various regional water authorities as well as equalisation within the area of a water authority.

There was also the political concept that water supply, being a public service, should wherever possible be of an equal cost to a domestic consumer irrespective of where that domestic consumer was situated.

The criteria using the historic financing costs as prescribed in section 1 of the Act by which the Act seeks equalisation charges for unmeasured domestic consumers have been challenged as producing 'perverse, absurd and capricious effects' and to have failed in achieving the desired objectives of the Act; the Government has given notice that the Act will be repealed (*Hansard, House of Commons*, 18 December 1979, vol. 976, no. 90 columns 210/42).

1.06 The European Communities

In 1973 the United Kingdom joined the European Communities. The act of accession has had a signal impact on English Law. Community Legislation is as much a part of our law as it forms part of the Municipal Law of the other member states of the Community. The powers for Parliament to make subordinate legislation in order to achieve harmonisation between English law and Community legislation are conferred under section 2 of the European Communities Act 1972.

1.07 The Water Act 1981

On the 15 April 1981 an inconspicuous Act received the Royal Assent. The Water Act 1981 is described in its preamble as "An Act to provide for increasing the borrowing powers of the British Waterways Board and to make further provision relating to water supply".

Section 1 of the W.A. 1981 increases the borrowing powers of the British Waterways Board; the further provisions affecting water supply are contained in the remaining sections 2 - 7 inclusive and in no small measure have financial and operational consequences for statutory water undertakers in England and Wales.

NOTE: Readers interested in a general introduction to Water Authorities and their functions in relation to Local Government are referred to Circular 100/73 dated 16 August 1973 issued by the Department of the Environment.

Chapter 2

INTERPRETATION

2.01 Statutory Abbreviations

In the chapters which follow, references to Acts of Parliament and their sections (and statutory instruments) are given at the beginning of each headed paragraph and to avoid repetition of their full titles the statutes and instruments are abbreviated as follows—

C.L.A. 1977	Criminal Law Act, 1977
C.P.A. 1974	Control of Pollution Act, 1974
D.A. 1976	Drought Act, 1976
L.G.A. 1972	Local Government Act, 1972
L.G.A. 1974	Local Government Act, 1974
L.G.A. 1978	Local Government Act, 1978
L.G.(MP)A. 1953	Local Government (Miscellaneous Provisions) Act 1953
L.G.(MP)A. 1976	Local Government (Miscellaneous Provisions) Act, 1976
L.G.,P.& L.A. 1980	Local Government, Planning and Land Act 1980
R.A. 1975	Reservoirs Act, 1975
R.(SP)A. 1930	Reservoirs (Safety Provisions) Act, 1930
W.A. 1945	Water Act, 1945
W.A. 1948	Water Act, 1948
W.A. 1973	Water Act, 1973
W.A. 1981	Water Act, 1981
W.C.A. 1976	Water Charges Act, 1976
W.C.E.A. 1977	Water Charges Equalisation Act, 1977
W.R.A. 1963	Water Resources Act, 1963
W.R.A. 1968	Water Resources Act, 1968
W.R.A. 1971	Water Resources Act, 1971

2.02 Terms commonly used in the Water Act, 1945 (s.59)

The following terms and expressions and their definitions are in use throughout the W.A. 1945, **except** in the Third Schedule to that Act—

CONTRAVENTION — includes failure to comply, and "contravene" is to be construed accordingly.

CUT OFF — in relation to a supply of water, means stop the supply, whether by operating a tap, by disconnecting pipes, or otherwise.

ENACTMENT — means any Act of Parliament, whether public general, local or private, any statutory order, or any provision in an Act of Parliament or statutory order.

LAND — includes any interest in land and any easement or right in, to or over land.

LIMITS OF SUPPLY — in relation to any water undertaking, means the limits within which the undertakers are for the time being authorised to supply water.

LOCAL ENACTMENT — means any local Act of Parliament, any public general Act of Parliament relating to the supply of water in Greater London and the surrounding area, any statutory order or any provision in any such Act of Parliament or statutory order.

OWNER — means (except in schedule 2 to the W.A. 1945) the person for the time being receiving the rackrent of the premises in connection with which the word is used, whether on his own account or as agent or trustee for any other person, or who would so receive the same if those premises were let at a rackrent.

PREMISES — includes land. Premises refer to property with a sufficient degree of permanency on the site it occupies, thus premises include a permanently moored houseboat (*West Mersea U.D.C. v. Fraser* [1950] 2 K.B. 119).

PRESCRIBED — means prescribed by regulations made by the Secretary of State under the W.A. 1945.

SECRETARY OF STATE — means the Secretary of State for the Environment.

STATUTORY ORDER — means an order or scheme made under an Act of Parliament, including an order or scheme confirmed by Parliament.

STREET — includes any highway, including a highway over any bridge, and any road, lane, footway, square, court, alley or passage, whether a thoroughfare or not.

SUPPLY OF WATER IN BULK — means a supply of water for distribution by the undertakers taking the supply.

WATERCOURSE — includes all rivers, streams, ditches, drains, cuts, culverts, dykes, sluices, sewers (other than sewers vested in a local authority or a water authority) and passages, through which water flows.

WATER FITTINGS — includes pipes (other than mains), taps, cocks, valves, ferrules, meters, cisterns, baths, water-closets, soil-pans and other similar apparatus used in connection with the supply and use of water.

2.03 Expressions used in the Third Schedule to the Water Act 1945 (3rd Sched, Pt. I, s.1)

Certain of the expressions found in the Third Schedule to the W.A. 1945, have the following definitions—

AUTHORISED — means authorised by the special Act.

BUILDING — includes a part of a building if that part is separately occupied.

BUSINESS — does not include a profession.

COMMUNICATION PIPE — means (a) where the premises supplied with water abut on the part of the street in which the main is laid, and the service pipe enters those premises otherwise than through the outer wall of a building abutting on the street and has a stopcock placed in those premises and as near to the boundary of that street as is reasonably practicable, so much of the service pipe as lies between the main and that stopcock; (b) in any other case, so much of the service pipe as lies between the main and the boundary of the street in which the main is laid, and also (i) where the communication pipe ends at a stopcock, that stopcock; and (ii) any stopcock fitted on the communication pipe between the end thereof and the main.

CONSUMER — means a person supplied, or about to be supplied, with water by the undertakers.

ENACTMENT — means any Act of Parliament, whether public general, local or private, any statutory order or any provision in an Act of Parliament or statutory order.

HIGHWAY AUTHORITY — means, in the case of a highway maintainable at the public expense, the authority in whom the highway is vested.

HOUSE — means a dwellinghouse, whether a private dwellinghouse or not, and includes any part of a building if that part is occupied as a separate dwellinghouse. Terraced houses with a continuous roof occupied as private dwellings held to be separate buildings and not inside the same curtilage (*Weaver v. Family Housing Association (York) Ltd.* [1976] R.A. 25 H.L.).

LIMITS OF SUPPLY — in relation to any water undertaking, means the limits within which the undertakers are for the time being authorised to supply water.

MAIN — means a pipe laid by the undertakers for the purpose of giving a general supply of water as distinct from a supply to individual consumers and includes any apparatus used in connection with such a pipe.

OWNER — means the person for the time being receiving the rackrent of the premises in connection with which the word is used, whether on his own account or as agent or trustee for any other person, or who would so receive the same if those premises were let at a rackrent.

SECRETARY OF STATE — means the Secretary of State for the Environment.

SERVICE PIPE — means so much of any pipe for supplying water from a main to any premises as is subject to water pressure from that main, or would be so subject but for the closing of some tap.

SPECIAL ACT — means the enactment with which any provisions of this Schedule are incorporated, with or without modifications, and includes those provisions as so incorporated.

STATUTORY ORDER — means an order or scheme made under an Act of Parliament, including an order or scheme confirmed by Parliament.

STATUTORY UNDERTAKERS — means any person

authorised by an enactment to construct, work or carry on any railway, canal, inland navigation, dock, harbour, tramway, gas, electricity, water or other public undertaking.

STREET — includes any highway, including a highway over a bridge, and any road, lane, footway, square, court, alley or passage, whether a thoroughfare or not.

A SUPPLY OF WATER FOR DOMESTIC PURPOSES — means a sufficient supply for drinking, washing, cooking and sanitary purposes, but not for any bath having a capacity (measured to the centre line of the overflow pipe, or in such other manner as the Secretary of State may by regulations prescribe) in excess of fifty gallons, and includes (a) a supply for the purposes of a profession carried on in any premises the greater part whereof is used as a house; and (b) where the water is drawn from a tap inside a house and no hosepipe or similar apparatus is used, a supply for watering a garden, for horses kept for private use and for washing vehicles so kept; provided that it does not include a supply of water for the business of a laundry or a business of preparing food or beverages for consumption otherwise than on the premises.

The meaning of "Domestic Purposes" has been a fruitful field for litigation. There is an extremely useful discussion of this phrase in *Metropolitan Water Board v. Avery* [1914] A.C. 118 where it was held that water supply to the Licensee of a Public House where luncheons were served was used for domestic purposes. Lord Atkinson said, at pages 126 and 127,

"I take it that water supplied for domestic purposes would mean water supply to satisfy or help satisfy the needs, or perform or help in performing services, which, according to the ordinary habits of civilised life, are commonly satisfied and performed in peoples homes, as distinguished from those needs and services which are satisfied or performed outside those homes, and are not connected with, nor incident to, the occupation of them."

The test, to determine whether or not a water supply is for "domestic purposes", is whether the user of the water is in its nature domestic. The concept of what is "domestic" is farily flexible and is a reflection of the customs and social priorities of society. Thus in the following cases the courts have held that the supply was for domestic purposes:—

(a) *Pidgeon v. Great Yarmouth Waterworks Company* [1902] 1 K.B. 301: the occupier of a dwelling house carried on the business of a boarding house keeper therein, receiving persons to board and lodge who used the water of the Company. It was used in the house for cleansing, cooking, drinking and sanitary purposes. It was held that the water was used for domestic purposes.

(b) *South West Suburban Water Company v. St. Marylebone Union* [1902] 1 K.B. 310: water supply was for domestic purposes at a school.

(c) *Frederick v. Bognor Water Company* [1909] 1 Ch,149: water supply was domestic at a Boarding School.

(d) *Grand Junction Waterworks Company v. Davies* [1897] 2 Q.B.209: domestic when watering a garden at the house.

(e) *Harrogate Corporation v. Mackay* [1907] 2 K.B. 611 water supply was domestic when washing horses, carriages and cars kept for private use.

On the other hand in *Barnard Castle Urban District Council v. Wilson* [1902] 2 Ch.746 it was held that a swimming pool or bath attached to a school was not a mere domestic appendage of the school but was educational and was used for the purposes of education and that therefore the water supply to the bath was **not** a domestic supply. In *Metropolitan Water Board v. London, Brighton and South Coastal Railway Company* [1910] 2 K.B.890 it was held that water supply to sanitary conveniences at a railway station was not a domestic supply. School premises where a school caretaker lives in are not considered to be used partly for domestic purposes in assessing water rates

— *Welsh National Water Development Authority v. Mid Glamorgan County Council* (1975) 73 L.G.R.180.

In *Oddenino v. Metropolitan Water Board* [1914] 2 Ch.734; it was held, under the provisions of section 20 of the Metropolitan Water Board (Charges) Act 1907, that the Board was not bound to afford a supply of water otherwise than by measure (*i.e.* a meter) to a house used as a restaurant notwithstanding that its use to which the water is put is in its nature domestic. The issue before the Court was whether under its construction of section 20, the supply of water was to a house or building which is used for a trade or manufacturing purpose for which water is used; the test to determine whether it is so used within section 20 the Court held lay in the character of the house or building and not in the use to which the water is put.

SUPPLY OF WATER IN BULK — means a supply of water for distribution by the undertakers taking the supply.

SUPPLY PIPE — means so much of any service pipe as is not a communication pipe.

TRUNK MAIN — means a main constructed for the purpose of conveying water from a source of supply to a filter or reservoir, or from one filter or reservoir to another filter or reservoir, or for the purpose of conveying water in bulk from one part of the limits of supply to another part of those limits, or for the purpose of giving or taking a supply of water in bulk.

UNDERTAKERS — means the persons whose water undertaking is authorised or regulated by the special Act.

WATERCOURSES — includes all rivers, streams, ditches, drains, cuts, culverts, dykes, sewers (other than sewers vested in a local authority or water authority) and passages, through which water flows.

WATER FITTINGS — includes pipes (other than mains), taps, cocks, valves, ferrules, meters, cisterns, baths, waterclosets, soilpans and other similar apparatus used in connection with the supply and use of water.

2.04 Definitions used in the Water Resources Act, 1963

Given below are definitions assigned to some of the expressions in use in provisions of the W.R.A. 1963—

ABSTRACTION — in relation to water contained in any source of supply in a water authority area, means the doing of anything whereby any of that water is removed from that source of supply and either (a) ceases (either permanently or temporarily) to be comprised in the water resources of that area, or (b) is transferred to another source of supply to that area, and "abstract" is to be construed accordingly.

AGRICULTURE — includes horticulture, fruit farming, seed growing, dairy farming, the breeding and keeping of livestock (including any creature kept for the production of food, wool, skins or fur, or for the purpose of its use in the farming of land), the use of land as grazing land, meadow land, osier land, market gardens and nursery grounds, and the use of land for woodlands where that use is ancillary to the farming of land for other agricultural purposes, and "agricultural" is to be construed accordingly.

ENGINEERING OR BUILDING OPERATIONS — includes the construction, alteration, improvement or maintenance of any reservoir, watercourse, dam, weir, well, borehole or other works, the construction, alteration, improvement, maintenance or demolition of any building or structure, and the installation, modification or removal of any machinery or apparatus.

FIRE-FIGHTING PURPOSES — means the purposes of the extinction of fires and the protection of life and property in case of fire.

IMPOUNDING WORKS — see para. 7.17.

INLAND WATER — means any of the following — (a) so much of any river, stream or other watercourse, whether natural or artificial and whether tidal or not, as is within any of the water authority areas; (b) any lake or pond, whether natural or artificial, and any reservoir or dock, in so far as these do not fall within (a) above and is within any of the water authority areas; and (c) so much of any channel, creek, bay, estuary, or arm of the sea as does not fall within any of the water authority areas, and any reference in the W.R.A. 1963, to an inland water includes a reference to part of an inland water.

LAND — includes land covered by water.

LAND DRAINAGE — includes defence against water (including sea water), irrigation other than spray irrigation, warping and the provision of flood warning systems.

LICENCES OF RIGHT — see para. **7.07**.

LOCAL ENACTMENT — means a local or private Act, a public general Act relating to London, an order or scheme made under an Act or confirmed by Parliament or brought into operation in accordance with special parliamentary procedure, or an enactment in a public general Act amending a local or private Act or any such order or scheme.

SECRETARY OF STATE — means the Secretary of State for the Environment.

SOURCE OF SUPPLY — in relation to any area, means either (a) so much of an inland water (other than a lake, pond or reservoir or a group thereof not discharging to another inland water) as is situated in that area, and (b) any underground strata in that area.

SPRAY IRRIGATION — means the irrigation of land or plants (including seeds) by means of water or other liquid emerging (in whatever form) from apparatus designed or adapted to eject liquid into the air in the form of jets or spray.

STATUTORY PROVISION — means a provision, whether of a general or a special nature, contained in, or in any document made or issued under, any Act, whether of a general or a special nature.

UNDERGROUND STRATA — means strata subjacent to the surface of any land and any reference to water contained in any underground strata is a reference to water so contained otherwise than in a sewer, pipe, reservoir, tank or other underground works constructed in any such strata.

WATER RESOURCES — in relation to any area, means water for the time being contained in any source of supply in that area.

WATERCOURSE — includes all rivers, streams, ditches, drains, cuts, culverts, dykes, sluices, sewers and passages through which water flows, except (a) mains and water fittings within the meaning of schedule 3 to the W.A. 1945, and (b) water authority sewers, and (c) adits and passages constructed in connection with a well, borehole or similar work for facilitating the collection of water in the well, borehole or work.

2.05 Definitions used in the Water Act 1973

Given below are definitions of some of the terms used in the W.A. 1973—

COUNTY, DISTRICT, COUNTY COUNCIL and DISTRICT COUNCIL — means respectively a county, district, county council and district council established by the Local Government Act, 1972.

LOCAL AUTHORITY — means a county council,* the Greater London Council,* a district council, a London borough council or the Common Council of the City of London.

LOCAL STATUTORY PROVISION — means a provision of a local Act (including an Act confirming a provisional order) or a provision of a public general Act passed with respect to some area or a provision of an instrument made under any such local or public general Act or of an instrument in the nature of a local enactment made under any other Act.

PUBLIC SEWER — has the same meaning as in the Public Health Act, 1936.

UNDERGROUND STRATA, INLAND WATER, WATERCOURSE and WATER RESOURCES have the same meaning respectively as in the Water Resources Act, 1963.

---

* Except for the purpose of Section 16 — Requisitioning of sewers for domestic purposes.

STATUTORY WATER COMPANY — means a company authorised immediately before the passing of the Water Act, 1973, by any local statutory provision to supply water or a company in whom the assets of any company so authorised have subsequently become vested.

STATUTORY WATER UNDERTAKERS — References in any enactment or instrument to statutory water undertakers as such are construed as references to water authorities, statutory water companies, joint water boards and joint water committees and to no other body.

Chapter 3

POLICY PLANNING AND ORGANISATION

3.01 Synopsis

This chapter refers to the Government departments primarily concerned with promoting the national policy for water and who are responsible for the overall supervision of water functions. The Ministers execute their policy through the regional water authorities, and both the Ministers and the authorities are advised and assisted by central agencies such as the National Water Council and the Water Space Amenity Commission. The water authorities are responsible for public supplies of water and the statutory water companies supply water within their limits of supply as the agents of the water authorities. Each water authority is required to survey the water resources and needs of its area, estimate future demands for water and prepare and periodically review plans and programmes to meet requirements. The Ministers may issue directions to water authorities about the performance of their functions and the Secretary of State may, if required, exercise default powers where there is a failure by a water authority in respect of the supply of water.

DEFINITIONS OF CERTAIN EXPRESSIONS USED IN THE WATER ACT 1973 THROUGHOUT PARTS (A) AND (B) OF THIS CHAPTER ARE GIVEN IN PARA. 2.05 DEFINITIONS OF CERTAIN EXPRESSIONS USED IN THE WATER ACT 1945 THROUGHOUT PART (C) OF THIS CHAPTER ARE GIVEN IN PARA. 2.02.

(A) CENTRAL ORGANISATION
(For definitions of certain expressions used in this part, see para. **2.05**)

3.02 National Policy for Water
(WA 1973, s.1)

It is the duty of the Secretary of State and the Minister of Agriculture, Fisheries and Food ("the Minister") to promote jointly a national policy for water in England and Wales and so to discharge their respective functions under the Act as to secure the effective execution of that policy by the relevant responsible bodies. Subject to the constitutional law doctrine that the office of the Secretary of State is one and indivisible, the ministerial responsibility for national policy is shared between the Secretary of State for the Environment in England and the Secretary of State for Wales in Wales, notwithstanding that part of the Severn-Trent Water Authority is in Wales and part of the Welsh Water Authority is in England. It is the duty of the Secretary of State to execute the national policy as it relates to:—

(a) the conservation, augmentation, distribution and proper use of water resources, and the provision of water supplies;

(b) sewerage and the treatment and disposal of sewage and other effluents;

(c) the restoration and maintenance of the wholesomeness of rivers and other inland water;

(d) the use of inland water for recreation;

(e) the enhancement and preservation of amenity in connection with inland water; and

(f) the use of inland water for navigation.

It is the duty of the Minister to secure the effective execution of so much of the national policy as it relates to land drainage and fisheries in inland and coastal waters.

The Secretary of State is required to collate and publish information from which assessments can be made of the actual and prospective demands for water and of actual and prospective resources in England and Wales, and he may collaborate with others in doing so whether in England and Wales and elsewhere.

The relevant bodies responsible for the various water functions so as to secure the effective execution of the national policy for water promoted by the Ministers are:—

(i) The ten regional water authorities, nine in England and one in Wales;

(ii) The National Water Council;

(iii) The Water Space Amenity Commission;

(iv) Statutory water companies, (as agents for the regional water authorities);

(v) Other authorities who participate to a limited or specialised extent *eg* local authorities who have specific statutory duties to ascertain from time to time the sufficiency and wholesomeness of water supplies within the area of that local authority, and with permissive power to appoint a specified number of members of water authorities, and drainage authorities (*eg* water authorities pursuant to their land drainage functions and internal drainage boards).

NOTE: 1. The ten regional water authorities are listed in paragraph **3.07**.

2. Land Drainage includes works of irrigation other than spray irrigation, (*Land Drainage Act* 1976, s. 116).

3.03 National Water Council
    (W.A. 1973, s.4)

The National Water Council was created by the W.A. 1973, to consider and advise any Minister on matters relating to the national policy for water, to advise any Minister and the water authorities on any other matter of common interest to them, to promote and assist water authorities in the efficient performance of their functions and as to research and the preparation, review and provision of plans (*see* para. **3.09**), to advise Ministers on matters on which the Council are consulted under a requirement imposed by the W.A. 1973, to establish after consultation a national scheme for the testing and approval of water fittings, to prepare after consultation a scheme for the training and education of water employees, and if authorised to perform services for or on behalf of two or more water authorities and other bodies in relation to matters of common interest.

The Council is composed of (a) a chairman appointed by the Secretary of State, (b) the chairman of the water authorities, and (c) up to ten other members with special knowledge of matters relevant to the functions of water authorities, of whom eight are appointed by the Secretary of State and two by the Minister.

The Council may furnish to any person or body for the benefit of any country or territory outside the United Kingdom technical assistance in connection with training and education in relation to any services corresponding to those provided in England and Wales by the Water Authorities.

The appropriate Minister or Ministers acting together may, after consultation with the Council, give to the council:—

(a)   Directions of a general character as to the exercise and performance by the council of their functions in relation to matters which appear to the appropriate Minister or Ministers to affect the execution of the national policy for water or otherwise they affect the national interest; and

(b)   Directions to discontinue any activity, either wholly or to a specified extent, or not to extend any activity or not to extend it beyond any specified limits.

Any direction given to the council shall be given by statutory instruments, of which a draft must be laid before Parliament.

The council is a body corporate. The Third Schedule to the Water Act 1973 defines the duties imposed by way of administrative and financial requirements on water authorities and of the National Water Council; these requirements are considered in Chapters 8 and 9.

3.04 Water Space Amenity Commission
(W.A. 1973, s.23)

The Water Space Amenity Commission was another specialist body set up under the W.A. 1973, with terms of reference to advise the Secretary of State on promoting the national policy for water and the National Water Council and water authorities on the discharge of their respective functions, all so far as relating to recreation and amenity. The Commission is composed of a chairman appointed by the Secretary of State, the chairmen of the water authorities and up to ten other members appointed by the Secretary of State after consultation with specified organisations and associations, see below. As to the recreational functions of water authorities and their duties regarding nature conservation and amenity *see* paras. **4.25** and **4.27**.

Of the members of the Commission other than the Chairman, appointed by the Secretary of State:—

(a) One should be appointed after consultation with the Countryside Commission;

(b) One should be appointed after consultation with the English Tourist Board;

(c) One should be appointed after consultation with the Sports Council or some other organisation appearing to the Secretary of State to be concerned with the encouragement of sport and recreation and prescribed for the purposes of the Water Act 1973 by order made by the Secretary of State;

(d) The remainder shall be appointed after consultation with such associations of local authorities, such bodies representing persons interested in the use of water and of any land associated with the water for the purposes of recreation or in the enhancement and preservation of amenity, as the Secretary of State considers desirable, and with the Greater London Council.

The Commission may collate and publish information and report on matters relating to recreation and amenity in connection with water.

The Commission is under a statutory duty to report to the Ministers, as soon as possible after each financial year, on the discharge by the Commission of its functions during that year and of its policy and programme.

The Commission has the statutory duty to formulate, promote and execute a national policy for water in relation to recreation and amenity. In the exercise of this duty the Commission must:—

(a)   advise the National Water Council and the water authorities on the discharge of their respective functions in relation to the recreational and amenity use of water;

(b)   submit to water authorities any proposals that the Commission considers appropriate for the discharge of the water authorities functions in respect of the recreational and amenity use of water;

(c)   assist water authorities in the preparation of plans and programmes under Section 24 of the 1973 Act (*see* para. **3.09**) insofar as those plans and programmes relate to the recreational and amenity use of water.

3.05 Directions to Water Authorities
(W.A. 1973, s.5)

The Minister of Agriculture, Fisheries and Food may give water authorities directions of a general character as to the exercise of their functions relating to fisheries and land drainage, and the Secretary of State may similarly give directions in relation to the exercise of their other functions, so far as the exercise of those functions appears to affect the execution of the national policy for water or otherwise to affect the national interest. A direction may be given either to a particular water authority or to water authorities generally and in the latter case the appropriate Minister is required to consult the National Water Council before giving a direction.

Land drainage includes irrigation other than spray irrigation (*Land Drainage Act* 1976, s.116).

3.06 Default Powers of the Secretary of State and of Water Authorities
(W.A. 1945, s.13 as substituted by W.A. 1973, sch.4, Part I)

If a complaint is made to the Secretary of State that a water authority has failed (a) to give an adequate supply of water, either as respects quantity or quality, to any part of its area, or to give a supply which it has been lawfully required to give, or (b) to take such steps as are reasonably practicable to obtain new powers or to extend its existing powers for the purpose of remedying any such failure, or (c) to do anything which it is required to do by or under the W.A. 1945, or the Secretary of State is of the opinion that an investigation should be made as to whether a water authority has failed in any of the matters mentioned in (a) to (c) above, he may hold a local inquiry into the matter.

Where a statutory water company is supplying water on behalf of a water authority and a complaint is made to the water authority that the company has failed (a) to give an adequate supply of water, either as respects quantity or quality, to any part of the water authority area which it is supplying, or to give a supply which it has been lawfully required to give, or (b) to take such steps as are reasonably practicable to obtain new powers or to extend its existing powers for the purpose of remedying any such failure, or (c) to do anything which it is required to do by or under the W.A. 1945, or a water authority is of the opinion that an investigation should be made as to whether a statutory water company through whom the authority is supplying water has failed in any of the matters mentioned in (a) to (c) above, the authority may hold a local inquiry into the matter.

Following a local inquiry if it appears to the Secretary of State or as the case may be the water authority, that there has been such a failure on the part of the statutory water undertakers in question, the Secretary of State or the water authority may make an order declaring the undertakers to be in default and directing them for the purpose of remedying the default to discharge such of their functions in such manner and within such time or times as specified in the order or to take such steps within such time or times as specified to obtain new powers or to extend their existing powers.

If a water authority declared to be in default fails to comply with any requirement of the order within the time limit specified, the Secretary of State, in lieu of enforcing the order by mandamus or otherwise, may by order transfer such of the functions of the water authority to himself as he thinks fit. Similarly, if a statutory water company in default fails to comply with any requirement of the order within the time limit, the water authority, in lieu of enforcing the order by mandamus or otherwise, may by order suspend all or any part of the arrangements made within the company under s.12 of the W.A. 1973 (see para. 3.08) and transfer such of the functions of the company to itself as it thinks fit. Expenses incurred in discharging functions so transferred are recoverable by the Secretary of State or the water authority from the body in default. An order may provide for the property and liabilities of the body in default to be transferred to the Secretary of State or water authority as may be necessary or expedient. The procedure for the making and confirmation of an order by a water authority is set out in the W.A. 1973, Schedule 4, Part II. — see Chapter 9 "ADMINISTRATION".

Section 250 of the Local Government Act 1972 applies in relation to any local inquiry held either by the Secretary of State or the water authority. This section makes general provisions with regard to public inquiries held on behalf of Ministers or, as amended by the Water Act 1973, on behalf of Water Authorities. Students of Administrative Law interested in the application of the principles of natural justice are referred to such leading cases as *Local Government Board v Arlidge* [1915] A.C.120; *Errington v Minister of Health* [1935]1K.B. 249 and *Miller v Minister of Housing and Local Government* [1968] 2. All E.R.633''

(B) REGIONAL ORGANISATION

(For definitions of certain expressions used in this Part, see para. 2.05)

3.07 Water Authorities

(W.A. 1973, ss.2, 3, 6, 25, Schs. 1 & 3)

The water authorities are—

the Anglian Water Authority
the Northumbrian Water Authority
the North-West Water Authority
the Severn-Trent Water Authority
the Southern Water Authority
the South-West Water Authority
the Thames Water Authority
the Wessex Water Authority
the Yorkshire Water Authority
the Welsh Water Authority

The water authorities were established by individual constitution orders made by the two Ministers under s.2 of the W.A. 1973, and on 1st April, 1974, the authorities assumed or took over the functions in respect of water supply, water resources, sewerage and sewage disposal, land drainage, fisheries, the control of pollution, water recreation and amenities and navigation (where applicable). The orders referred to the number of members appointed by the Ministers and local authorities and defined the boundaries of the water authority areas.

Paragraphs 42 and 43 of Schedule 3 to the Act impose a duty on the Severn-Trent Water Authority to consult the Welsh Water Authority on any substantial development or matter of policy arising from the exercise of the former's functions, insofar as the development or matter affects so much of their area as is within Wales. It is the statutory duty of the Welsh Water Authority to keep the Secretary of State informed of their views on all matters about which they are in consultation with the Severn-Trent Water Authority.

Where the Severn-Trent Water Authority acquires an estate or interest in land in Wales or in connection with the construction and operation of a reservoir, it shall convey the estate or interest in the land to the Welsh Water Authority who shall grant the Severn-Trent Water Authority, for the purpose for which the latter originally acquired the estate or interest, a lease or sub-lease of the land or such other interest in it as may be appropriate. If there is a failure to agree between the two water authorities on the terms of any such conveyance or grant then the terms may be settled by the Secretary of State.

Insofar as the subject matter of this book is concerned, the Water Act 1973 (*Section* 25) makes special provision relating to the discharge of the recreational and amenity functions in and around the Greater London area. A duty is imposed on the Thames Water Authority to transfer to the Greater London Council the recreational and amenity functions of water authorities as prescribed in the Water Act 1973, in respect of the full or part of the following water courses and land associated with those water courses. Namely:—

(1)   So much of the River Thames as lies within Greater London;

(2)   Every watercourse, other than the River Thames, which is for the time being a "main metropolitan water course" (for the meaning of main metropolitan water course see the London Government Act 1963, Schedule 14);

(3)   So much of the River Bean, the River Ingrebourne and the River Roding as lies within the area of Greater London;

(4)   So much of any other watercourse situated wholly or partly within, or adjoining the boundary of, the area of Greater London as lies within the flow and re-flow of the tides of the River Thames.

Subject to special arrangements for appointing members to certain water authorities, the membership of a water authority normally comprises—

(a)   a chairman appointed by the Secretary of State;

(b)   between two to four members appointed by the Minister of Agriculture, Fisheries and Food with experience of, and capacity in, agriculture, land drainage or fisheries;

(c)   members appointed by the Secretary of State with experience of, and capacity in, some matter relevant to the functions of water authorities;

(d) members appointed by the local authorities; it is considered desirable that they should be familiar with the requirements and circumstances of the authority's area, and the order must be framed so that the total number of ministerial appointments is less than the number of members appointed by local authorities.

With regard to members appointed by local authorities, where a quarter or more of the population of a metropolitan county resides within the area of a water authority, the county council appoints two members and the district councils within the county between them appoint two members, of the water authority. In the case of a non-metropolitan county where a quarter or more of the population lives within the area of a water authority, the county council appoints one member and the district councils within the county between them appoint one member, of the water authority. And if one-sixth or more but less than one-fourth of the population of a county is resident within that area, the county council, after consultation with the district councils within the county and wholly or partly within that area, may appoint one member of the water authority. The person appointed by a local authority need not necessarily be one of their own members.

NOTE 1: The Constitution Orders establishing the water authorities are:—
North West Water Authority (S.I. 1973 No. 1287)
Northumbrian Water Authority (S.I. 1973 No. 1288)
Yorkshire Water Authority (S.I. 1973 No. 1289)
Anglian Water Authority (S.I. 1973 No. 1359)
Thames Water Authority (S.I. 1973 No. 1360)
Southern Water Authority (S.I. 1973 No. 1361)
Wessex Water Authority (S.I. 1973 No. 1306)
South West Water Authority (S.I. 1973 No. 1307)
Severn-Trent Water Authority (S.I. 1973 No. 1437)
Welsh National Water Development Authority (S.I. 1973 No. 1345)

NOTE 2: The name of the Welsh National Water Development Authority was changed by Ministerial Order in March 1978 to the Welsh Water Authority.

NOTE 3: The Constitution Orders were amended in 1979 by the Constitution (Amendment) Orders increasing the number of members of water authorities appointed by local authorities.

3.08 Local Organisation for Water Supply
(W.A. 1973, ss. 11, 12 and 33)

As stated earlier the responsibility for the public supply of water is vested in the Water Authorities. Local authorities have ceased to have a responsibility for the supply of water whether under special statutory powers or under Part IV of the Public Health Act 1936. Joint water boards and committees ceased to exist unless their membership included one or more statutory water companies. Under the terms of various Transfer of Property Orders, made under the Local Government Act 1972 and the Water Act 1973, the assets and liabilities and personnel of the bodies whose functions as statutory water undertakers had ceased to exist were transferred to the Water Authorities.

Statutory water companies continue in existence as separate entities from water authorities but subject to the provision of any order made under section 254 of the L.G.A. 1972,* so much of the enactments relating to a statutory water company as imposed any duty on that company to supply water cease to have effect subject to one important exception. Where the provisions of Part VIII of the Third Schedule to the Water Act 1945 had been applied to a water company or where any local statutory provision contained similar provisions to Part VIII of the Third Schedule, and that local statutory provision applies to the company, the duty to supply in accordance with those provisions remains with the statutory water company. Part VIII of the Third Schedule to the Water Act 1945 imposes the duty on a statutory water undertaker to fix and maintain fire hydrants on its mains and supply water in respect of those fire hydrants. There is also the additional obligation on the statutory water undertaker, where a hydrant has been fixed to a pipe of the undertakers, to provide a supply of water for cleansing sewers and drains, for cleansing and watering highways and for supplying any public pumps, baths or wash houses.

---

* This section (based on Section 84 of the London Government Act 1963) enables Ministers, including the Secretary of State, to make orders covering incidental, consequential, transitional and supplementary matters which are not specifically dealt with in the Water Act 1973.

Where the area of a Water authority includes the whole or part of the limits of supply of a statutory water company, the Authority is required to discharge its water supply duties through the company in accordance with arrangements made between the Authority and the company whereby the company undertakes to supply water on behalf of the Authority. These arrangements may include:—

(1)   the management or operation of sources of supply

(2)   the supply of water in bulk by or to the company

(3)   the company's charges for the supply of water

Any such arrangement can be varied by agreement or by the Secretary of State in default of agreement; however the Secretary of State cannot vary any agreement as to oblige the company to fix their charges at a level which will endanger their ability, so long as their undertaking is managed efficiently, to provide a reasonable return on their paid-up capital, having regard to their probable future expenditure and to the need to provide for any contributions which they may lawfully carry to any reserved fund or contingency fund, to make good depreciation and to make all other costs, charges and expenses properly chargeable to revenue.

It is the duty of the water authority on whose behalf water is being supplied by a statutory water company to take all reasonable steps for making water available to that company to meet the foreseeable demands to their consumers.

Each local authority within the area of a Water Authority is under a duty to periodically check the sufficiency and wholesomeness of water supplies within their area and to notify the water authority of any deficiency.

If the local authority notify the water authority that the supply of water for domestic purposes to specified premises is such as to endanger health by reasons of insufficiency or being unwholesome, and it is not practicable to provide a pipe supply, it is the duty of the water authority to provide some other means of supply to within a reasonable distance of the premises concerned if such can be done at a reasonable cost. The Secretary of State is to determine:

(a)   any dispute between the local authority and the water authority as to the insufficiency or unwholesomeness of any supply of water or whether it causes a danger to health;

(b)   on the requisition of the local authority, parish or community council or ten or more local government electors, whether a supply of water can be provided at a reasonable cost.

3.09 Periodical Reviews, Plans and Programmes
(W.A. 1973, s.24)

Each water authority has the duty in consultation with any water authority or authorities likely to be affected—

(a)   to carry out a survey of the water in its area, the existing management of water, the purposes for which it is being used and its quality in relation to its existing and likely future uses, and to prepare a report setting out the results of the survey;

(b)   to prepare an estimate of the future demand for the use of the water for the next twenty years or other period as the Secretary of State for the Environment and the Minister of Agriculture, Fisheries and Food may direct;

(c)   prepare a plan of action to be taken during that period by the authority (whether by way of executing works or securing the execution of works by other persons or otherwise) for the purpose of securing more efficient management of water in the area, including meeting future demands for water and the use of water and restoring or maintaining the wholesomeness of rivers and other inland or coastal waters in the area.

Where a statutory water company supply water in a water authority area, the authority may require the company to carry out a survey and estimate and formulate proposals for meeting water supply requirements in that part of the area within the company's limits of supply and to submit a report to the authority.

The water authority has to keep under review its report or estimate and plan and revise these either by way of amendment or by making a further survey, estimate and plan at intervals of not more than seven years or as appropriate having regard to when similar revisions are proposed to be carried out by other water authorities. Land drainage functions are, however, excepted from such review and are subject to a survey by the water authority at such times as the Minister of Agriculture, Fisheries and Food may direct.

In the light of its most recent survey and plan, the water authority must from time to time prepare one or more programmes of a general nature for discharging its functions over a period of up to seven years and submit this for the approval of the Secretary of State and the Minister. A programme which relates to the supply of water must take account of any proposed operations by a statutory water company or joint water board or joint water committee if extant and involving a substantial outlay on capital account.

In carrying out its duty under the above provisions a water authority has to consult every local authority whose area is wholly or partly included in the water authority area, and have regard to structure plans, local plans or development plans prepared for any part of the area pursuant to the Town and Country Planning Act, 1971. A water authority or other statutory water undertaker must, in carrying out a project involving substantial outlay on capital account, act in accordance with any approved programme applicable to the discharge of its functions or the carrying out of its operations.

Each water authority is required to make arrangements for carrying out research and related matters (whether by the authority or by others) in respect of matters affecting its functions and may subscribe to research organisations.

(C) STATUTORY ORDERS—THE WATERWORKS CODE
(For definition of certain expressions used in this Part, see para. **2.02**)

3.10 Water Orders

Apart from the issue of directions or the possession of default powers, the Secretary of State can exercise a variety of other powers in relation to water undertakers, such as being the confirming authority for the making of byelaws or compulsory purchase orders. Another important ministerial act in this category is the making of an order, on the application of statutory water undertakers or other persons, which confers statutory powers upon the applicants. He may by order—

(1)   Combine or transfer undertakers (W.A. 1945, s.9) — *see* para. **3.11**;

(2)   Vary the limits of supply of undertakers (s.10) — *see* para. **6.12**;

(3)   Require the giving and taking of a supply of water in bulk (s.12 as substituted) —*see* para. **6.10**;

(4)   Confer specific powers on undertakers, *ie* to construct waterworks, raise capital, etc (s.23) — *see* para. **5.06**;

(5)   Repeal or amend local enactments relating to the supply of water by the undertakers (s.33) — *see* para. **3.12**.

Any power conferred on the Secretary of State to make orders is deemed to include a power to vary or revoke an order (s.50).

The Secretary of State may also by order made under ss. 9, 10, 12 or 23 of the W.A. 1945, apply to a water undertaking to which the order relates any provisions of the Waterworks Code contained in the Third Schedule to that Act (*see* para. **3.13**).

3.11 Combination and Transfer of Undertakers
(W.A. 1945, s.9; W.A. 1948, ss. 2, 3; W.A. 1973, Sch. 9)

On the application of the water undertakers concerned, the Secretary of State may make an order providing for—

(a)   the joint furnishing by two or more statutory water undertakers, by agreement, of a supply of water;

(b)   the constitution, by agreement, of a joint board or joint committee of two or more statutory water undertakers for the purpose of exercising all or any of their functions relating to the supply of water;

(c) the amalgamation, by agreement, of the undertakings or parts of the undertakings of two or more statutory water undertakers; or

(d) the transfer, by agreement, to statutory water undertakers of the undertaking or part of the undertaking of any other water undertakers, whether statutory or not.

Where it appears to the Secretary of State to be expedient for the purpose of securing a more efficient supply of water to provide for any of the matters for which, if the undertakers concerned agreed thereto, provision could be made as above, he may by order provide compulsorily for any of those matters. An order may contain such incidental, consequential and supplementary provisions as the Secretary of State thinks necessary or expedient for the purposes of the order, and in particular may provide for the transfer of property and liabilities and for the amendment or repeal of a local enactment relating to any of the undertakers. Schedule 1, Part I to the W.A. 1945, deals with the making of orders on the application of undertakers and Part II of the same schedule deals with orders made by the Secretary of State.

An order which provides for the matters mentioned in (b) or (c) of this provision above may include the matters mentioned in s.23 of the W.A. 1945 (*see* para. **5.06**), so as to avoid having to make separate orders under ss. 9 and 23, and such an order may contain such incidental, consequential and supplementary provisions as the Secretary of State thinks necessary or expedient for the purpose, including provisions for the amendment or repeal of any local enactment and for the transfer of property and liabilities; but the order cannot empower the undertakers to acquire land compulsorily or vary the amount of compensation water required by an enactment to be discharged into a watercourse or the periods during which or the manner in which the compensation water is required to be discharged.

An order under this provision which authorises the construction or alteration of waterworks or works connected therewith may authorise the compulsory acquisition of land required for the construction or alteration of such works, being land whichcould be acquired compulsorily under s.24 of the W.A. 1945 (*see* para. **5.02**), and the Schedule to the W.A. 1948 applies to a compulsory purchase order which authorises such an acquisition.

3.12 Repeal and Amendment of Local Enactments
(W.A. 1945, s.33; W.A. 1973, Sch. 9)

On the application of statutory water undertakers the Secretary of State may by order repeal or amend a local enactment relating to the supply of water by the undertakers, provided that (a) an order cannot vary the quantity of compensation water required by a local enactment to be discharged into a watercourse or the period during which or the manner in which the compensation water is required to be discharged; (b) the Secretary of State must not make an order as to a matter which in his opinion could be more appropriately dealt with under another provision of the W.A. 1945.

3.13 Modernisation of Waterworks Code by Incorporation of Third Schedule
(W.A. 1945, s.32; W.A. 1973, Sch. 9)

The Secretary of State may by any order made under ss. 9, 10, 12 or 23 of the W.A. 1945, apply to a water undertaking to which the order relates the appropriate provisions contained in the Third Schedule to the 1945 Act, subject to such modifications and adaptations as may be specified in the order. The Secretary of State may also at any time by order apply the provisions of the Third Schedule or any of them to the undertaking of any statutory water undertakers, subject to such modifications and adaptations as may be specified in the order, and may by the order repeal any provision previously applicable to the undertaking to the extent to which, having regard to the provisions of the 1945 Act which apply or are applied by the order to the undertaking, appear to be no longer required, or amend any provision previously applicable to the undertaking to any extent which appears necessary to bring it into conformity with the provisions of the 1945 Act. Part I of Sch. 1 to the 1945 Act applies to orders made on the application of the undertakers and Part II of Sch. 1 applies to orders made without application.

Apart from provisions of the Third Schedule to the W.A.

1945, being incorporated by order made under s.32, the whole or parts of the Third Schedule have been applied by certain Acts and statutory instruments throughout water authority areas or water supply areas subject to various exceptions or modifications, namely—

Local Government (Miscellaneous Provisions) Act 1953, s.12, as substituted by the Water Act 1973, Sch.8, para. 66 — Subject to any provision to the contrary contained in any instrument made under or by virtue of the W.A. 1973, **Part XIII** of the Third Schedule to the W.A. 1945 (*Provisions for preventing waste of water*), **except** s.61, applies throughout every water authority area except in the limits of supply of a statutory water company within the meaning of the W.A. 1973 — ss.41(3) and 64 of Sch. 3 are modified.

Water Act 1973, s.11(7)(b) — Subject to any provision to the contrary contained in any instrument made under or by virtue of the W.A. 1973, **Parts VII and IX** of the Third Schedule to the W.A. 1945 (*Supply of water for domestic purposes,* and *Duties as to Constancy of supply and pressure*) apply throughout every water authority area, whether or not applied by or under any other enactment.

The Water Authorities etc (Miscellaneous Provisions) Order, 1974 (S.I. 1974 No. 607), Art. 8 provides that where in relation to any area forming part of a water authority's water supply area there was in operation immediately before 1st April 1974 a local statutory provision which (a) applied with modifications some or all of the provisions of Parts VII and IX, or (b) comprised provisions substantially to the like effect as any such last-mentioned provisions, notwithstanding anything in s.11(7)(b) of the 1973 Act, that local statutory provision continues to have effect in relation to the first-mentioned area instead of the corresponding provisions as originally enacted of Part VII or IX.

Water Authorities etc (Miscellaneous Provisions) Order 1974 (S.I. 1974 No. 607), Art. 9 provides that **the Third Schedule** to the W.A. 1945, **except** s.2 (*Permissible limits of deviation*), s.7 (*Power to acquire easements for underground works*) and Part XV (*Financial Provisions applicable to Water Companies*), applies in relation to any area which forms part of the water supply area of a water authority and within which, immediately before 1st April 1974, a supply of water was furnished by former statutory water undertakers under powers conferred by part IV (*Water Supply*) of the Public Health Act, 1936, and the Third Schedule is thereby incorporated with the 1974 Order and has effect, as so applied, as if it had been applied by virtue of s.32 of the 1945 Act, but Art. 9 does not apply to the Welsh National Water Development Authority — ss. 3, 5, 19, 41, 42, 64 and 70 of the Third Schedule are modified.

Local Authorities etc (Miscellaneous Provisions) Order 1977 (S.I. 1977 No. 293), Art. 7 — **Section 19** (*Power to lay mains*) of the Third Schedule to the W.A. 1945 applies throughout the water supply area of any water authority (other than the Welsh National Water Development Authority) subject to the substitution of subs.(1)(b) for the original wording and any local statutory provision ceases to have effect in so far as it applies s.19 in any such water supply area.

Fire Services Act 1947, s.14 — **Sections 32 to 34** of the Third Schedule to the W.A. 1945 apply to all statutory water undertakers in substitution for any other provision having effect for the purposes of those sections by virtue of any enactment.

Water Act 1981, s.3 — **Sections 35 to 38** of Part VIII of the Third Schedule to the W.A. 1945 (*Supply of water for public purposes*) apply throughout every water authority area, and accordingly any local statutory provision applying those sections with or without modifications ceased to have effect from 15 April 1981.

Water Act 1981, s.4 — Without prejudice to any modification made by any local statutory provisions, **Section 42 (1) to (6)** of the Third Schedule to the W.A. 1948 (*Power of undertakers to require separate service pipes*) apply throughout every water authority area whether or not applied by or under any other enactment. *See* para. **5.13** p. 119 *post*. Sub-sections (7) and (8) of Section 42 are repealed.

The above statutes and statutory instruments which apply parts of the Third Schedule to the W.A. 1945 to water authority areas, statutory water undertakers, etc are summarised in the following table—

Parts of Third Schedule which are applied	Enactment authorising application	Area covered by application	Areas where application of sch.3 does not apply
Part XIII (except s.61) with modifications to ss.41(3) and 64	L.G. (Miscellaneous Provisions) Act 1953, s.12 as substituted by the Water Act 1973, sch.8, para.66	Throughout every water authority area	(1) Where there is any provision to the contrary contained in an instrument made under or by virtue of the Water Act 1973 (2) Limits of supply of statutory water company
Part VII Part IX	Water Act 1973, s.11(7) Water Authorities etc. (Miscellaneous Provisions) Order 1974 (S.I. 1974, No. 607) Art.8	Throughout every water authority area	(1) Where there is any provision to the contrary contained in an instrument made under or by virtue of the Water Act 1973 (2) Part of a water supply area of a water authority where immediately before 1/4/1974 there was in operation a local statutory provision which (a) applied Parts VII and IX with modifications, or (b) comprised provisions substantially to the like as those (Here the local statutory provision continues to have effect in such area instead of Parts VII and IX as originally enacted)
All of Third Schedule (except ss. 2, 7 and Part XV) with modifications to ss. 3, 5, 19, 41, 42, 64, 70	Water Authorities etc (Miscellaneous Provisions) Order 1974 (S.I. 1974, No. 607) Art.9	Every area forming part of the water supply area of a water authority and within which immediately before 1/4/1974 a supply of water was furnished by former statutory water undertakers under Part IV of the Public Health Act 1936	Welsh National Water Development Authority
s.19 as modified	Local Authorities etc. (Miscellaneous Provisions) Order 1977 (S.I. 293). Art.7	Throughout the water supply area of any water authority	Welsh National Water Development Authority
ss. 32-34	Fire Services Act, 1947, s.14	All statutory water undertakers	
ss. 35-38	Water Act 1981, s.3	Throughout every water authority area	
s. 42(1)-(6)	Water Act 1981, s.4	Throughout every water authority area	

Chapter 4

CONSERVATION AND PROTECTION OF WATER RESOURCES

4.01 Synopsis

Part III of the Water Act, 1945, originally contained provisions designed to prevent the unnecessary squandering of the nation's water resources, namely by—

(a) conserving the quantity of water taken from underground strata by means of licensing the abstraction of water from wells, boreholes, etc;

(b) seeking to preserve the quality of water by preventing the gathering grounds and water being suplied from becoming polluted;

(c) ensuring that water is not wasted, misused or contaminated.

Whilst these powers remain, some slightly amended, they have been in part greatly expanded under the Water Resources Acts, 1963-71, as amended by the Water Act, 1973, in the following directions—

(1) Most abstractions from inland waters and underground strata are now licensed by the water authorities;

(2) Each water authority is required to take steps to conserve, redistribute or otherwise augment water resources within its area, to secure the proper use of such resources, or for transferring such resources to another area (*see* para. **4.12**);

(3) Each water authority must carry out a survey of the water resources in its area, prepare an estimate of future demands for water and a plan of the works required (*see* para. **3.09**);

To this chapter has been added a range of provisions from the Water Resources Act, 1963, dealing with the conservation and protection from pollution of water resources and water in supply. Reference is also made to Part XIV (ss.71-73) (*Pollution of water by manufacture, etc. of gas*) of the Third Schedule to the

Water Act, 1945. The licensing of abstraction has well outgrown its initial introduction in the Water Act, 1945, and due to its importance and length as now contained in the Water Resources Act, 1963, this subject is considered separately in Chapter 7.

This chapter further contains provisions dealing with the Drought Act, 1976, the statutes concerned with safety in reservoirs, and water recreation.

DEFINITIONS OF CERTAIN EXPRESSIONS USED IN THE WATER ACT 1945 THROUGHOUT PART (A) OF THIS CHAPTER ARE GIVEN IN PARA. **2.02.**

DEFINITIONS OF CERTAIN EXPRESSIONS USED IN THE THIRD SCHEDULE TO THE WATER ACT 1945 THROUGHOUT PART (A) OF THIS CHAPTER ARE GIVEN IN PARA. **2.03.**

DEFINITIONS OF CERTAIN EXPRESSIONS USED IN THE WATER RESOURCES ACT 1963 THROUGHOUT PART (B) OF THIS CHAPTER ARE GIVEN IN PARA. **2.04.**

(A) PROVISIONS FROM THE WATER ACT 1945

(For definitions of certain expressions used in the Water Act 1945, see para. **2.02**).

(For definitions of certain expressions used in the Third Schedule to the Water Act, 1945, see para **2.03**).

4.02 Prevention of Waste of Underground Water
(W.A. 1945, s.14; W.A. 1948, s. 5; W.R.A. 1963, Sch.14, Part II; W.A. 1973, Sch.8, para. 48; C.L.A. 1977, Sch. 6)

A person must not (a) cause or allow underground water to run to waste from a well, borehole or other work except for the purpose of testing the extent or quality of the supply or cleaning, sterilising, examining or repairing the well, borehole or other work; or (b) abstract from a well, borehole or other work water in excess of his reasonable requirements. But where underground water interferes or threatens to interfere with the execution or operation of underground works (whether waterworks or not) it is not an offence to cause or allow the water to run to waste so far as may be necessary to enable the works to be executed or operated, if no other method of disposing of the water is reasonably practicable. A person who contravenes any of the above provisions is, in respect of each offence, liable on summary conviction to a fine not exceeding £200 and the court may, on the conviction of a person, order that the well, borehole or other work shall be effectively sealed or may make such order as is necessary to prevent waste of water. If a person fails to comply with an order of the court, the court may, on the application of the water authority within whose area the well, borehole or other work is situated, authorise the authority to take necessary steps to execute the order and any expenses so incurred are recoverable summarily as a civil debt from the person convicted.

An officer of a water authority authorised for the purpose by the authority (on producing his authority if required) is entitled at reasonable hours (i) to enter any premises in the water authority area for the purpose of ascertaining whether there is or has been on or in connection with the premises a contravention of the above provisions; or (ii) to enter any premises in which the authority has been authorised to execute an order of the court for the purpose of executing that order; Section 48 of the W.A. 1945, relating to entry of premises (*see* para. **10.07**) applies to such right of entry.

4.03 Agreements as to Drainage, etc of Land
(W.A. 1945, s.15; W.A. 1973, Sch.8, para. 49)

Statutory water undertakers may enter into agreements with the owners and occupiers of land, or with a local authority, as to the execution of any necessary works for the purpose of draining the land, or for more effectually collecting, conveying or preserving the purity of water which the undertakers are authorised to take. Where the execution of such works would result in the discharge of water into a watercourse otherwise than thrugh public sewers, the undertakers must before entering into an agreement consult (a) any water authority exercising functions in relation to the watercourse; and (b) if the watercourse is subject to the jurisdiction of a navigation authority, consult that authority.

4.04 Power to Prohibit or Restrict Temporarily the use of Hosepipes
(W.A. 1945, s.16; W.A. 1948, s.6; C.L.A. 1977, Sch.6)

If statutory water undertakers consider that a serious deficiency of water available for distribution by them exists, or is threatened, they may prohibit or restrict as respects the whole or part of their limits of supply the use, for the purpose of watering private gardens or washing private motor cars, of water supplied by them and drawn through a hosepipe or similar apparatus, for such period as they think necessary.

Before the prohibition or restriction comes into force, the undertakers must give public notice in two or more newspapers circulating in the area affected of the prohibition or restriction and of the date when it comes into force. A person who contravenes the provisions of the prohibition or restriction while it is in force is liable on summary conviction to a fine not exceeding £200.

Where a prohibition or restriction is imposed, charges made by the undertakers for the use of a hosepipe or similar apparatus are subject to a reasonable reduction to be settled in case of dispute by the magistrates court and where a charge is paid in advance any necessary repayment or adjustment must be made by the undertakers.

Whilst a prohibition or restriction is in force, an officer of the undertakers (on producing his authority if required) is entitled at reasonable hours to enter any premises to which the prohibition or restriction applies for the purpose of ascertaining whether there is or has been a contravention of the prohibition or restriction; and section 48 of the W.A. 1945, relating to entry of premises (*see* para. **10.07**) applies to such right of entry.

As to making orders for meeting serious deficiencies in water supplies due to exceptional shortage of rain, see the Drought Act, 1976 (referred to in paras. **4.19-4.22**).

4.05 Byelaws for Preventing Waste, Misuse or Contamination of Water
(W.A. 1945, s.17)

Statutory water undertakers may make byelaws for preventing waste, undue consumption, misuse or contamination of water they supply, and the byelaws may include provisions (a) prescribing the size, nature, materials, strength and workmanship, and the mode of arranging, connection, disconnection, alteration and repair, of the water fittings to be used; and (b) forbidding the use of water fittings which are of such a nature or are so arranged or connected as to cause or permit, or be likely to cause or permit, waste, undue consumption, misuse, erroneous measurement or contamination of water, or reverberation in pipes. If a person contravenes the provision of a byelaw, the undertakers may (without prejudice to their right to take procedings for a fine) cause water fittings belonging to or used by that person which are not in accordance with the requirements of the byelaws to be altered, repaired or replaced, and can recover the expenses reasonably incurred by them in doing so from the person in default summarily as a civil debt. No account must be taken of radioactivity in the exercise, performance or enforcement of this provision (*Radioactive Substances Act,* 1960).

For procedures relating to the making, implication and confirmation of Byelaws, *see* para **9.08** *post.*

NOTE: The Health and Safety at Work etc Act 1974, sect. 61 enables the Secretary of State to make buidling regulations with respect to the design and construction of buildings and the provisions of services, fittings and equipment in or in connection with the buildings. Such regulations may include regulations preventing waste, undue consumption, mis-use or contamination of water; see also Schedule 5 of the Act in relation to the subject matter of such Building Regulations. The scope of the enabling powers is widened; the Regulations may prescribe the manner in which the work is to be carried out.

4.06 Byelaws for Preventing Pollution of Water of Undertakers (W.A. 1945, s.18)

Statutory water undertakers may for the purpose of protecting against pollution water (surface or underground) belonging to them or which they are authorised to take by byelaws (a) define the area necessary for exercising control; and (b) prohibit or regulate the doing within the area of any act specified in the byelaws. Byelaws may contain different provisions for different parts of the area. Where an area has been defined by byelaws, the undertakers may by notice require either the owner or occupier of premises within the area to execute and keep in good repair such works as they consider necessary for preventing pollution of their water, and failure to comply with such requirement renders him liable to the same penalties as if he had committed an act prohibited by the byelaws. An owner or occupier who considers that a requirement is unreasonable may, within 28 days after service of the requirement on him, appeal to the Secretary of State, and there is a right of compensation against the undertakers in specified circumstances. Where a person has failed to comply with a requirement and either he has not appealed to the Secretary of State and the time for appealing has expired, or his appeal has been dismissed or the requirement has been modified and he has failed to comply with the requirement as modified, the undertakers may (without prejudice to their right to take proceedings for a fine) execute and keep in good repair the works specified in the requirement, and may recover the expenses they have reasonably incurred in default summarily as a civil debt.

The Radioactive Substances Act, 1960, provides that no account must be taken of radioactivity in the exercise, performance, or enforcement of this provision.

For the procedures relating to the making, publication and confirmation of Byelaws, *see* para. **9.08** *post*.

NOTE: Section 18 Water Act 1945 and Section 79(1)(2) and (7) and in part (8) of the Water Resources Act 1963 are repealed from a date or dates to be appointed by the Secretary of State pursuant to Section 108 and Schedule 4 of the Control of Pollution Act 1974. Statutory powers for the prevention of pollution of waters including specified underground water are provided in Part II of the Control of Pollution Act 1974.

4.07 General Provisions as to Byelaws
(W.A. 1945, s.19; W.A. 1973, sch.8, para.50; C.P.A. 1974, sch.2, para.15)

The Secretary of State is the confirming authority as respects byelaws made under ss.17 or 18 of the W.A. 1945, and Part II of Sch.7 to the W.A. 1973, applies to the making and confirming of such byelaws (*see* para. **9.08** *post*). It is the duty of the undertakers by whom the byelaws are made to enforce the byelaws. The byelaws may provide for imposing on a person contravening the byelaws a fine recoverable on summary conviction not exceeding £400 for each offence and in the case of a continuing offence a further fine not exceeding £50 for each day during which the offence continues after conviction therefor. Where statutory undertakers consider that the operation of any byelaw would be unreasonable in relation to any particular case, they may with the consent of the Secretary of State relax the requirements of the byelaws or dispense with compliance therewith.

4.08 Power of Secretary of State as to Byelaws
(W.A. 1945), s.20)

The Secretary of State may by notice require statutory water undertakers to make byelaws under paras. **4.05** or **4.06** *ante* in relation to such matters as he specifies and, in the case of byelaws under para. **4.06**, he shall specify the area for which the byelaws are to be made, and if the undertakers do not within three months after the requirement make specified byelaws satisfactory to him, he may himself make the byelaws. In the same manner, if the Secretary of State considers that byelaws made by statutory water undertakers under the above paras. **4.05** or **4.06** or similar byelaws or regulations made by undertakers under any other enactment are unsatisfactory, he may require the undertakers to revoke such byelaws or regulations and to make new byelaws as he considers necessary.

4.09 Penalty for polluting water used for human consumption
(W.A. 1945, s.21; C.P.A. 1974, sch.2, para.16;
C.L.A. 1977, s.28(2); W.R.A. 1963; W.A. 1973)

If a person is guilty of any act or neglect whereby a spring, well, borehole or adit, the water from which is used or likely to be used for human consumption or domestic purposes, or for manufacturing food or drink for human consumption, is polluted or likely to be polluted, he is guilty of an offence and is liable in respect of each offence (a) on summary conviction to a fine not exceeding £1,000 and in the case of a continuing offence to a further fine not exceeding £50 for every day during which the offence is continued after conviction; (b) on conviction on indictment to a fine or to imprisonment for a term not exceeding two years or to both a fine and such imprisonment. Nothing in this provision is to prohibit or restrict the cultivation of land according to the principles of good husbandry or the reasonable use of oil or tar on a highway maintainable at public expense. Officers of statutory water undertakers are empowered to enter premises for the purpose of ascertaining whether there is any contravention of this provision to the spring, well, borehole or adit (As to entry of premises, *see* para. **10.07**). The Radioactive Substances Act, 1960, provides that no account must be taken of radioactivity in the exercise, performance or enforcement of this provision.

NOTE: The Water Resources Act, 1963, introduced the word "borehole" but that modification to s.21 W.A. 1945 is excluded from the Thames Catchment area, the Lee Catchment area and the London excluded area — as defined in sections 125 and 136. That exclusion of the modification has been repealed by the Water Act 1973, s.40 and sch.9 thereto.

Under this head it is convenient to mention a number of powers possessed by local authorities under the Public Health Act, 1936. S.124 provides that all public pumps, wells, cisterns, reservoirs, conduits and other works used for the gratuitous supply of water to the inhabitants of any part of the district of a local authority shall vest in and be under the control of the authority, and the local authority may cause works to be maintained and supplied with wholesome water or may construct, maintain and supply with wholesome water other works equally convenient. If the local authority are satisfied that such works are no longer required, or that the water obtained from any such works is polluted and that it is not reasonably practicable to remedy the cause of the pollution, they may close those works or restrict the user of the water obtained therefrom. The liability of a local authority for subsequent flooding ceases when its undertaking vests in a water board (*Gibson v. Kerrier District Council* [1976] 1 W.L.R.904).

Under s.125 of the Public Health Act, 1936, a parish council may utilise a well, spring or stream within their parish and provide facilities for obtaining water therefrom and may execute any works including those of maintenance or improvement incidental thereto. S.141 of the same Act enacts that wells, tanks cisterns or water-butts used for the supply of water for domestic purposes which are so place, constructed or kept as to render the water therein liable to contamination prejudicial to health are statutory nuisances for the purposes of Part III of the Act. By s.140 of the 1936 Act a local authority may apply to a magistrates court to order the closing or restriction of a polluted source of supply from which water is used for domestic purposes or in preparing food or drink for human consumption.

The term "prejudicial to health" is defined in Section 343 of the Public Health Act 1936 as meaning injurious or likely to cause injury to health. The question whether the particular wells, tanks, systems or water butts are injurious, or likely to cause injury, is a question of fact; "health" is not to be confused with comfort or with a physical injury — there must be a real or potential threat of disease or the wells, tanks, systems or butts must be in such a state that they are likely to attract vermin.

If the reader wishes to pursue the phrase "prejudicial to health" as used in the Public Health Act 1936, Part III, he is referred to the *National Coal Board v. Thorne* [1976] 1 W.L.R. 543 and *Coventry City Council v. Cartwright* [1975] 1 W.L.R. 845.

4.10 Acquisition of land and execution of works for protection of water
(W.A. 1945, s.22; W.A. 1973, Sch.8, para.51)

Where the W.A. 1945, confers power on statutory water undertakers to acquire land for the purposes of their undertaking (*see* para. **5.02**), those purposes are deemed to include the purpose of protecting against pollution of water (surface or underground) which belongs to the undertakers or which they are authorised to take. Statutory water undertakers may on land belonging to them or over or in which they have acquired the necessary easements or rights, construct and maintain drains, sewers, watercourses, catchpits and other works for intercepting, treating or disposing of foul water arising or flowing upon the land, or for otherwise preventing water which belongs to the undertakers or which they are authorised to take from being polluted.

Before constructing any such works the undertakers must, if the proposed works will affect a watercourse (a) consult any water authority exercising functions in relation to the watercourse; and (b) if the watercourse is subject to the jurisdiction of a navigation authority, consult that authority. But this does not authorise the undertakers to intercept or take water which a navigation authority is authorised to take or use for the purposes of its undertaking, without the consent of the navigation authority.

Statutory water undertakers proposing to construct a drain, sewer or watercourse for the above purposes may with the consent of the highway authority (which may be given subject to conditions), carry the drain, etc under, across or along any street whether within or outside their limits of supply and Part VI of sch.3 to the W.A. 1945, as amended by the Public Utilities Street Works Act, 1950 relating to the breaking open of streets apply accordingly. But the consent of the highway authority is not required for the carrying by the undertakers of a drain, etc under a street maintainable at the public expense which is within the limits of supply of the undertakers. Any consent as above is not to be unreasonably withheld nor may an unreasonable condition be attached to a consent, and any question whether or not a consent is unreasonably withheld or whether a condition is unreasonable must be referred to an arbitrator to be appointed in default of agreement by the Secretary of State.

The provisions of the Arbitration Act 1950 apply to any arbitration proceedings.

4.11 Pollution of Water by Manufacture of Gas
(W.A. 1945, Third Schedule Part XIV (ss.71-73))

This Part of the Third Schedule to the W.A. 1945, concerns the pollution of water and waterworks of water undertakers caused by the manufacture or supply of gas and its provisions may be applied to a water undertaking by order made under the W.A. 1945.

The provisions of Part XIV are summarised below.

Provisions as to pollution by liquids resulting from manufacture of gas (Section 71)

A person manufacturing or supplying gas who—

(a) causes or suffers any washing or other liquid produced in, or resulting from, the manufacture or supply of gas, or the treatment of any residual products of the manufacture of gas, to run or be conducted (i) into, or into any drain communicating with, a spring, stream, reservoir, aqueduct or other waterworks belonging to the undertakers; or (ii) into a depression in the ground or excavation in such proximity to a spring, well or adit belonging to any such undertakers that contamination of water therein is reasonably probable; or

(b) wilfully does any other act connected with the manufacture or supply of gas, or the treatment of any such residual products as a foresaid, whereby any water of the undertakers is fouled,

is liable on summary conviction to a fine not exceeding £200 and to a further fine not exceeding £20 for each day during which his offence continues after the expiration of 24 hours from the service on him by the undertakers of notice of his offence.

NOTE 1: For other provisions relating to pollution from gas waste or gas operations, see s.68 of the P.H.A. 1875, and s.15 of the Gas Act, 1965.

NOTE 2: S.71 has been modified and amended by the Criminal Law Act, 1977, Sch.1, para.8, and Sch.13.

NOTE 3: S.15 of the Gas Act 1965 defines the responsibilities of gas authorities, i.e. the area boards, for interference with a water supply; such is without prejudice to their criminal liability under section 71 of the Third Schedule to the Water Act 1945.

Provision as to pollution by gas (Section 72)

If water belonging to the undertakers is fouled by gas belonging to a person manufacturing or supplying gas, he is liable to a fine not exceeding £50, and to a further fine not exceeding £10 for each day during which his offence continues after the expiration of 24 hours from the service on him by the undertakers of notice of his offence.

Power to examine gas pipes to ascertain source of pollution (Section 73)

For the purpose of ascertaining whether water belonging to them is being fouled by gas belonging to a person manufacturing or supplying gas, the undertakers may open the ground, and examine the pipes and other works of that person; but before proceeding to do so, they must give 24 hours' notice of the time at which the examination is intended to take place both to that person and also to the persons having the control or management of the street or other place where they propose to open the ground, and they are subject to the like obligations and liable to the same penalties in relation to reinstatement, maintenance and other matters as those to which they are subject and liable when breaking open streets for the purpose of laying water pipes.

If, upon examination, it appears that water of the undertakers has been fouled by gas belonging to the said manufacturer or supplier of gas, the undertakers may recover from him summarily as a civil debt the expenses reasonably incurred by them in connection with the examination and the repair of the street or place disturbed in the examination, but otherwise the undertakers must pay all expenses of the examination and repair, and must also make good to the said person any injury which may be occasioned to his pipes or other works by the examination. The amount of the expenses of such examination and repair, and of any injury so occasioned, shall, in default of agreement, be referred to arbitration.

NOTE: Arbitrations under the Third Schedule of the Water Act 1945 shall, except where otherwise expressly provided, be conducted by a single arbitrator to be appointed by agreement between the parties, or in default of any such agreement, by the Secretary of State. Such arbitration proceedings are governed by the Arbitration Act 1950 (W.A. 1945, Third Schedule, s.91).

(B) PROVISIONS FROM THE
WATER RESOURCES ACT 1963

(For definitions of certain expressions used in this Part, see para. **2.04**)

4.12 Duty of Water Authorities as Regards Water Conservation (W.A. 1973, s.10)

It is the duty of each water authority to take all such action as the authority may from time to time considers necessary or expedient, or as directions under the W.A. 1973 (*see* para. **3.05**) or the W.R.A. 1963, may require it to take, for the purpose of conserving, redistributing or otherwise augmenting water resources in its area, of securing the proper use of water resources in its area, or of transferring any such resources to the area of another water authority. Action for the purpose of augmenting water resources includes action for the purpose of treating salt water (whether taken from the sea or elsewhere) by any process for removing salt or other impurities.

A similar duty was imposed on the former River Authorities by Section 4 of the Water Resources Act 1963 except that to that section was silent on the question of salinity. Section 4 of the W.R.A. 1963 was repealed and replaced by Section 10 of the Water Act 1973.

In addition to the powers to give directions under the Water Act 1973, the Secretary of State and the Minister have power to give directions in relation to specific statutory functions under Section 107 of the Water Resources Act 1963 and under Section 108 of the W.R.A. 1963 for remedying of the faults. An Order given under Section 108 need not, by virtue of Section 134(4) of that Act be exercised by statutory instruments.

The functions referred to in section 107 of W.R.A. 1963 are:

(1) "new functions", *i.e.* the functions assigned by or under the W.R.A. 1963 to the former river authorities, other than—

    (a) land drainage functions;

    (b) functions of river authorities with respect to navigation, conservancy or harbour authorities;

(c) pollution prevention, in particular the exercise of functions under the Rivers (Prevention of Pollution) Acts, 1951/61;

(d) fisheries functions, or,

(e) any other statutory provision not contained in, or made or issued under, the River Boards Act 1948.

(2) "transferred functions" are the functions listed above in (a), (b), (c), (d), or (e).
See also section 82 of W.R.A. 1963.

Section 9 of W.A. 1973 transferred to the water authorities with effect from 1 April 1974 all the functions previously exercised by the river authorities, subject only to special provisions relating to land drainage in the London area or to the provisions of any instrument made under the W.A. 1973.

4.13 Control of Abstraction

S.14 of the W.A. 1945, originally provided that in areas which had been defined in a conservation order a borehole, well or other work for the purpose of abstracting underground water could only be constructed in accordance with a ministerial licence, although a licence was dispensed with in certain cases, *i.e.* where water was abstracted solely and to the extend necessary for a supply of domestic household water, or for experimental boring if the work was carried out with Ministry consent.

That provision has been replaced and greatly extended by Part IV of the W.R.A. 1963, under which (subject to certain exemptions) a person can abstract water from a source of supply, that is from an inland water or from underground strata, only in pursuance of a licence granted by the water authority (the licensing system is described in Chapter 7).

4.14 Inspection of Records kept by Water Authority
(W.R.A. 1963, s.16; W.A. 1973, sch.8, para.77, sch.9)

Each water authority must provide reasonable facilities for the inspection of any records it keeps of the rainfall, the evaporation of water and the flow, level and volume of inland water and water in underground strata in its area, and for taking copies of, and extracts from, such records. These facilities shall be available free of charge to all local authorities and internal drainage boards wholly or partly comprised within the water authority area, and shall also be available to all other persons on payment of such reasonable fees as the authority may determine.

NOTE: See the Civil Evidence Act 1968, ss.4, 5, and 6 re the admisibility of statements and records produced by or held on computers, microfilm etc. But see also *R. v. Pettigrew, R. v. Newark* (1980) *The Times* January 22, 1980 C.A. re inadmisability of evidence in criminal proceedings of certain computer produced statements where there was a lack of "personal knowledge of the matter" processed by the computer, Criminal Evidence Act 1965, s.1.

4.15 Gauges and Records Kept by Other Persons
(W.R.A. 1963, s.17)

A person, other than a water authority, who proposes to install a gauge for measuring and recording the flow, level or volume of an inland water (other than a lake, pond or reservoir or groups thereof which do not discharge into other inland waters) must (1) notify the authority of his proposal and not begin the work of installing it within the period of three months from the date of service of the notice or such shorter period as the authority may allow, and (2) not more than one month after the work is completed to notify the water authority where the records obtained by means of the gauge are to be kept; this provision does not apply to a gauge installed solely for the benefit of fishermen, nor to a gauge which is removed within 28 days after it is installed.

A water authority is entitled at reasonable hours to inspect records kept by any other person of the flow, level or volume of inland waters in the area of the authority and to take copies of and extracts from the records. A person who contravenes the provisions for installing a gauge, or who without reasonable excuse refuses or fails to permit inspection or copying of records, is guilty of an offence and liable on summary conviction to a fine not exceeding £20.

4.16 Minimum Acceptable Flows
(W.R.A. 1963, ss.19-22, sch.7; W.A. 1973, sch.9)

Each water authority is required to consider (a) for which inland waters in its area (other than lakes, ponds or reservoirs or groups thereof which do not discharge into other inland waters) minimum acceptable flows ought to be determined, and (b) whether, for the purpose of determining minimum acceptable flows, they ought to be dealt with simultaneously or successively, and if successively, how they should be grouped or arranged and in what order. Following this consideration, the water authority has to prepare and submit to the Secretary of State a draft statement or a series of draft statements indicating with respect to each inland water for which minimum acceptable flows are to be determined (i) the control points at which the flow of water is to be measured and the method of measurement to be used at each point, and (ii) the intended minimum acceptable flow at each control point.

Before preparing a draft statement for a particular inland water the water authority must consult (1) any statutory water undertakers having the right to abstract water from the inland water; (2) any other statutory water undertakers entitled to abstract from underground strata where it appears that the level of water in the strata depends on the flow of the inland water and the exercise of the right to abstract may be substantially affected by the draft statement; (3) any internal drainage boards from whose drainage district water is discharged into the inland water or in whose district any part of it is situated; (4) any navigation, harbour or conservancy authority having functions in relation to the inland water, or any such authorities having functions in relation to another inland water, or any such authorities having functions in relation to another inland water where changes in the flow of the inland water in question may affect the flow of the other inland water, or if the inland water is tidal and thee are no such authorities, the Secretary of State for Transport; and (5) the Central Electricity Generating Board.

In determining the flow to be specified in relation to an inland water, the water authority must have regard to the character of the inland water and its surroundings (and, in particular, any natural beauty which the water and its surroundings may possess) and to the flow of the water therein from time to time. The flow so specified shall not be less than the minimum which in the opinion of the water authority is needed for safeguarding the public health and for meeting (in respect both of quantity and quality) the requirements of existing lawful uses of the inland water, whether for agriculture, industry, water supply or other purposes, and the requirements of land drainage, navigation and fisheries, both in relation to the inland water and other inland waters whose flow may be affected by changes in the flow of that inland water.

The procedure relating to statements of minimum acceptable flows is set out in Schedule 7, Parts I and IV to the W.R.A. 1963.

Each water authority has to keep under review any approved statement of minimum acceptable flows relating to inland waters in its area and at intervals not exceeding seven years must submit to the Secretary of State a draft statement in substitution for the current statement, or proposals for amending the current statement, as the authority considers appropriate in consequence of the review. Each river basin in a water authority area has to be dealt with separately, but all inland waters comprised in on basin have to be taken together.

The Secretary of State may at any time himself prepare proposals for amending a statement of minimum acceptable flows after consulting the water authority in whose area the inland water is situated, except where he is acting on the application of the water authority.

Where it appears to a water authority, in the case of a particular inland water, that it would be appropriate to measure the level or the volume, either instead of, or in addition to, the flow, the authority may determine that the previous provisions relating to statements of minimum acceptable flows and their review shall apply in relation to the inland water.

The advantages of having minimum acceptable flows or notional such flows will be more apparent in considering the licensing provisions relating to abstraction where, in determining an application for a licence to abstract water from an inland water for which a minimum acceptable flow has been determined, the water authority in dealing with the application must have regard to the need to secure that the flow at any control point will not be reduced below the minimum acceptable flow at that point, or if no minimum acceptable flow has yet been determined, the authority must have regard to the considerations by reference to which a minimum acceptable flow would fall to be determined (*see* para. **7.10**).

The expressions "shall consult" and "have regard to" frequently appear in legislation. Whilst there is no case law directly bearing on the use of these words in the Water Resources Act, the courts have examined their implication in other legislation. In *Rollo v Minister of Town and Country Planning* (1948), Bucknill, L.J., defined a consultation as the provision of sufficient information to those bodies who are required to be consulted, and the giving of sufficient opportunity to those bodies to tender their advice. Providing these formalities are compiled with consultation will be deemed to have taken place.

The above interpretation of consultation (where there is a duty to consult) were upheld by the Privy Council in 1954 in the *Union of Benefices of Whippingham and East Cowes, St. James, re Derham v. Church Commissioners for England.* The expression "due regard" was examined by Harman, J., in *Proctor v Avon and Dorset River Board* (1953) in respect of fishery interests and the duty to pay "due regard" under the Land Drainage Acts.

When exercising its functions under the Water Resources Act, a Water Authority must take into account its duty under Section 28 of the Salmon and Freshwater Fisheries Act 1975 to maintain, improve and develop salmon fisheries, trout fisheries, freshwater fisheries and eel fisheries within their area.

The Water Resources Act 1963, Section 135(5), provides that for the purposes of any provision of that Act relating to existing lawful uses of an inland water, or of water from underground strata, a water authority shall be entitled, but shall not be bound, to treat as lawful any existing use thereof unless, by a decision given in any legal proceedings, it has been held to be unlawful, and that decision has not been quashed or reversed.

4.17 Special Provisions for Protection of Water Against Pollution
(W.R.A. 1963, ss.65 and 68; W.A. 1945, s.22)

Section 65 of the Water Resources Act 1963 enables a water authority to acquire either by agreement or compulsorily any land which is required for any purpose in connection with the performance of its functions — subject to the authorisation of the appropriate Minister.

Section 68 of the W.R.A. 1963 contains special provisions relating to the protection of water against pollution. Without prejudice to the generality of Section 65, land is defined in Section 68 to include such land as the authority require for the purpose of protecting against pollution water in:—

(a) any reservoir owned or operated by the authority or proposed to be acquired or constructed by the authority for the purposes of its being operated by the authority, or

(b) any underground strata within the area of the authority from which the authority has for the time being to abstract water in pursuance of a licence granted or due to be granted under the Water Resources Act 1963.

Section 22 of the Water Act 1945 conferred powers to acquire land for the protection against pollution of water, whether on the surface or underground, belonging to the authority or which the authority is permitted to abstract.

4.18 Byelaws for Protection of Water Resources
(W.R.A. 1963, s.79; W.A. 1973, sch.8, para.82; C.P.A. 1974, sch.2, para.15)

S.18 of the W.A. 1945, which empowers statutory water undertakers to make byelaws for the purpose of protecting water against pollution (*see* para. **4.06**) is applied to enable a water authority to make byelaws for the purpose of protecting against pollution (1) water in a reservoir owned or operated by the authority or proposed to be acquired or constructed by the authority for the purpose of it being operated by the authority, or (2) water in underground strata in its area from which the authority is currently authorised to abstract water under a licence granted or deemed to be granted under the W.R.A. 1963. Such byelaws must not conflict or interfere with the operation of byelaws made by the navigation, harbour or conservancy authority.

Where it appears to a water authority to be necessary or expedient to do so for the purposes of its functions relating to water resources or land drainage or fisheries, the authority may make byelaws prohibiting inland waters in its area from being used for poating (whether with mechanically propelled boats or otherwise), swimming or other recreational purposes, or regulating the way in which such inland water may be used for any of those purposes. Byelaws made in respect of inland waters may include provision prohibiting the use of the inland water by boats which are not registered with the water authority and authorising the authority to make reasonable charges in respect of the registration of boats. Such byelaws shall not apply to (a) tidal waters; (b) inland waters where functions are exercisable by a navigation, harbour or conservancy authority other than the water authority.

A person who contravenes or fails to comply with any byelaw is guilty of an offence and liable on summary conviction to a fine not exceeding £400, and if the contravention or failure to comply is continued after the conviction, he is guilty of a further offence and liable on summary conviction to a fine not exceeding £50 for each day on which it is so continued.

For procedure relating to the making, publication and confirmation of Byelaws, *see* para. **9.08** *post*.

(C) THE DROUGHT ACT 1976

4.19 Provision for Meeting Water Shortages — General
(D.A. 1976, s.1)

Upon an application being made to the Secretary of State for the Environment by a water authority or statutory water company (the applicant is hereafter referred to as "the authority"), if he is satisfied that, by reason of an exceptional shortage of rain, a serious deficiency of supplies of water in an area (in which the authority supplies water) exists or is threatened, he may by order make provision with a view to meeting the deficiency. An order may provide as follows—

(a) authorise the authority (or persons authorised to do so by the authority) to take water from a source subject to any conditions or restrictions;

(b) authorise the authority to prohibit or limit the use of water for any purpose, and this may affect consumers generally or a class of consumer (in which case this may affect a particular consumer within that class);

(c) authorise the authority (or persons authorised to do so by the authority) to discharge water to a place subject to any conditions or restrictions;

(d) authorise the authority to prohibit or limit a person (including other water authorities or statutory water companies) taking water from a source if the authority is satisfied that taking water from that source seriously affects the supplies available to the authority;

(e) suspend or modify (subject to any conditions) any restriction or obligation to which the authority or any person is subject as respects (i) the taking of water from a source; (ii) the discharge of water; (iii) the supply of water (whether in point of quantity, pressure, quality, means of supply or otherwise); or (iv) the filtration or other treatment of water;

(f) authorise the authority to suspend, vary or attach conditions to any consent for the discharge within the authority's area (whether by the authority or any other person) of sewage or trade effluent;

and the order may also contain such supplemental, incidental and consequential provisions as appear expedient to the Secretary of State.

An order does not affect the right of the authority, in the event of an interruption or diminution of the supply of water, to raise, charge and levy a water rate or minimum charge which might have been raised, charged and levied if there had been no interruption or diminution.

The purpose for which the use of water may be prohibited or limited in an order under provision (b) above must be one which is prescribed by the Secretary of State in an direction given to water authorities and statutory water companies generally and he may by a further direction revoke or vary a direction given by him. An authorisation given, prohibition or limitation imposed and suspension or modification effected by or under an order does not have effect longer than six months beginning with the day when the order came into operation. The procedure for making orders is contained in schedule 1 to the D.A. 1976, and Part I of schedule 2 to that Act, has effect as to the payment of compensation by the authority to persons affected by orders.

4.20 Provision for Meeting Water Shortages in an Emergency (D.A. 1976, s.2)

Upon an application being made to the Secretary of State by a water authority or statutory water company (the applicant is hereafter referred to as "the authority"), if he is satisfied that, by reason of an exceptional shortage of rain, a serious deficiency of supplies of water in an area (in which the authority supplies water) exists or is threatened, and is further satisfied that the deficiency is such as to be likely to impair the economic or social well-being of persons in the area, he may by order make provision with a view to meeting the deficiency. An order may provide as follows—

(a) any provision which could be included in an order under s.1 of the D.A., 1976 (see para. **4.19**) except one authorised under provision (b) thereof;

(b) authorise the authority to prohibit or limit the use of water for such purposes as the authority thinks fit;

(c)   authorise the authority to supply water in its area or in any place within its area by means of stand-pipes or water tanks and to erect or set up and maintain stand-pipes or water tanks in any street in that area;

and the order may also contain such supplemental, incidental and consequential provisions as appear expedient to the Secretary of State.

The Secretary of State is empowered to give such directions as he considers necessary or expedient to an authority on whom powers have been conferred by an order as to the manner in which or the circumstances in which a power is or is not to be exercised, and an authority to whom a directon has been given is bound to comply with it.

An authorisation given, a prohibition or limitation imposed and a suspension or modification of a restriction or obligation effected by or under an order does not have effect longer than three months beginning with the day on which the order came into operation. The procedure for making orders is contained in schedule 1 to the D.A. 1976, and Part II of schedule 2 to that Act has effect as to the payment of compensation by the authority to persons affected by orders.

Any works carried out under the authority of an order are included in the definition of emergency works in s.39(1) of the Public Utilities Street Works Act, 1950.

4.21 Supplementary Provisions as to Orders
(D.A. 1976, ss.3, 5(4)-(6))

These provisions apply to orders under ss.1 or 2 of the D.A. 1976 (*see* paras. **4.19** and **4.20**).

In an order (a) authorising the taking of water from a source from which water is supplied to an inland navigation; or (b) suspending or modifying (i) a restriction as respects the taking of water from a source from which water is supplied to an inland navigation; or (ii) an obligation to discharge compensation water into a canal or into a river or stream which forms part of, or from which water is supplied to, an inland navigation; the

Secretary of State may include provision for prohibiting or imposing limitations on the taking of water from the inland navigation or for the suspension or modification of any obligations to which the navigation authority is subject as respects the discharge of water from the inland navigation.

A prohibition or limitation on the taking of water from a source may be imposed so as to have effect in relation to a source from which a person to whom the prohibition or limitation applies has a right to take water whether by virtue of an enactment or instrument, an agreement or the ownership of land.

An order may authorise the authority, subject to any conditions and restrictions, to execute works required for the discharge of its functions under the order and (a) may authorise the authority for that purpose to enter upon land and to occupy and use the land to such extent and in such manner as requisite for the execution and maintenance of the works; and (b) may apply in relation to the execution of the works such provisions of the Waterworks Code as appear appropriate to the Secretary of State subject to any modifications and adaptations.

In an order which authorises the authority to enter on land the Secretary of State must include provisions requiring the authority to give the occupier and such other persons concerned with the land as specified in the order at least seven days notice of intended entry. The Secretary of State may require an authority on whom powers have been conferred by an order to furnish him with such information relating to the exercise by the authority of any of the powers as he considers necessary to enable him to discharge his functions under the D.A. 1976.

The power to make an order is exercisable by statutory instrument and the Secretary of State may by order in a statutory instrument revoke an order made by him. The power to make an order includes power (a) from time to time to extend a period specified in a previous order, but not to extend beyond a year the period of six months mentioned in s.1 of the D.A. 1976 (*see* para. **4.19**) or beyond five months the period of three months mentioned in s.2 of that Act (*see* para. **4.20**); (b) to vary a previous order in any other respect.

4.22 Offences
(D.A. 1976, s.4; C.L.A. 1977, s.28(2))

If a person (a) takes or uses water in contravention of a prohibition or limitation imposed by or under an order under s.1 or 2 of the D.A. 1976, or takes or uses water otherwise than in accordance with a condition or restriction so imposed; or (b) discharges water otherwise than in accordance with a condition or restriction imposed by or under such an order, he is guilty of an offence.

If a person (a) fails to construct or maintain in good order a gauge, weir or other apparatus for measuring the flow of water which he was required to construct or maintain by an order under s.1 or 2; or (b) fails to allow some person authorised for the purpose by or under such an order to inspect and examine such apparatus or any records made thereby or kept by that person in connection therewith or to take copies of such records, he is guilty of an offence.

A person who is guilty of an offence as above is liable on summary conviction to a fine not exceeding £1,000, or on conviction on indictment to a fine. In any proceedings for an offence it is a defence for the accused person to prove that he took all reasonable precautions and exercised all due diligence to avoid the commission of such an offence.

NOTE: The maximum fine on Summary conviction is the prescribed sum of £1,000 or such sum as is for the time being substituted therefore by an order in force as made by the Secretary of State pursuant to the powers contained in Section 61(1) of the Criminal Law Act 1977. Section 61 enables the Secretary of State when there has been a change in the value of money since the last occasion when the prescribed sum was fixed, whether by the coming into force of the appropriate provision of the C.L.A. 1977 or by any order made under Section 61, to make an order by which such other sums or sums as appear to the Secretary of State to be justified by the change in the value of money is substituted for the prescribed sum. Any order made under Section 61 by the Secretary of State must be made by statutory instrument and such statutory instrument is subject to annulment by a resolution of either House of Parliament.

(D) SAFETY OF RESERVOIRS

4.23 The Reservoirs (Safety Provisions) Act 1930

This Act, which at some time will be replaced by the Reservoirs Act, 1975, continues in force for the time being.

DEFINITIONS — "Large reservoir" means one designed to hold or capable of holding more than five million gallons of water above the natural level of any part of the land adjoining the reservoir. "Undertakers" means the persons carrying on any undertaking comprising or intended to comprise a reservoir, or when a reservoir is not used or intended to be used for the purposes of an undertaking the owners or lessees thereof, or in the case of a reservoir managed and operated by a water authority but not owned or leased by them, the water authority. (R(SP)A 1930, s.10).

CONSTRUCTION OF RESERVOIRS — A large reservoir cannot be constructed unless a qualified civil engineer is employed to design and supervise the construction thereof. The engineer gives a preliminary certificate specifying the level up to which the reservoir may be filled and with any conditions when the construction has reached a stage at which the reservoir can properly be filled wholly or partially with water. When the engineer is satisfied that the reservoir is sound and satisfactory and may safely be used for the storage of water he gives a final certificate to that effect. A reservoir cannot be filled with water either wholly or partially or used for the storage of water (a) before the issue of a preliminary certificate, (b) between the issue of a preliminary certificate and the final certificate otherwise than in accordance with the preliminary certificate or any variations thereof, (c) after the issue of the final certificate otherwise than in accordance with it.

When giving the final certificate the engineer must furnish detailed drawings and descriptions of the works constructed which form part of the final certificate and this is delivered to and kept by the undertakers (R(SP)A 1930, s.1).

INSPECTIONS — large reservoirs are subject to periodic inspections at intervals of not more than 10 years or such shorter period should a report recommend that the next inspection should be made within a shorter time period.

The Act provides full references to an independent qualified Engineering Arbitrator (as defined by Section 2(8) and (9)) in the event of a dispute arising between the undertaker and the Panel Engineer.

If the undertakers alter a large reservoir in such a manner that whilst the alteration does not increase the capacity of the larger reservoir that affects or may affect the safety of the larger reservoir, then, unless a qualified Civil Engineer, as defined by the Act, is employed to design and supervise the carrying out of the alterations, the undertakers must have the reservoir inspected and reported on by a qualified Civil Engineer as soon as possible after the alterations have been completed (R(SP)A 1930, Section 2).

RECORDS — The undertakers must keep records giving information about large reservoirs as to—

(a)   water levels and depth of water, with the flow of water over the waste weir or overflow;

(b)   leakages, settlements of walls and other works and repairs;

(c)   such other matters as may be prescribed by regulations (*see* the Reservoir Regulations, 1930 (S.R. & O. 1930 No. 1125) (R(SP)A 1930, s.3).

ALTERATIONS TO RESERVOIRS — When a reservoir is altered so as to increase its capacity and the reservoir is a large reservoir, or will when altered become a large reservoir, then the above provisions of the Act apply—

(a)   references to the construction of reservoirs includes references to such alterations as aforesaid:

(b)   in s.1 references to a reservoir are construed as references to that part of the reservoir which will provide the added capacity. (R(SP)A 1930, s.6).

APPLICATIONS TO CROWN COURT FOR AN ORDER— The Act also makes provisions for a local authority (county council or district council) or interested person to apply to the Crown Court for an Order if it is alleged that the provisions of the Act have not been observed. The local authority must be the Authority that is likely to be affected by the escape of water from the reservoir and the "interested person" is defined as any person resident in or interested in property in any area likely to be affected (R(SP)A 1930 s.4).

QUALIFICATIONS OF ENGINEERS — There is a panel of civil engineers for the purposes of the Act and a civil engineer may apply to be placed on the panel and the Secretary of State if satisfied after consultation with the President of the Institution of Civil Engineers that the applicant is qualified and fit to be placed on the panel appoints him a member of the panel (R(SP)A 1930, s.4).

LIABILITY FOR DAMAGE AND INJURY — The Reservoirs (Safety Provisions) Act 1930 provides that, in the case of reservoirs constructed after the 1 January 1931, in pursuance of statutory powers granted after 1 August 1930, a statutory water undertaker has an absolute liability for the escape of water **without proof of negligence**. In other words where damage or injury is caused by the escape for water the fact that the reservoir was constructed pursuant to statutory powers does not exonerate the undertakers from any indictment, action or other proceedings to which they would have otherwise been liable; the effect of this statutory provision is to make the undertaker liable to the rule in *Rylands v Fletcher* (1868) L.R.3 H.L.330 (*see* para. **5.10**). This provision prevents the undertaker from establishing what would otherwise have been a good defence, namely that the collection and keeping of the water had been authorised by statute and that either the statute concerned created a statutory means of redress or that the escape was not caused by negligence.

4.24 The Reservoirs Act 1975

The Reservoirs (Safety Provisions) Act 1930 was repealed by the Reservoirs Act 1975 which received the Royal Assent on the 8 May 1975. This Act will come into force on such day or days as may be appointed by Order of the Secretary of State as made by Statutory Instrument and the day appointed may differ with different provisions of the Act or for different purposes of the same provision. The objective of the act is to prevent escapes of water from large reservoirs or from lakes or lochs artificially created or enlarged.

Parliament passed the Reservoirs Act 1975 after a period of nearly 10 years of intense pressure from the Institution of Civil Engineers for tighter legislation. To a great extent the 1975 Act was modelled on the Institution of Civil Engineers' Reservoirs Committee Report of 1966. In that Report great play was made on the necessity to separate the functions of "policemen" from the undertaker — and on the designation in the 1975 Act of County Councils as the "enforcement authority".

DEFINITIONS — For the purposes of the Act "reservoir" means a reservoir for water as such and does not include (a) a mine or quarry lagoon which is a tip within the meaning of the Mines and Quarries (Tips) Act, 1969; or (b) a canal or inland navigation; a "raised reservoir" is one designed to hold or capable of holding water above the natural level of any part of the land adjoining the reservoir, and a "large raised reservoir" is one designed to hold or capable of holding more than 25,000 cubic metres above that level. Unless otherwise stated the provision made by the Act in relation to reservoirs extend to any place where water is artificially retained to form or enlarge a lake or loch, whether or not use is or is intended to be made of the water, and references to a reservoir are to be construed accordingly.

In relation to a reservoir "undertakers" means (a) in the case of a reservoir that is or, when constructed, is to be managed and operated by a water authority, that authority; and (b) in any other case (i) if the reservoir is used or intended to be used for the purposes of any undertaking, the persons carrying on the undertaking; or (ii) if the reservoir is not so used or intended to be used, the owners or lessees of the reservoir (RA 1975, s.1).

The Act does not *per se* confer on any person a claim to damages in respect of a breach by "undertakers" of their obligations under the Act but the Act, in addition to preserving civil liability for escapes of water, (the rule in *Rylands v Fletcher*), for the first time introduces the concept of criminal liability.

The Act extends to England, Wales and Scotland but not to Northern Ireland.

ADMINISTRATION — Each local authority (these are county councils in England and Wales) must establish and maintain for their area a register showing the large raised reservoirs situated in their area and giving information about them as prescribed by regulations. The register and copies of it have to be available for inspection by any persons at reasonable times. The local authority in whose area a reservoir is situated, if they are not themselves the undertakers, must secure that the undertakers observe and comply with the requirements of the Act and there is provision made where a reservoir extends into the areas of more than one local authority. "Enforcement authority" means the local authority charged with securing that the undertakers observe and comply with the statutory requirements and, where the context so requires, the authority so charged if the reservoir were a large raised reservoir; the provisions of the Act relating to an enforcement authority do not apply to a reservoir if a local authority are the undertakers and the reservoir is situated wholly in the area of that authority (R.A. 1975, s.2).

Each local authority must at intervals report to the Secretary of State on the steps they have taken as enforcement authority to secure that undertakers observe and comply with the requirements of the Act or on the steps they have taken as undertakers to observe and comply with such requirements for any reservoir situated wholly in their area. The Secretary of State may hold an inquiry into the question whether a local authority have failed to perform any of their functions undr the Act in a case where they ought to have performed them, and if satisfied that there has been a failure, he may by order declare the authority to be in default and direct the authority to perform such functions as may be specified in the order and the manner and time within which such functions are to be performed (R.A. 1975, s.3).

For the purposes of the Act there are panels of civil engineers and a civil engineer may apply to be placed on a panel and appointed if the Secretary of State is satisfied after consultation with the President of the Institution of Civil Engineers that the applicant is qualified and fit to be placed on the panel. An appointment is for a term of five years and there is provision for payment of expenses incurred by the Institution and for the removal of engineers from a panel (R.A. 1975, s.4).

NEW AND ALTERED RESERVOIRS — A large raised reservoir cannot be constructed (whether as a new reservoir or by altering an existing reservoir that is not a large raised reservoir) or altered so as to increase its capacity, unless a qualified civil engineer (referred to as "the construction engineer") is employed to design and supervise the construction or alteration. An abandoned reservoir which is brought back into use after alteration to increase its capacity is treated as the construction of a new reservoir. A large raised reservoir which is constructed as a new reservoir cannot be used for the storage of water, or be filled wholly or partially with water, except in accordance with the certificate of the construction engineer responsible for its construction.

A large raised reservoir which is constructed by altering an existing reservoir that is not a large raised reservoir cannot have the addition to the reservoir used for the storage of water, or be filled wholly or partially with water, except in accordance with the certificate of the construction engineer responsible for the construction of the reservoir. Where a large raised reservoir is altered so as to increase its capacity, then from the time when the construction engineer responsible for the alteration gives a certificate for the reservoir, it cannot be used for the storage of water, or be filled wholly or partially with water, except in accordance with the certificate. Where the construction or alteration of a reservoir is required to be supervised by a construction engineer, the reservoir is under his supervision until he gives his final certificate for the reservoir (R.A. 1975, s.6).

CERTIFICATE OF CONSTRUCTION ENGINEERS —
As soon as the construction engineer responsible for any reservoir or addition thereto considers that the construction or addition has reached a stage at which it can properly be filled wholly or partially with water, he is required to give a preliminary certificate specifying the level up to which it may be filled and any conditions subject to which it may be filled. A preliminary certificate may be superseded from time to time by the issue of a further preliminary certificate varying the previous certificate, whether as to water level or conditions.

Where the construction engineer responsible for an addition to a large raised reservoir considers during the carrying out of the alteration that the reservoir ought not to be filled with water up to the level or subject to the conditions that would be lawful apart from this provision, he may give an interim certificate specifying the level up to which it may be filled until the issue of a preliminary certificate and any conditions subject to which it may be filled.

Three years after a preliminary certificate is first issued for a reservoir or addition thereto or at any time thereafter, if the construction engineer is satisfied that the reservoir (or the reservoir with the addition) is sound and satisfactory and may safely be used for the storage of water, he must give a final certificate to that effect which specifies the level up to which mater may be stored and any conditions subject to which it may be stored. If the construction engineer has not issued his final certificate five years after issuing a preliminary certificate for a reservoir or additon thereto, he must give the undertakers a written explanation of his reasons for deferring the issue of the final certificate.

The construction engineer for a reservoir or addition thereto must after completion of the works and not later than the giving of the final certificate, give a certificate that the works have been efficiently executed in accordance with the drawings and descriptions annexed to the certificate, and shall annex to the certificate detailed drawings and descriptions giving information of the works actually constructed with dimensions and levels and details of the geological strata or deposits encountered or excavations made (R.A. 1975, s.7).

POWERS OF ENFORCEMENT AUTHORITY FOR NON-COMPLIANCE — Where it appears to the enforcement authority either (a) that a large raised reservoir is being constructed (whether as a new reservoir or by altering an existing reservoir that is not a large raised reservoir) or is being altered so as to increase its capacity; or (b) that, a large raised reservoir having been so constructed or altered, no final certificate has yet been given for the reservoir on the construction or alteration, but that no qualified civil engineer is responsible for the reservoir or addition as construction engineer, the authority may by written notice served on the undertakers require them within 28 days after the date of service to appoint a qualified civil engineer for the purposes of this provision, unless an appointment has already been made, and to notify the authority of the appointment.

An engineer must be so appointed to inspect the reservoir and report on the construction or alteration, and to supervise the reservoir until he gives a final certificate therefor. The report is to include any recommendations the engineer sees fit to make as to measures to be taken in the interests of safety. An engineer acting under this provision has the same powers and duties (subject to the modifications under s.8(5)-(7)) relating to the giving of preliminary, interim and final certificates as if he were the construction engineer for the reservoir or addition thereto (R.A. 1975, s.8).

RE-USE OF ABANDONED RESERVOIRS — Where the use of a large raised reservoir as a reservoir has been abandoned it must not again be used as a reservoir unless a qualified civil engineer has been employed to inspect the reservoir and report on it, and to supervise the reservoir until he gives a final certificate. Where a large raised reservoir is brought back into use as a reservoir after that use had been abandoned, it must not be used for the storage of water, or be filled wholly or partially with water, except in accordance with the certificate of the engineer. The report of the engineer shall include in it any recommendations he sees fit to make as to measures to be taken in the interests of safety, and the reservoir must not be used as such if those recommendations have not been carried into effect. These provisions do not apply to a reservoir, if before it is brought back into use, it is either (a) altered in such manner as to be treated as the construction of a new reservoir; or (b) it is altered under the supervision of a qualified civil engineer so as not to be a large raised reservoir when brought back into use.

Where it appears to the enforcement authority (a) that a large raised reservoir has been brought back into use as a reservoir after such use had been abandoned but that a report has not been obtained as required above; or (b) that a report obtained on a reservoir includes a recommendation as to measures to be taken in the interests of safety that has not been carried into effect, the authority may serve notice on the undertakers requiring them within 28 days after service to appoint a qualified civil engineer for the above purposes or requiring them to carry the recommendation into effect (R.A. 1975, s.9).

INSPECTIONS — The undertakers are required to have any large raised reservoirs inspected periodically by an independent qualified civil engineer (referred to as "the inspecting engineer") and obtain from him a report of the result of his inspection. Unless it is being supervised by a construction engineer, a large raised reservoir must be inspected —

(a) within two years from the date of any final certificate given for the construction of the reservoir or for any alteration to it;

(b) as soon as practicable after alterations to the reservoir which do not increase its capacity but might affect its safety and which have not been designed and supervised by a qualified civil engineer;

(c) at any time when the supervising engineer so recommends;

(d) within ten years from the last inspection or within a less interval as may be recommended in the report of the inspecting engineer on the last inspection.

As soon as practicable after an inspection, the inspecting engineer must report on the result of the inspection with any recommendations made as to the time of the next inspection or about measures to be taken in the interests of safety; a note must be included of any matters that need to be watched by the supervising engineer during the period before the next inspection of the reservoir. When making his report, an inspecting engineer has to give a certificate stating whether or not the report includes recommendations as to measures to be taken in the interests of safety and a recommendation as to the time and period of the next inspection. As soon as practicable the undertakers shall carry the recommendations into effect under the supervision of a qualified civil engineer.

Where it appears to the enforcement authority in the case of a large raised reservoir (a) that an inspection and report thereon have not been made as required; or (b) that the latest report of the inspecting engineer includes a recommendation as to measures to be taken in the interests of safety that has not been carried into effect as so required, the authority may serve written notice on the undertakers requiring them within 28 days after the service to appoint an independent qualified civil engineer to carry out an inspection and notify the authority of the appointment or require them to carry the recommendation into effect within a specified time (R.A. 1975, s.10).

RECORDS — For every large raised reservoir the undertakers must keep a record in a form prescribed by regulations of (a) water levels and depth of water, including the flow of water over the waste weir or overflow; (b) leakages, settlements of walls or other works and repairs; (c) such other matters as may be prescribed. The undertakers must install and maintain the necessary instruments to provide the information to be recorded (R.A. 1975, s.11).

SUPERVISION OF LARGE RAISED RESERVOIRS — Whenever a large raised reservoir is not being supervised by a construction engineer, a qualified civil engineer ("the supervising engineer") shall be employed to supervise the reservoir and keep the undertakers advised of its behaviour in any respect which might affect safety and to draw the attention of the undertakers to breaches of specified provisions of the R.A. 1975. Where a large raised reservoir is not under the supervision either of a construction engineer or of a supervising engineer, the enforcement authority may serve written notice on the undertakers requiring them within 28 days after service to appoint a supervising engineer (R.A. 1975, s.12).

DISCONTINUANCE OF LARGE RAISED RESERVOIRS — A large raised reservoir cannot be altered in order to render it incapable of holding more than 25,000 cubic metres of water above the natural level of any part of the land adjoining the reservoir, unless a qualified civil engineer is employed to design or approve and to supervise the alteration. An engineer so employed must give a certificate that the alteration has been completed and has been efficiently executed and a local authority will then remove the reservoir from their register of large raised reservoirs, but for the purposes of the R.A. 1975, the reservoir continues to be a large raised reservoir unless the alteration is made and a certificate given as above. (R.A. 1975, s.13).

ABANDONMENT OF LARGE RAISED RESERVOIRS — Where the use of a large raised reservoir is to be abandoned, the undertakers shall obtain a report from a qualified civil engineer on any measures that ought to be taken in the interests of safety to secure that the reservoir is incapable of filling accidentally or naturally with water above the natural level of any part of the land adjoining the reservoir or is only capable of doing so to an extent that does not constitute a risk. Before the use of the reservoir as a reservoir is abandoned or as soon as practicable afterwards the undertakers must carry into effect any recommendations as to measures to be taken in the interests of safety. In the case of a large raised reservoir where it appears (a) that the use of the reservoir as a reservoir has been abandoned but that a report has not been obtained as above; or (b) that a report includes a recommendation as to measures to be taken in the interests of safety that has not been carried into effect as required above, the enforcement authority may serve a written notice on the undertakers requiring them within 28 days after service to appoint a qualified civil engineer to make the report or requiring them to carry the recommendation into effect within a specified time (R.A. 1975, s.14).

RESERVE POWERS — Where undertakers are required by a notice from the enforcement authority under ss.8, 9, 10, 12 or 14 to appoint an engineer for any purpose of the R.A. 1975 and the undertakers fail to make the appointment, the authority may appoint an engineer and the provisions of the Act apply to him and to anything done by him as if he had been duly appointed by the undertakers. Likewise, where undertakers are required by a notice from the enforcement authority under ss.9, 10 or 14 to carry into effect any recommendation as to measures to be taken in the interests of safety and the undertakers fail to comply with that requirement, the authority may cause the recommendation to be carried into effect under the supervision of a qualified civil engineer appointed by them. Where an enforcement authority makes an appointment or exercises powers as above, the undertakers must pay them the expenses they have reasonably incurred by reason of the appointment or in the exercise of those powers (R.A. 1975, s.15).

EMERGENCY POWERS — Where it appears to the enforcement authority that a large raised reservoir is unsafe and immediate action is needed to protect persons or property against an escape of water from the reservoir, they may take such measures at the reservoir as they consider proper to remove or reduce the risk or to mitigate the effects of an escape. Also, where it appears to the enforcement authority that the use of a large raised reservoir as a reservoir has been abandoned, but there may from time to time be an undue accumulation of water there and immediate action is needed to protect persons or property against an escape of water, they may take there such measures as they consider proper to remove or reduce the risk or to mitigate the effects of an escape.

An enforcement authority who propose to exercise the powers conferred above shall appoint a qualified civil engineer to make recommendations as to the measures to be taken, and the measures so taken shall be carried into effect under the supervision of a qualified civil engineer appointed by the authority. As early as practicable the enforcement authority must serve notice on the undertakers giving full information of the measures being or to be taken in the exercise of such powers, but notice is not required if the authority are unable after reasonable enquiry to ascertain the name or address of the undertakers. The undertakers shall pay the enforcement authority the expenses they reasonably incur in exercising the powers (R.A. 1975, s.16).

OTHER PROVISIONS — An enforcement authority is empowered to enter upon land on which a reservoir is situated for the purposes of carrying out surveys or inspections or for carrying into effect a recommendation as to measures to be taken for various purposes of the Act (R.A. 1975, s.17).

Compensation is payable by an enforcement authority for damage or disturbance to land in exercising powers conferred by s.17 (R.A. 1975, s.18).

Undertakers who are aggrieved by a recommendation made by an engineer as to measures to be taken in the interests of safety etc. may refer their complaint to a referee (R.A. 1975, s.19).

Certificates or reports of engineers acting for the purposes of the Act must comply with certain provisions (R.A. 1975, s.20).

Undertakers are required to provide information in connection with reservoirs (R.A. 1975, s.21).

Undertakers are liable for criminal offences arising out of certain provisions (R.A. 1975, s.22).

Where damage or injury is caused by the escape of water from a reservoir constructed after 1930 under statutory powers granted after July, 1930, the fact that the reservoir was so constructed does not exonerate the persons for the time being having the management and control of the reservoir from any indictment, action or other proceedings to which they would otherwise have been liable (R.A. 1975, sch.2); the effect of this is to continue the operation of the rule in *Rylands v Fletcher* (*see* para. **5.10**).

(E) RECREATION

4.25 General Provisions as to Recreation
(W.A. 1973, s.20)

The 1973 Act provides water authorities and all other statutory water undertakers with the permissive power to take steps to secure the use of water and land associated with water for the purposes of recreation. The Act further imposes a positive duty on all statutory water undertakers (that definition includes water authorities) to make the best possible use of their rights to the use of water and of any land associated with water for recreational purposes.

Statutory water undertakers, other than water authorities, when discharging their duties with respect to recreation must consult the water authority for the area in which the water or land in question is situated and must take account of any proposals formulated by the water authority for discharging their own duty.

Previous legislation conferred the powers on water undertakers to provide recreational facilities in respect of inland waters. Section 80 of the Water Resources Act 1963 empowered the former River Authorities to provide recreational facilities, if it appeared to the former River Authorities reasonable so to do, at any reservoir owned or managed by the River Authority and certain other inland waters. Section 22(1) of the Countryside Act 1968 enabled statutory water undertakers to provide recreational facilities at their reservoirs. Neither of the Acts of 1963 or 1968 imposed any duty but gave only permissive powers; those permissive powers have been repealed (W.A. 1973, s.40 and sch.9).

The water authorities may, and with the consent of the owner of the inland water, secure the right to use water for the purposes of recreation; this right also applies to inland associated with the inland water.

In exercising its function in respect of recreation, a water authority must not obstruct or otherwise interfere with navigation which is subject to the control of a Harbour or Navigation Authority without the consent of that Harbour or Navigation Authority (W.A. 1973, s.20(4)).

In addition to the powers expressly granted by Section 20 of the 1973 Act, water authorities may exercise their powers, through Section 65 and 66 of the Water Resources Act 1963, to acquire, by agreement or by compulsory purchase, any land or rights in interested land which the water authority require for the discharge of its functions in respect of recreation. "Land" further the purposes of the 1963 Act includes land covered by water (W.R.A. 1963, s.135(1)).

Section 20(5) of the Water Act 1973 provides that where the Secretary of State makes an order authorising a water authority to carry out works of an engineering or building nature (Section 67 of the 1963 Act), or an order under Section 23 of the Water Act 1945, in relation to the construction or operation of a reservoir or conferring compulsory powers for that purpose on a water authority, and such powers are likely to permanently affect the area in which the works are situated and are not primarily intended to benefit the inhabitants of that area, the Secretary of State may include in the relevant Order specific provisions in respect of facilities for recreation or other leisure time occupation for the benefit of the inhabitants of that area.

Because of the special relationship, as prescribed by the 1973 Act, between the Welsh and Severn-Trent Water Authorities, the Welsh Water Authority is under a duty, after consultation with the Severn-Trent Water Authority, to prepare a plan for the purposes or recreation of the rights of both authorities to the use of water and land associated with water in Wales. The Severn-Trent Authority shall carry out such parts of the plan as affects their area in accordance with the agreed plan or as may be directed by the Secretary of State in default of any agreement. This is in addition to the duties imposed on water authorities under Section 20 of the Act to take steps for putting their rights to use of water to the best possible use for recreational purposes.

In addition to any powers conferred on water authorities by the Water Resources Act 1963 for the acquisition of land or interests or rights over land either by agreement or compulsory, the Welsh Water Authority are given specific powers under Section 21 of the 1973 Act to acquire by agreement rights to use water and associated land in any part of Wales for the purposes of recreation. Where such rights are acquired in the area of the Severn-Trent Authority, the Welsh Water Authority may instead of using it themselves for the purposes of recreation, grant the Severn-Trent Water Authority such derivitive estate, interest or rights as may be appropriate for enabling the Severn-Trent Water Authority to use the water or land associated therewith for recreation.

Where a water authority carry out works for or in connection with the construction of operation of a reservoir in Wales and those works permanently affect one or more communities and are not primarily intended by the water authority to benefit the inhabitants of that authority or those communities affected, the water authority concerned is under a duty to provide, or assist others to provide, the facilities for recreation or other leisure type occupation for the benefit of those inhabitants. This statutory duty is independent of any Order which the Secretary of State may make under Section 23 of the Water Act 1945 or Section 67 of The Water Resources Act 1963.

In discharging its duty in this connection, the water authority concerned must consult with the district council and the community councils of the communities affected.

The nature of the duty imposed by the 1973 Act on statutory water undertakers is to "take such steps as are reasonably practicable for putting their rights to the use of water and any land associated with the water to the best possible use" for recreation. That duty can be discharged either directly by the statutory water undertaker by itself establishing and maintaining recreational activities or indirectly by the statutory water undertaker through an agent.

The terms "recreation" and "recreational facilities" are not defined in the statute; they should therefore be given their normal and everyday meaning.

4.26 Recreational Facilities and Services
(Countryside Act, 1968, s.22; W.A. 1973, Sch.8, para.92, Sch.9; C.P.A. 1974, Sch.4)

For the purposes of s.20(1) of the W.A. 1973, relating to recreation (*see* para. **4.25**) statutory water undertakers may set apart any land held by them and provide, improve, alter, renew and maintain such buildings and other works and do such other things as may be necessary or expedient.

They may also—

(1) make such reasonable charges as they may determine with respect to the use for the purposes of recreation of any waterway or land held therewith and the use of any facilities or services made available by the water undertakers;

(2) let any works constructed by them for the purposes of providing such facilities or services;

(3) make byelaws with respect to any waterway owned or managed by them and any land held therewith for the purposes of order, for preventing damage to land held with the waterway or anything on or in the waterway or such land and for securing that persons resorting to the waterway or such land will so behave themselves as to avoid undue interference with the enjoyment of the waterway or land by other persons, including (a) regulating sailing, boating, bathing, fishing and other forms of recreation; (b) prohibiting the use of the waterway by boats not currently registered with the undertakers as provided by the byelaws; (c) requiring the provision of such sanitary appliances as may be necessary for the purpose of preventing pollution, and authorising the making of reasonable charges in respect of the registration of boats in pursuance of the byelaws.

4.27 Duties with Regard to Nature Conservation and Amenity (W.A. 1973, s.22)

In formulating or considering proposals relating to the discharge of any of their functions, the water authority and the appropriate Minister or Ministers must have regard to the desirability of—

(a) preserving natural beauty, conserving flora, fauna and geological or physiographical features of special interest and protecting buildings and other objects of architectural or historic interest and take into account any effect which the proposals would have on the beauty of, or amenity in, rural or urban areas or on such flora, fauna, features, buildings or objects;

(b)   preserving public rights of access to areas of mountains, moor, health, cliff, foreshore and other places of natural beauty and take into account any effects which the proposals would have on the preservation of such rights of access.

Where the Nature Conservancy Council are of opinion that an area of land, not being land managed as a nature reserve, is of special interest by reason of its flora, fauna or geological or physiographical features, and may be affected by schemes, operations or activities of a water authority, the Council must notify the water authority in whose area the land is situated.

F

Chapter 5

LANDS AND WORKS

5.01 Synopsis

This chapter relates firstly to the powers which enable statutory water undertakers to obtain water orders authorising the construction of waterworks and works in connection therewith, the supply of water (by non-statutory water undertakers) and the raising of capital or borrowing of money for any purposes of the undertaking. Secondly, land may be acquired compulsorily or by agreement for the purposes of the undertaking, and land may be surveyed before purchase to ascertain that it is suitable for the purpose for which it is to be acquired. Lastly, the essential "nuts and bolts" of the subject-matter is discussed, such as the powers for undertakers to execute works on land, obtain easements and lay mains under streets and across private property, work minerals and break open streets, by reference to those sections of the Waterworks Code (*refer back to* para 3.13) which are appropriate to this chapter, namely —

Part II (ss 2-9) — Works and Lands
Part IV (ss 11-18) — Minerals underlying waterworks
Part V (ss 19-21) — Power to lay mains, etc
Part VI (ss 22, 25, 27, 28) — Breaking open streets, etc
Part X (ss 40-44) — Laying and maintenance of supply
pipes and communication pipes
Part XI (s 45) — Stopcocks

DEFINITIONS OF CERTAIN EXPRESSIONS USED IN THE WATER ACT 1945 THROUGHOUT THIS CHAPTER ARE GIVEN IN PARA **2.02**. DEFINITIONS OF CERTAIN EXPRESSIONS USED IN THE THIRD SCHEDULE TO THE WATER ACT 1945 THROUGHOUT THIS CHAPTER ARE GIVEN IN PARA **2.03**.

(A) LAND AND MINERALS

5.02 Power of Statutory Water Undertakers to Acquire Land
(W.A. 1945, s.24; W.A. 1948, s.3; W.A. 1973, sch 9; Compulsory Purchase Act 1965, s.38)

The Water Act 1945, as amended, confers the power on any statutory water undertaker to acquire land by agreement, whether by way of purchase, lease or exchange, for any of the purposes of their undertaking, including acquisition of land for either the erection of housing accommodation for employees or for use as a recreational ground for employees. The requirement contained in The Water Act 1945 for the prior consent of the Secretary of State in respect of the acquisition of land by agreement is removed by virtue of Section 22(1)(2)(4) and Schedule 4 of the Town and Country Planning Act 1959.

The purpose of protecting water against pollution is a purpose for which statutory water undertakers may acquire land; Section 22 of the 1945 Act. The purposes for which land may be acquired compulsorily do not include the acquisition of land for the purpose of erecting houses and other buildings thereon for the use of employees or the acquisition of land to be used as recreational ground for their employees.

A statutory water undertaker, which by definition includes a water authority, may also acquire land by means of a Compulsory Purchase Order, subject to the procedural code of the Acquisition of Land (Authorisation Procedure) Act 1946 and the confirmation of the Secretary of State for any other purposes of the undertaking other than for the use of subsequent housing accommodation or recreational facilities for employees.

The Secretary of State, by Order, may authorise the construction, acquisition by agreement, or alteration of any water works connected therewith. Such an Order may contain such incidental, consequential and supplementary provisions, including provisions for the amendment or repeal of any local enactment, as the Secretary of State considers necessary or expedient including:—

(a) authorisation to acquire compulsorily any land required in the construction or alteration of those works;

(b) the application including modifications, if any, of the provisions of the Third Schedule of the Water Act 1945.

Special procedures, termed Special Parliamentary Procedure and as defined by the Statutory Orders (Special Procedures) Act 1945 applies to any order relating to the compulsory purchase of land belonging to the National Trust, "common land" which includes any land subject to the enclosed under the Inclosure Acts 1845 to 1882, and any town or village green, "open space" which means any land laid out as a public garden or use for purposes of public work recreation and any disused burial ground, or "allotment" which means an allotment set out as a fuel allotment or a village green allotment under an Inclosure Act or an ancient monument as defined in Section 15 of the Ancient Monuments Act 1931, as amended by the Ministry of Works (Transfer of Powers) (No. 1) Order, 1945 (S.R. & O. 1945, No. 991.)*

Water authorities have powers in relation to acquisition of land and execution of works under Part VI of the Water Resources Act 1963. Those powers include powers to acquire land or an interest right in on or over land either by agreement or by means of a Compulsory Purchase Order. Those powers, it is submitted, relate only to the functions of the former river authorities and do not apply to a water authority, when the water authority is discharging its functions as a statutory water undertaker.

Water authorities, like all statutory bodies, are children of the statute and must operate within the scope of the statute under which they seek to derive the necessary statutory powers; what is done beyond the scope of such powers is *ultra vires* and void. If the reader is interested in pursuing this particular subject he is referred to such interesting cases as *National Guaranteed Manure Company* v *Donald* (1859) or the *Attorney General* v *Smethwick Corporation* (1932).

Water authorities may provide housing accommodation for

---

* The responsible Minister is now the Secretary of State for the Environment.

their employees under the powers conferred by paragraph 13 of Part I to Schedule 3 of The Water Act 1973. The power to provide housing accommodation can be exercised by constructing, converting, enlarging or acquiring any building and whether by selling such accommodation or letting it or permitting it to be occupied with or without requiring the payment of rent or other charges. Furthermore, a water authority may permit a person for whom the authority provides accommodation while employed by the authority to occupy such accommodation after ceasing to be so employed.

It is important to note that water authorities do not have any general powers comparable to the general powers contained in the Local Government Act 1972 and the Town and Country Planning Act 1971. The power of a water authority to acquire land compulsorily must always stem from a particular statute and, as stated above, must be limited to a particular function. A water authority cannot exercise the statutory power of compulsory acquisition in any particular case unless and until it receives a specific authorisation so to do. The Acquisition of Land (Authorisation Procedure) Act 1946 prescribes the procedural code for such authorisation; the code applies wherever compulsory powers are conferred on local or public authorities by statutes existing at the time the 1946 Act was passed and by any subsequent statute which incorporates powers which have devolved upon water authorities.

Water authorities have power to appropriate land vested in them for one statutory purpose to some other statutory purpose; (Town and Country Planning Act 1959, s.23 and 4th Sch.).

The exercise of the statutory power of land appropriation is subject to the constraint that the power referred to must be vested in the authority by another statutory enactment; in other words, Section 23 of the Town and Country Planning Act 1959 regulates the manner in which the statutory permissive power to appropriate is exercised. Provisions contained in any statute, in whatever terms the provision is expressed, that a power to appropriate land for any purpose, (whether the purpose is so defined in a statute specifically or by reference to some other power exercisable by the water authority) is not to be exercised without the consent of the Minister, is by virtue of Section 23 of the Town and Country Planning Act 1959 freed from the requirement to obtain ministerial consent.

The exercise by the water authority of any power of appropriation is subject to the following provisions:—

(a)   land which consists or forms part of an open space (not being land which consists or forms part of a common or of a fuel or field garden allotment) shall not be appropriated except with the consent of the Secretary of State for the Environment;

(b)   land which has been acquired by the authority and has been so acquired in the exercise (directly or indirectly) of compulsory powers, and has not subsequently been appropriated by that authority for any purpose other than that for which it was so acquired, shall not be appropriated by that authority for any other purpose except with the consent of the Minister who, at the time of the appropriation is the Minister concerned with the function for the purposes for which the land was acquired by the authority.

Statutory water undertakers may apply for an Order under Section 23 of The Water Act 1945 to authorise them to acquire by agreement water works and works connected therewith, and an order made under Section 9 or 23 of the 1945 Act which authorises the construction or alteration of works or works connected therewith may also authorise the compulsory acquisition of any land required for the construction or alteration of such works, being land which could be authorised by means of a Compulsory Purchase Order made under Section 24 of the 1945 Act.

See also the Water Act (Compulsory Purchase) Regulations 1945.

5.03 Power of Statutory Water Undertakers to Hold and Dispose of Land
(W.A. 1945, s.25)

Statutory water undertakers may hold and use for the purposes of their undertaking land belonging to them and may with the consent of the Secretary of State sell, lease, exchange or otherwise dispose of land in such manner, for such consideration and on such terms and conditions as they think fit. In certain circumstances ministerial consent for the disposal of land can be dispensed with; see the Town and Country Planning Act, 1959, s.22(4), 26, sch.4.

5.04 Power to Survey and Search for Water on Land to be Purchased
(W.A. 1948, s.8; W.A. 1973, sch.9)

When a statutory water undertaker proposes to acquire land for the purposes of its water undertaking, or proposed water undertaking, the Secretary of State may authorise the statutory water undertaker to survey that land subject to:—

(a) Notice of the application having been given by the statutory water undertaker to the owner or occupier of the land;

(b) The Secretary of State has considered any representation made to him by the owner or occupier within thirteen days of the receipt of the Notice.

The Act further provides that where the statutory water undertaker is authorised by the Secretary of State to survey land, the power to survey shall include the power to carry out experimental borings or other works for the purpose of ascertaining the nature of the sub-soil or the presence of underground water thereunder, or the quality or quantity of such water.

No works can be carried out on land which is occupied unless at least 24 hours notice has been given to the occupier of the land; the land is held by statutory undertakers and those undertakers object to the proposed works on the grounds that the carrying out thereof would be seriously detrimental to the carrying on of their undertaking, the works shall not be carried out without the authorisation of the appropriate minister.

The 1948 Act provides that compensation is payable to any person interested in the land when the land has been damaged. The Act further provides that where in consequence of the exercise of the right of entry and the power to survey land, any person is disturbed in his enjoyment of the land, such person may recover compensation in the respect of the disturbance from the statutory water undertaker. Any question of disputed compensation shall be determined by arbitration; such arbitration shall be by a single arbitrator to be appointed by agreement between the parties concerned, or in default of agreement, by the Secretary of State.

If any damage or injury is caused by the escape of water from any land on which works have been carried out in pursuance of the statutory power conferred by Section 8 of the Water Act 1948, and such damage is not damage in respect of which compensation is payable under the parameter of the immediately preceding paragraph, nothing in Section 8 of the 1948 Act shall be construed as exonerating the statutory water undertaker from any liability, in respect of that damage, to which the undertaker would have been subject if such works had not been carried out by virtue of the statutory power.

Included amongst the purposes for which a statutory water undertaker (*ie* a Water Authority or a statutory water company) may acquire land for the purposes of their undertaking is the right to take protective measures against pollution of water; such measures may include the construction and maintenance of drains, sewers, watercourses, catchpits and other works for the interception, treatment or disposal of any foul water rising or flowing on that land.

A statutory water company must consult with the Water Authority, if the proposed works would affect any watercourse over which the Water Authority exercises functions or, if the watercourse is subject to the jurisdiction of a Navigation Authority, that Navigation Authority. Likewise it is necessary to consult with the Highway Authority if the proposed works affect the highway.

Consent from Water Authorities, Navigation Authorities or Highway Authorities must not be unreasonably withheld nor should unreasonable conditions be attached to any consent granted. Section 22 of the Water Act 1945 provides for an arbitrator to be appointed to make a determination regarding the reasonableness of withholding consent or the reasonableness of conditions attached to consent granted.

5.05 Minerals Underlying Waterworks
(W.A. 1945, Third Schedule, Pt. IV, (ss.11-18))

The following provisions of the Third Schedule to the W.A. 1945 may be applied to a water undertaking by means of an order made under the W.A. 1945—

Undertakers not entitled to underlying minerals unless expressly purchased (Section 11)

Where the undertakers purchase land they become entitled to such parts of any mines of coal, ironstone, slate or other minerals under the land necessary to be dug, carried away or used in the construction of waterworks authorised by the appropriate Act or order, but otherwise their purchase of the land does not entitle them to such mines and minerals which are deemed to be excepted from the conveyance of the land unless expressly conveyed.

Map of underground works to be prepared and kept up to date (Section 12)

Within six months from laying any underground works the undertakers shall mark the course and situation of all existing pipes (excluding service pipes) or other conduits for the collection, passage or distribution of water and underground works belongong to them on a map (of not less than six inches to one mile). The map must be corrected from time to time and kept at the offices of the undertakers and be open to inspection by any person interested free of charge.

Mines lying near works not to be worked without notice to undertakers (Section 13)

Unless agreed to the contrary the owners, lessee or occupier of mines of coal or other minerals lying under the reservoirs or buildings of the undertakers, or their pipes, other conduits or underground works shown on the map of underground works, or lying within forty yards or other prescribed distance therefrom, who desires to work the mines or minerals must give thirty days notice to the undertakers.

If undertakers unwilling to pay compensation, mines may be worked in usual manner (Section 14)

Having received a notice under s.13 and inspected the mines and minerals, the undertakers may consider that the working thereof is likely to damage their works (surface or underground) and to pay compensation to the owner, lessee or occupier thereof not to work the mines and minerals, and the amount of compensation in case of dispute is determined by arbitration. If the undertakers are not willing to treat with the owner, lessee or occupier for the payment of compensation, he may work the mines and minerals and drain them as if the appropriate Act or order had not been passed and he must make good any damage or obstruction occasioned to the property or works of the undertakers by working the mines or minerals in an unusual manner.

Power to make mining communications where continuous working is prevented (Section15)

If the working of mines and minerals lying under the property or works of the undertakers is prevented by reason of apprehended injury thereto, the respective owners, lessees and occupiers of the mines and minerals may make mining communications through the mines, measures or strata for ventilating, draining and working mines and minerals on each or either side thereof, but no communication may exceed the prescribed dimensions or sections or be made or cut so as to cause injury to the property or works of the undertakers.

Undertakers to pay compensation for expenses incurred by reason of severance (Section 16)

Unless otherwise agreed the undertakers are liable to pay compensation to the owner, lessee or occupier of mines and minerals lying on both sides of property or works of the undertakers for severance of the lands above the mines and minerals and for other specified reasons.

Undertakers may enter and inspect the working of mines (Section 17)

For the purpose of ascertaining whether any mines or minerals (which are subject to the restrictions of s.13 of the Third Schedule) are worked so as to damage any of their works, the undertakers, after giving twenty-four hours notice and on producing a document of authority, may enter upon lands in, on or near which the works are situated and under which they know or suspect mines are being worked, and may enter such mines and works connected therewith and inspect the same.

Undertakers not exempted from liability for injury to mines (Section 18)

Nothing in the special Act exempts the undertakers from liability to an action or other legal proceeding to which they would have been liable in respect of any damage or injury done or occasioned to any mines by means or in consequence of their waterworks, if the works had been constructed or maintained otherwise than by virtue of the special Act.

5.05.1 General Notes on Minerals Underlying Waterworks

Where land is purchased by a statutory water undertaker, either by agreement or by way of a compulsory purchase order, pursuant to a Ministerial Order which has incorporated part IV of the Third Schedule to the Water Act 1945, the statutory water undertaker, unless the contrary is established in the contract of sale, conveyance or Order, is entitled to dig, carry away or use in the construction of any works authorised by the Order all minerals underlying the land which have to be removed for the purposes of construction. Certain minerals are by Statute excluded from this particular right such as coal, iron ore, uranium, oil.

It is a question of fact in each particular case whether a substance is a mineral or not. The test that was advanced by Janes, L. J. in *Hext v Gill* (1872) 7 Ch.App. at page 719 has been firmly established by subsequent decisions; see *Glasgow Corporation v Farie* (1888) 13 A.C. 657 and *Waring v Foden* [1932] 1 Ch. 276. In essence what is meant by mines and minerals, depends on what those particular words mean in the vernacular of the mining world, the commercial world and land-owners at the time of the acquisition of the land or the right or interest in the land.

Part IV of the Third Schedule, Water Act 1945 introduced a
code in respect of waterworks constructed on or after 1 October
1945 (the date on which that Act came into operation); that code
can be applied by an order made under the 1945 Act to a
statutory water undertaker — *see* para. **5.06.**

Except as provided for in section 61 of the W.A. 1945, an
Order made under section 32 of that Act shall not abrogate or
affect the protection afforded to the owners, lessees or occupiers of mines or minerals lying under reservoirs or buildings or
pipes or other underground works constructed prior to the
Third Schedule being applied. It is therefore necessary to consider the "old mining codes" in relation to such waterworks.

The "mining codes" are incorporated in

(a)   The Railway Clauses Consolidation Act 1845 and Mines
       (Working Facilities and Support) Act 1923.

(b)   The Waterworks Clauses Act 1847, replaced by and incor-
       porated in the Water Act 1945, in relation to waterworks
       constructed after 1 October 1945 — and dealt with in para.
       5.05 *ante*.

(c)   The Public Health Act 1875 (Support of Sewers) Amend-
       ment Act 1883.

The Atomic Energy Act 1946 empowers the Secretary of State
to acquire compulsorily the right to work certain minerals. The
right to work coal is vested in the National Coal Board by the
Coal Industry Nationalisation Act 1946. The Coal Mining (Subsidence) Act 1957 requires the National Coal Board to repair or
compensate for damage to all works of a statutory water undertaker in respect of damage resulting from the underground
working of coal. The National Coal Board must remedy or provide compensation for subsidence damage to property including
houses; the Act covers damage to land drainage, ancient
monuments and certain cases where subsidence causes injury
resulting in death or disablement.

Railway Clauses Consolidation Act 1845 provided the earliest
mining code of general application. This Act provides that
railway companies are not entitled to the minerals under land

purchased by them unless they expressly purchased the minerals. The Act then provides that anyone proposing to work the minerals under or within a prescribed distance of the railway must give 30 days notice of his intention to do so. If the railway company decides it requires the minerals needed for support of the railway to be left unworked the company serves a "counter notice" and the railway company pays compensation for the minerals sterilised in order to provide support.

If no counter notice is served, the mineral operator is free to work the minerals in the usual manner of working such materials in the district.

The mining code incorporated by the Railway Clauses Consolidation Act 1845 is not restricted to railways; it is usually incorporated into compulsory purchase orders. The inclusion of sections 77, 78 to 85 inclusive of the 1845 Act in a compulsory purchase order means that the acquiring Authority need not purchase any minerals under the land to be acquired unless the acquiring Authority so desires. The inclusion of section 77 excludes minerals from the conveyance, unless such minerals are expressly named therein and conveyed. Sections 77 to 85 inclusive, the "mining code" regulates the relationship between the acquiring authority and any mineral owner, ie the requirement to give notice of approach before minerals can be worked. Compensation is then payable if the acquiring authority, as the surface owner, then decides that minerals should not be worked.

The Waterworks Clauses Act 1847 applied to all waterworks the construction of which was authorised by any Act passed between the 23 April 1847 and the 1 October 1945 which declares that the 1847 Act is incorporated therein.

The mining code under the 1847 Act operates in a similar way to the code under the Railway Clauses Consolidation Act 1845; 30 days notice of approach is required and compensation has to be paid for minerals sterilised in consequence of the counter notice having been given. If no counter notice is given the mineral operator may work the minerals provided that he does not do so in an unusual manner and provided he does no wilful damage. Unlike the code in the 1845 Act, the code in the 1847 Act provides that if a counter notice is not given the minerals may be worked "as if this Act . . . had not been passed". The effect of this is that the mineral undertaker is subject to the common law rules even within the area of protection. Thus the right to withdraw support may be restricted or prohibited by some provision in the deeds relating to the surface land. Accordingly where sufficient protection is afforded by the deeds a statutory water undertaker may choose not to give a counter notice but to rely upon its common law rights of support.

It is important to note that for the purposes of the 1847 Act the statutory water undertakers are required to keep and make available up to date maps of any pipes, conduits or underground works.

The Public Health Act 1875 (Support of Sewers) Amendment Act 1883 regulates the right of a statutory water undertaker to subjacent support of any sanitary works (such as sewers or water pipes) vested in the statutory water undertaker or under the control of that undertaker. The Act was passed following judicial determination that the Public Health Act 1875 imposed on the owners of land through which a sewer was laid an obligation to preserve subjacent support to the sewer and so entitle the owners to compensation for being prevented from working their minerals. This right to compensation was immediate upon the sewer being constructed. The objective of the 1883 Act is to provide for payment of compensation only upon a statutory water undertaker serving a counter notice for the sterilisation of minerals. This applies to all "sanitary works" and is not limited solely to the support of sewers but includes water pipes.

The 1883 Act provides for the statutory water undertaker to pay compensation for such minerals as are not worked because of the counter notice or alternatively the undertaker may specify and define a limited nature and extent of support which the undertaker requires to be left; the quantum of compensation would be reduced accordingly. Such compensation would be assessed in accordance with the Land Compensation Act 1961.

The onus is upon the water undertaker to serve notice upon the owner of the subsoil as to the action to be taken; such notice must be served within 30 days. In the absence of such a notice, the owner of the subsoil may work the minerals but by virtue of section 4 of the 1883 Act, the owner or worker of a mine shall not be liable for damage to a sanitary work caused in or consequent upon the working of any mines in a reasonable and proper manner.

In order to call in aid the 1883 Act, the statutory procedures contained therein must be followed; the statutory water undertaker must have made and deposited maps showing the course of its mains or pipes.

(B) CONSTRUCTION OF WORKS: GENERAL POWERS

5.06 Orders Conferring Powers on Water Undertakers
(W.A. 1945, s.23; W.A. 1948, ss.2, 3, 14(7); W.A. 1973, sch.9)

The Secretary of State is empowered, on the application of existing or proposed statutory water undertakers, to make an order—

(a) authorising them to construct, acquire by agreement, alter or continue, and to maintain, waterworks and works connected therewith;

(b) if the applicants are not statutory water undertakers, authorising them to supply water in any area;

(c) authorising the applicants to raise capital or borrow money for any purposes of the undertaking;

(d) transferring to the applicants by agreement or compulsorily the undertaking or part of the undertaking of any water undertakers, whether statutory or not.

An order made under head (a) above cannot empower the applicants to acquire water rights or vary the quantity of compensation water required by any enactment to be discharged into a watercourse or the periods during which or the manner in which such compensation water is required to be discharged. The making of applications and orders is dealt with under Part I of Sch.1 to the W.A. 1945, and orders have effect subject to the licensing provisions of Part IV of the W.R.A. 1963 (see Chapter 7).

A combined order may be made either under ss.9 or 23 of the W.A. 1945 in order to avoid the inconvenience of making separate orders relating to the matter contained in those sections. An order under ss.9 or 23 of the 1945 Act authorising the construction or alteration of waterworks can authorise the compulsory acquisition of land for such purposes, being land which could be authorised by a compulsory purchase order under s.24 of the W.A. 1945 (see para. 5.02) and the schedule to the W.A. 1948, has effect for such purposes.

The powers of the Secretary of State are extended by the Water Act 1973, Section 20(5) whereby in certain circumstances the Secretary of State may make provision in the order for recreational facilities. The Secretary of State may by an order under this section apply to any water undertaking to which the order relates such of the provisions in Schedule 3 as appear to the Secretary of State to be appropriate and subject to such modifications and adaptations as may be specified in the Order. Power to revoke or vary Orders is contained in section 50 of the 1945 Act.

Planning permission for any development of land, such as the construction and alteration of waterworks, is required by the Town and Country Planning Act 1971, section 23, but certain developments by statutory water undertakers such as the laying of underground pipes may be undertaken without permission; see the general notes on Planning Legislation contained in Chapter 9.

5.07 Works and Lands
(WA 1945, Sch 3, Part II, (ss 2-9))

Where the provisions of Part II of the Third Schedule to the WA 1945 are applied to a water undertaking the following sections take effect —

Permissible limits of deviation (Section 2)

In the construction of any authorised works the undertakers may deviate laterally to any extent not exceeding the limits of deviation shown on the plans submitted to the Secretary of State and, where on a street no limits are shown, the boundaries of the street (including any verge or roadside waste adjoining it) are deemed to be the limits, and they may also deviate vertically from the levels shown on the plans to any extent, provided that (a) an embankment for a reservoir must not be constructed at a greater height above the general surface of the ground than that shown on the plans and six feet in addition thereto; and (b) a pipe or other conduit or aqueduct must not be raised above the surface of the ground otherwise than in accordance with the plans, except for the purposes of crossing a watercourse or railway or of crossing land where the consent of all persons having a legal interest therein has been given.

NOTE: Where Art 9 of the Water Authorities etc (Miscellaneous Provisions) Order 1974 (S.I. 1974 No 607) applies (*see* para **3.13**), s.2 is excluded by Art 9(5).

Limit on powers of undertakers to take water (section 3)

The undertakers must not construct works for taking or intercepting water (other than works for intercepting foul water) from lands acquired by them, unless the works are authorised by, and the lands on which the works are to be constructed are specified in, the special Act or some other enactment.

NOTE: Where Art 9 of the Water Authorities etc (Miscellaneous Provisions) Order 1974 (S.I. 1974 No 607) applies (*see* para **3.13**), words are added to the end of s 3 by Art 9(6)(a).

General power to construct subsidiary works (Section 4)

Subject to s 3 and to any other provisions of the special Act limiting the powers of the undertakers to abstract water, the undertakers, in addition to any works specifically authorised, may in, on or over land held by them in connection with their water undertaking, construct, lay or erect for the purposes thereof, or in connection therewith, and may maintain such reservoirs, sluices, tanks, cisterns, aqueducts, tunnels, culverts, mains, pipes, engines, pumps, machinery, filters, treatment plant, buildings and things for, or in connection with, the supply of water as they deem necessary. Electrical works or apparatus executed under this provision must not interfere with telegraphic lines or communication of the Post Office.

Power of undertakers to lay or erect telephone wires, etc (Section 5)

The undertakers may lay and erect across a highway and with the consent of the owners and occupiers across land telegraphic, telephonic or other electrical communication between their offices and any part of their works or between different parts of their works and the provisions of Part VI of the Third Schedule to the WA 1945 (*see* para **5.08**) relating to the breaking open of streets apply as respects a highway in relation to the laying, erection and maintenance of wires, posts, conductors or other apparatus.

NOTE: Where Art 9 of the Water Authorities etc (Miscellaneous Provisions) Order 1974 (S.I. 1974 No 607) applies (*see* para **3.13**), s.5(6) is added by Art 9(6)(b).

Penalty for obstructing construction of works (Section 6)

A person who wilfully obstructs a person engaged by the undertakers in setting out the line, level or site of authorised works, or knowingly pulls up a peg or stake driven into the ground for the purpose of setting out lines, etc, or knowingly defaces or destroys anything made or erected for that purpose, is liable to a fine not exceeding £25.

NOTE: The amount of the fine was increased to £25 by CLA 1977, s.31.

Power to acquire easements for underground works (Section 7)

Where the undertakers are authorised by the special Act to acquire land compulsorily for the purpose of executing underground works, they may, instead of purchasing the land, purchase easements and rights over or in the land sufficient for the purpose.

NOTE: Where Art.9 of the Water Authorities etc (Miscellaneous Provisions) Order 1974 (S.I. 1974 No. 607) applies (*see* para. **3.13**), s.7 is excluded by Art.9(5).

Persons under disability may grant easements, etc (Section 8)

Persons who are empowered to sell and convey and release any land may, subject to the provisions of the special Act, grant the undertakers any easement or right required for the purposes of the special Act over or in such land.

Extinction of private rights of way (Section 9)

A private right of way over land which the undertakers are authorised to acquire compulsorily is, if they so resolve and give notice to the owner of the right, extinguished as from their acquisition of the land, or from the expiration of one month from service of the notice, whichever is the later. The undertakers must pay compensation to all interested persons in respect of the extinguished right and in case of dispute the compensation is determined by the Lands Tribunal.

5.08 Breaking Open Streets, etc
(W.A. 1945, Third Schedule, Part VI, (ss.22, 25, 27, 28))

Part VI of the Third Schedule to the W.A. 1945 and the Street Works Code contained in the Public Utilities Street Works Act, 1950, provide the necessary powers (when applied by order to statutory water undertakers) to enable the undertakers to break open streets for laying mains, service pipes, plant and apparatus. The provisions of the Public Utilities Street Works Act, 1950, are not given here.

The provisions of Part VI are summarised below:—

Powers to break open streets (Section 22)

The undertakers may within their limits of supply for the purpose of laying, constructing, inspecting, repairing, renewing or removing mains, service pipes, plant or other works, and outside those limits for the purpose of laying any mains which they are authorised to lay and of inspecting, repairing, renewing or removing mains, break open the roadway and footpaths of any street and of any bridge carrying a street, and any sewer, drain or tunnel in or under any such roadway or footpath, and may remove and use the soil or other materials in or under any such roadway or footpath. Provided that they must in the exercise of such powers cause as little inconvenience and do as little damage as may be, and pay compensation for damage done as determined, in case of dispute, by arbitration (*see* para. **10.15**, Section 91).

Protection for railway companies, navigation authorities, tramway undertakers, etc (Section 25)

Except in cases of emergency arising from defects in pipes, plant or works, the roadway or footpath of a street or bridge (not being a street or bridge maintainable at the public expense) which is under the control or management of, or maintainable by, a railway company or navigation authority must not be broken open without their consent, but consent must not be unreasonably withheld and any question whether or not consent is unreasonably withheld is referred to and determined by the Secretary of State.

Remedies where undertakers fail to comply with foregoing requirements (Section 27)

If the undertakers fail to comply with, or contravene, any of the foregoing provisions of this Part of the Third Schedule, they are, without prejudice to their civil liability, if any, to a person aggrieved, liable to a fine not exceeding £25, and to a further fine not exceeding £5 for each day on which the offence continues after notice has been given to them by, or by an officer or agent of, the persons aggrieved.

NOTE: Fine increased to £25 by C.L.A. 1977, s.31.

Application of Part VI to verges and streets and highways not maintainable at the public expense (Section 28)

The provisions of this Part of the Third Schedule apply in relation to any land within the limits of a street, but not included in a roadway or footpath thereof, as if that land were, or formed part of, a footpath of the street.

5.09 Temporary Discharge of Water into Watercourses
(W.A. 1945, s.34; W.A. 1973, Sch.8, para.52, Sch.9; C.L.A. 1977, Sch.1, para.7)

Statutory water undertakers carrying out the construction, alteration, repair, cleaning or examination of a reservoir, well or bore-hole, line of pipes or other work forming part of their undertaking may cause the water therein to be discharged into an available watercourse and for that purpose may lay and maintain in any street (inside or outside their limits of supply) all necessary discharge pipes and apparatus, and such statutory provisions as to the breaking open of streets applicable to the undertakers (*see* para. **5.08**) apply accordingly. Except in an emergency and except as may be otherwise agreed in writing between the undertakers and the authority concerned, before commencing to discharge water through a pipe exceeding nine inches in diameter, the undertakers must observe certain procedures with any water authority and navigation authority exercising functions in respect of a watercourse into which the water is to be discharged and with certain other interests. The undertakers must pay compensation to persons for any damage sustained by them or liability to which they may become subject by reason of the exercise of these powers. The undertakers must secure that any water discharged under this provision is as free as reasonably practicable from mud and silt, from solid, polluting, offensive or injurious matters, and from any matter prejudicial to fish or spawn, spawning grounds or food of fish, and, if they fail to do so, are guilty of an offence and liable on summary conviction to a fine not exceeding £200 and, where the offence continues after conviction, to a further fine of £20 for every day during which it so continues.

5.10 Liability for the Escape of Water

The liability of a statutory water undertaker for water escapes from its pipes or mains is dependent on negligence. The standard of care is what is reasonable in the prevailing circumstances to prevent escapes caused by foreseeable eventualities. The escape of water from a water undertaker's pipes or mains is *prima facie* evidence of negligence; the onus is upon the statutory water undertaker to rebut the alleged negligence; *Snook v Grand Junction Waterworks Company* (1886) 2 T.L.R. 308; *Green v Chelsea Waterworks Company* (1894) 70 L.T. 547.

If the pipes are constructed in accordance with the usual practice of a person skilled in such matters, it is not negligence to prove that if they had been constructed differently, an accident would not have happened because the statutory water undertaker is not "bound to ransack science in the hope of discovering some scientific specific against possible accident"; *Snook v Grand Junction Waterworks Company, supra.*

In *Manchester Corporation v Markland* [1936] A.C. 360, H.L., one of the Corporation's water pipes burst and caused a pool of water to form on the road. The pool remained for three days and then froze in consequence of which a motorcar skidded and killed a pedestrian. The Corporation had taken the usual precautions taken by water companies to discover bursts and also relied upon information being supplied by the police, public transport and the highway authorities. The court held that the Corporation was negligent in not discovering the burst in the main road sooner than they did and not having a better system of discovering bursts. It was also held that once it was established that the Corporation had a duty to take some care, then there was no obligation upon the plaintiff to indicate the precise steps which the Corporation should have taken to discover bursts.

Where a water undertaker which had statutory authority to maintain a stopcock in the highway was warned of an escape of water from a pipe and stopped the leak and replaced some paving stones which they had to take up near it, the Courts held that the water undertakers were liable to a person on the highway who tripped over another paving stone, which had not been taken up, loosened by the escape of water, when they neither knew or ought to have known such a stone was loose; *Longhurst* v *Metropolitan Water Board* [1948] 2 All E.R. 834, H.L.

Under a permissive power conferred by statute the inference is that the general powers so conferred should be exercised in strict conformity with private rights and that no nuisance may be caused; *Metropolitan Asylums Board* v *Hill* (1881) 44 L.T. 653.

Where undertakers act under a permissive statute and water escapes without negligence on their part, they are not liable under the rule in *Rylands* v *Fletcher* or in nuisance for the consequences of the escape; it was stated in *Dunne* v *North Western Gas Board* [1964] 2 Q.B. 806 that a person acting under a mandatory statutory obligation does not incur liability under *Rylands* v *Fletcher* or in nuisance, whether or not the statute contains a saving clause retaining liability for the nuisance, provided that what is done is that which was expressly required to be done or is reasonably incidental thereto and done without negligence. Note that this proposition was questioned by Rees J in *Pearson* v *North Western Gas Board* [1968] 2 All E.R. 669, at page 672.

The doctrine of strict liability in respect of an escape of water does apply however to a statutory water undertaker in respect of escapes of water from a reservoir constructed after the year 1930 under statutory powers granted after July 1930; section 28 and schedule 2, Reservoirs Act 1975, which slightly amended section 7 of the Reservoirs (Safety Provisions) Act 1930. Such liability, under the Rule in *Rylands* v *Fletcher*, is owed to all the world; any person injured may sue. The only constraint to an action is the ordinary rule governing the remoteness of damage; see *Charing Cross Electricity Supply Company* v *Hydraulic Power Company* [1914] 3 K.B. 772, and *Cattle* v *Stockton Waterworks Company* (1875) L.R. 10 Q.B. 453.

The damage must be caused by the escape of water from the land of the undertaker to a place outside the occupation or control of the undertaker; if there is no such "escape" from the reservoir then in the absence of negligence there will be no liability under the rule in *Rylands* v *Fletcher; Read* v *J. Lyons and Company Limited* [1947] A.C. 156.

It must not be forgotten that the liability of the statutory water undertaker for water escapes could be dependent upon the terms of any particular covenant contained in a Deed of Easement if any such deed had been executed between the undertaker and the landowner from whom the statutory water undertaker acquired the land or any interest in that land.

There are duties imposed under the Health and Safety at Work etc Act 1974 whereby statutory water undertakers, amongst others,

(1)   Have a general duty as an employer to ensure, so far as is reasonably practicable, the health, safety and welfare at work of all of their employees.

(2)   Have a duty to conduct their undertaking in such a way as to ensure, so far as is reasonably practicable, that persons not in the employment of the statutory water undertaker who may be affected thereby are not thereby exposed to risks to their health or safety. There is a converse duty on every self employed person to conduct himself in such a way as to ensure, so far as is reasonably practicable, that he and other persons, not being his employees, who may be affected thereby are not thereby exposed to risks to their health or safety.

(3) There is a duty on every statutory water undertaker, amongst others, who has, to any extent, control of premises (which by definition includes any installation on land including the foreshore and other land intermittently covered by water or any installation resting on land covered with water or the subsoil thereof or any vehicle, vessel, and/or moveable structure), or control of the means of the access or egress to or from such premises or of any plant or substance in such premises to take such measures as it is reasonable for a person in the position of the statutory water undertaker to take to ensure, so far as is reasonably practicable, that the premises, all means of access or egress to or from the premises available for use by persons using the premises, and any plant or substance in the premises or, as the case may be, provided for use there, is or are safe and without risks to health (*Health and Safety at Work etc.Act* 1974, ss.2, 3, 4 and 53).

It must not be forgotten that the liability of a statutory water undertaker for water escapes could also be dependent upon a contractual relationship, namely upon the terms of any particular covenant contained in a Deed of Easement if any such deed had been executed between the undertaker and the landowner from whom the statutory water undertaker acquired the land or any interest in that land.

As a result of increasing pressure from various vested interests, Parliament has now provided in Section 6 of WA 1981 that statutory water undertakers would no longer be able to claim the defence contained in *Green v. Chelsea Waterworks*.

Section 6 of the W.A. 1981 provides that where an escape of water, however caused, from a communication pipe or main of statutory water undertakers causes loss or damage, the undertakers shall be liable for the loss or damage. However, statutory water undertakers shall not incur any liability if the escape was due wholly to the person who suffered the loss or the damage. Furthermore, statutory water undertakers shall not incur any liability in respect of any loss or damage suffered by any excepted undertakers for which they would not have been liable apart from the provisions contained in Section 6. Excepted undertakers for the purpose of the Water Act 1981 are,

i) statutory undertakers within the meaning of section 290(1) of the Town and Country Planning Act 1971;

ii) any highway authority, within the meaning of the Highways Act 1980;

iii) any bridge authority, bridge managers, street authority or street managers within the meaning of section 39(1) of the Public Utilities Street Works Act 1950; and

iv) any person on whom a right to compensation under section 26 of the said Act of 1950 is conferred.

Section 6 of the W.A. 1981 further provides that the Law Reform (Contributory Negligence) act 1945, the Fatal Accidents Act 1976 and the Limitation Act 1980 shall apply in relation to any loss or damage for which statutory water undertakers are liable under the section, but which is not due to their fault, as if it were due to their fault.

Nothing in Section 6 affects any entitlement which statutory water undertakers may have to recover contribution under the Civil Liability (Contribution) Act 1978; and for the purposes of that Act, any loss for which statutory water undertakers are liable under that subsection shall be treated as if it were damage.

Where statutory water undertakers are liable, under any enactment or agreement passed or made before the coming into force of Section 6, to make a payment in respect of any loss or damage, they shall not incur liability under the Water Act 1981 in respect of the same loss or damage.

Section 6 of the Water Act 1981 shall come into force on such day as the Secretary of State may appoint by way of statutory instrument.

(C) MAINS LAYING —
COMMUNICATION AND SUPPLY PIPES

5.11 Introductory Note on Mains and Service Pipes

Water mains are provided by statutory water undertakers and may be laid either (a) in streets, subject to the code relating to the breaking open of streets (*see* para. **5.08**), or (b) across private property, provided proper notice is given the owners and occupiers and subject to the payment of compensation by the undertakers. It is common practice for undertakers to obtain an easement (which is registered as a land charge) for laying mains in private land with a condition attached not to erect structures over the main without permission.

The communication pipe (this is the section of service pipe between the undertakers' main and the street boundary or stopcock placed at the boundary of the premises being served) is laid at the cost of the consumer and when situate in a highway is laid by the undertakers who recover the expense from the consumer. The supply pipe (which runs from the boundary or stopcock to the premises being supplied) is paid for by the consumer and, again, when in a highway is laid by the undertakers. Once laid, communication pipes vest in the water authority who carry out any maintenance at their own expense, and the water authority is also liable to repair supply pipes in the highway at the expense of the consumer. There is power for stopcocks to be fitted on service pipes at boundaries of private premises or street boundaries.

5.12 Power to Lay Mains, etc

(W.A. 1945, Third Schedule, Part V (ss.19-21); S.I. 1974 No.607, Art 9(6)(c); S.I. 1977 No.293, Art.7)

Part V of the Third Schedule to the W.A. 1945 relating to water mains may be applied to a water undertaking by being incorporated in an order made under that Act. The provisions of Part V are summarised below—

Power to lay mains (Section 19)

The undertakers may within their limits of supply and also, outside those limits, lay a main—

(a) in any street subject to the provisions of Part VI of the Third Schedule as amended by the Public utilities street Works Act, 1950 relating to the breaking open of streets; and

(b) in, on or near any land not forming part of a street after giving reasonable notice to every owner and occupier of that land and with the consent of—

    (i) the highway authority concerned, if the main will be laid within 220 feet of any highway; and

    (ii) the electricity or gas board concerned, if the main will be laid in, on or over any land of that board being operational land within the meaning of the Town and Country Planning Act, 1971;

and may from time to time inspect, repair, alter or renew, or may at any time remove, any main they have laid; a consent required is not to be unreasonably withheld and any question whether it is or is not must be referred to and determined by the Secretary of State.

Where a proposed main will cross or interfere with a watercourse or works vested in or under the control of a land drainage authority (*ie* a water authority or internal drainage board), the undertakers shall notify their proposals to that authority, and if within 28 days that authority serves on the undertakers notice of objection to their proposals, the undertakers cannot proceed with their proposals until all objections are withdrawn or the Secretary of State after a local inquiry has approved the proposals with or without modifications. This provision does not apply to a proposed main to be laid in a bridge carrying a highway across a watercourse.

Where the undertakers lay a main in, on or over land not forming part of a street, or inspect, repair, alter, renew or remove a main laid across such land, they are liable to pay compensation to every person interested in the land for any damage done to, or injurious affection of, the land by reason of the inspection, etc. The undertakers may erect and maintain in a street notices indicating the position of underground water fittings used for controlling the flow of water through their mains, and the notices may be affixed to a house or other building, wall or fence. In this section a private street within a factory curtilage is deemed not to be, or form part of, a street.

NOTE 1: It is common practice for statutory water undertakers to obtain an easement from the owner and interested parties to enter upon private land for the purpose of laying a main with a condition or convenant that the owner etc will not erect any structure over the main without the prior consent of the undertakers.

NOTE 2: S.19 of the Third Schedule to the W.A. 1945, has been applied throughout the water supply area of any water authority (other than the Welsh National Water Development Authority) with paragraph (b) above substituted for the original wording by art.7 of the Local Authorities etc. (Miscellaneous Provisions) Order, 1977 (S.I. 1977, No. 293) and any local statutory provision ceased to have effect in so far as it applied to s.19 in any such water supply area. See also Art.9(6)(c) of the Water Authorities etc (Miscellaneous Provisions) Order, 1974 (S.I. 1974, No. 607) which applied the same modification to s.19 in any area which formed part of the water supply area of a water authority and within which, immediately before 1st April, 1974, a supply of water was furnished by former statutory water undertakers under Part IV (Water Supply) of the Public Health Act, 1936.

NOTE 3: Notice must be given to the fire authorities of proposed works affecting water supply and fire hydrants; Fire Services Act 1947, sect. 16.

Conditions as to laying mains outside limits of supply (Section 20)

Where the undertakers propose to lay a main outside their limits of supply, they must notify the land drainage authority as required by s.19 to the Third Schedule and in addition—

(a) publish an advertisement in a local newspaper circulating a notice in the district council area specifying the land affected, describing their proposals and naming a place where a plan of the proposals may be inspected free of charge; and

(b) serve, not later than the date of publication of the advertisement, a copy of the notice on the district council and on the highway authority for any highway in which they propose to lay a main.

If, within 28 days after the publication of the notice, notice of objection to their proposals is served on the undertakers by the district council or highway authority, they cannot proceed with their proposals unless all objections are withdrawn or the Secretary of State has approved the proposals with or without modification.

The above provisions do not apply where the work which the undertakers propose to carry out outside their limits of supply consists of the laying of a main in a highway maintainable at the public expense and they have obtained the consent of the district council and of the highway authority.

Power to lay service pipes, etc (Section 21)

The undertakers may in any street within their limits of supply lay the necessary service pipes with stopcocks and other fittings for supplying water to premises within the limits, and may from time to time inspect, repair, alter or renew and may at any time remove a service pipe laid in a street. Where a service pipe has been lawfully laid across land not forming part of a street, the undertakers may from time to time enter upon the land and inspect, repair, alter or remove the pipe or lay a new pipe, and shall pay compensation for any damage they do.

5.12.1 The Effect of a Notice Under Section 19

Section 19 notices confer the statutory right to lay a water main in, on or over any land not forming part of the street, after having given reasonable notice to every owner and occupier of that land. The exercise of this power does not amount, and must not be construed as amounting, to a form of compulsory acquisition of land. There is no question of the procedure of the Compulsory Purchase Act 1965 being applied. The interest acquired is an interest in land in the form of a statutory easement and in this connection the principles contained in the Land Compensation Act 1961 apply thereto.

In the case of *Thurrock, Grays and Tilbury Joint Sewerage Board* v *Thames Land Company Limited* (1925) the Court held that there could be two heads of claim, namely one for the easement *per se* and one for damage; *see* also *Markland and*

Felthouse v *Cannock Rural District Council* (1973). Those cases were concerned with the construction of a public sewer that the principles are comparable to a water main laid pursuant to statutory powers. In *Newcastle-under-Lyme Corporation* v *Wolstanton* (1947), a case dealing with a gas main laid pursuant to section 6 of the Gas Works Clauses Act 1847, the Court of Appeal held that the corporation's exclusive right of occupation was limited to the space in the soil taken by the gas pipes and did not apply to any part of the soil on which the pipes rested.

The nature of the "statutory easement" which was examined in some depth in the *Wolstanton* case is that a statutory water undertaker has, by virtue of the enabling legislation, an exclusive right to occupy the space or cavity occupied by the actual pipes themselves. Unless the procedures contained in Part IV of the Third Schedule or of the earlier legislation examined in this book regarding minerals is observed, there would appear to be no legal authority which will permit a statutory water undertaker to bring an action for trespass if some person, not authorised by the statutory water undertaker, removed all the soil around a portion of the undertaker's mains. Obviously an action for trespass would lie if that person physically damaged the mains.

The right of the statutory water undertaker in respect of the statutory easement amounts to a beneficial occupation in the rating sense and it is an encumbrance on the ownership of the land in or through which the main runs.

The powers to lay a main in on or over any land not forming part of the street, after giving reasonable notice to every owner and occupier of that land (pursuant to the powers contained in section 19, as modified, of the Third Schedule to the W.A. 1945, includes the power to do that which is inescapable if the power is to be exercised. In *Hutton* v *Esher Urban District Council* (1973) the Court of Appeal held that the right to construct a public sewer under a section 15 notice (under the Public Health Act 1936) includes the right if so required to demolish any house or building that lies in the path of the intended sewer. That case was concerned with the construction of a public sewer but it is submitted that the principles contained therein are equally applicable to the powers contained in section 19, as modified, of the Third Schedule. See also *Roderick* v *Aston Local Board* (1877) 5 Ch. D. 328, a case concerned with the right to construct and lay sewers in or over land under the Public Health Act 1875, and *re Dudley Corporation and Earl of Dudley's Trustees* (1881) 8 Q.B.D. 86.

5.13 Laying and Maintenance of Supply Pipes and Communication Pipes
(W.A. 1945, Third Schedule, Part X (ss.40-44))

This Part of the Third Schedule to the W.A. 1945 regarding supply pipes and communication pipes may be applied to statutory water undertakings by means of an order made under that Act.

Laying of supply pipes etc (Section 40)

An owner or occupier of premises within the limits of supply desiring to have a supply of water for his domestic purposes from the waterworks of the undertakers must (a) give the undertakers 14 days notice of his intention to lay the necessary supply pipe and at or before giving notice pay or tender the sum payable in advance by way of water charge in respect of his premises; and (b) lay the supply pipe at his own expense, having first obtained in respect of land not forming part of a street the consent of the owners and occupiers thereof. Where part of the supply pipe is being laid in a highway, he must not himself break open the highway or lay that part of the pipe.

Laying of communication pipes, etc (Section 41)

On receiving a notice referred to in s.40, the undertakers shall lay the necessary communication pipe and any part of the supply pipe being laid in a highway and connect the communication pipe with the supply pipe. Where part of the supply pipe is being laid in a highway, the undertakers may elect to lay a main in the highway for such distance as they think fit in lieu of the supply pipe and then lay a communication pipe from the main and connect it with the supply pipe. If the undertakers fail to carry out the work within 14 days after the person by whom the notice was given has laid a supply pipe, they are liable to a fine not exceeding £25 and to a further fine not exceeding £2 for each day on which the default continues after the expiration of the 14 days, unless they show that the failure was due to unavoidable accident or other unavoidable cause. The expenses reasonably incurred by the undertakers in executing the work must be repaid to them by the person by whom the notice was given and may be recovered summarily as a civil debt, but where the undertakers lay a main in lieu of a supply pipe, the additional cost so incurred is borne by them. Within seven days of receiving a notice as above, the undertakers may require the person giving the notice either to pay them in advance the cost of the work as estimated by their engineer or give security for payment thereof to their satisfaction.

NOTE 1: S.41(3) is referred to in s.12(3) of the Local Government (Miscellaneous Provisions) Act 1953, (as substituted by the W.A. 1973, Sch.8, para.66) (*see* para. **3.13**).

NOTE 2: Where Art.9 of the Water Authorities etc (Miscellaneous Provisions) Order 1974 (S.I. 1974, No. 607) applies (*see* para. **3.13**), s.41(1) proviso is substituted by Art.9(6)(d) and s.41(3) is substituted by Art.9(6)(e).

NOTE 3: The amount of the fine was increased to £25 by C.L.A. 1977, s.31.

Power of undertakers to require separate service pipes
(Section 42)

The undertakers may require the provision of a separate service pipe for each house or other building supplied by them with water. If, in the case of a house or other building already supplied with water but not having a separate service pipe, the undertakers notify the owner of the house or building that a pipe is required, the owner must within three months lay so much of the required pipe as constitutes a supply pipe and is not required to be laid in a highway, and the undertakers shall within 14 days after he has done so lay so much of the required pipe as constitutes a communication pipe or a supply pipe to be laid in a highway and make all necessary connections. If an owner fails to comply with a notice served on him, the undertakers may themselves execute the work. The expenses reasonably incurred by the undertakers in executing the work of laying a pipe in a highway and making connections, or in executing the work themselves where an owner fails to comply with a notice, shall be repaid by the owner of the house or building and may be recovered by them summarily as a civil debt. If the undertakers default in laying a pipe in a highway and making the necessary connections, they are liable to a fine not exceeding £25 and to a further fine not exceeding £2 for each day on which the default continues after the expiration of the 14 days.

A further limit to the discretionary power of statutory water undertakers under Section 42 of the Third Schedule has been introduced by Section 4 of the Water Act 1981 and since the passing of that Act on 15 April 1981 they may not require the provision of separate service pipes for those houses until either —

a) The existing supply pipe becomes so defective as to require renewal or is no longer sufficient to meet the requirements of the houses; or

b) a payment in respect of the supply of water to any of the houses remains unpaid after the end of the period for which it is due; or

c) the houses are, by structural alterations to one or more of them, converted into a larger number of houses; or

d) the owner or occupier of any of the houses has interfered with or allowed another person to interfere with the existing service pipe or the stopcock fixed to it and thereby caused the supply of water to any house to be interfered with or the undertakers have reasonable grounds to believe that such interference is likely to take place.

NOTE 1: The amount of the fine was increased to £25 by C.L.A. 1977, s.31.

Power to break open streets forming boundary of limits of Supply (Section 43)

Where premises which are within the limits of supply abut on, or are situated near to, a street which is, as to the whole or a part of its width, outside the limits, the undertakers may, for the purpose of supplying water to the owner or occupier of the premises, exercise with respect to the whole width of the street the like powers of laying, inspecting, repairing, altering, renewing and removing service pipes with any necessary stopcocks and fittings and of breaking open streets for the purpose as are exercisable by them with respect to streets within the limits of supply (as to breaking open streets, *see* para. **4.08**).

Vesting of communication pipes and repair of such pipes and of supply pipes in highways (Section 44)

All communication pipes vest in the undertakers who shall at their own expense carry out any necessary work of maintenance, repair or renewal of such pipes and any work on their mains incidental thereto. The undertakers must also carry out any such necessary works in the case of so much of a supply pipe laid in a highway and may recover the expenses reasonably incurred by them summarily as a civil debt from the owner of the premises supplied by the pipe. If the undertakers fail to carry out any such necessary work with reasonable despatch after the owner or occupier of premises affected has served notice of complaint of a defect upon them, they are liable to a fine not exceeding £25 and to a further fine not exceeding £2 for each day on which the default continues.

NOTE: The amount of the fine was increased to £25 by C.L.A. 1977, s.31.

5.14 Stopcocks
(W.A. 1945, Third Schedule, Part XI (s.45))

Part XI of the Third Schedule to the W.A. 1945, which relates to the fitting of stopcocks on service pipes, can be incorporated with the legislation relating to statutory water undertakers by means of an order made under the 1945 Act.

Provisions as to position, etc. of stopcocks (Section 45)

On service pipes laid after the coming into force of this provision, the undertakers must, and on service pipes laid before that date the undertakers may, fix a stopcock enclosed in a covered box or pit of such size as may be reasonably necessary. Stopcocks fitted on service pipes after the coming into force of this provision must be placed in such position as the undertakers deem most convenient provided that (a) a stopcock in private premises must be placed as near as reasonably practicable to the street from which the service pipe enters such premises; and (b) a stopcock in a street must, after consultation with the highway authority concerned, be placed as near to the boundary thereof as reasonably practicable.

NOTE: "Coming into force"; Sect 32 of the W.A. 1945 empowers the Secretary of State to apply, by Order under ss.9, 10, 12 or 23 any of the provisions of the Waterworks Code contained in the Third Schedule to any statutory water undertaker to which the Order relates.

Chapter 6

SUPPLY OF WATER

6.01 Synopsis

This deals with the supply of water, as distinct from the powers and means of procuring, treating and distributing water (as to which see mainly chapter 3). The water authority is under the duty to supply water within its area, and where a statutory water company is supplying water on behalf of a water authority, the authority must make water available to the company to meet the foreseeable demands of its consumers. The supply must be sufficient and wholesome, and a constant supply and pressure shall be maintained in pipes on which fire hydrants are fixed or which are used for giving supplies for domestic purposes. Water authorities are under varying duties to supply water for (a) domestic purposes; (b) non-domestic purposes; and (c) public purposes.

The following aspects of the Waterworks Code are considered here:—

Part VII (ss.29-31) — Supply of water for domestic purposes

Part VIII (ss.32-38) — Supply of water for public purposes

Part IX (s.39) — Constancy and pressure of supply

Part XIII (ss.60-70) — Provisions for preventing waste etc of water and as to meters and other fittings

DEFINITIONS OF CERTAIN EXPRESSIONS USED IN THE WATER ACT 1945 THROUGHOUT THIS CHAPTER ARE GIVEN IN PARA 2.02. DEFINITIONS OF CERTAIN EXPRESSIONS USED IN THE THIRD SCHEDULE TO THE WATER ACT 1945 THROUGHOUT THIS CHAPTER ARE GIVEN IN PARA 2.03.

(A) SUPPLY FOR DOMESTIC PURPOSES

6.02 Supply Otherwise than in Pipes
(W.A. 1973, s.11)

Recalling the respective duties of the water authority to supply water within its area and of the local authority to monitor the sufficiency and wholesomeness of water supplies within its area, should (i) the local authority notify the water authority that the supply of water to specified premises in the local authority's area is insufficient or unwholesome to the extent of causing a danger to health; and (ii) a supply of wholesome water by the water authority for domestic purposes is required for the premises and it is not practicable to provide such a supply in pipes, although practicable to provide such a supply otherwise, at a reasonable cost, the water authority must provide a supply of wholesome water otherwise than in pipes (*eg* by tanker) for domestic purposes to or within a reasonable distance of the premises.

Any dispute between the local authority and the water authority as to the insufficiency or unwholesomeness of a water supply or whether it causes a danger to health is determined by the Secretary of State. Any question whether or not a supply of water can be provided at reasonable cost in the area of a local authority may be referred at the request of the local authority, or by a parish or community council, or by ten or more local government electors in that area to the Secretary of State, who shall, after consulting the local authority and the water authority, determine the question and the water authority must give effect to his determination.

6.03 Duty of Water Authority to Accept Guarantees from Local Authorities
(W.A. 1945, s.36; W.A. 1973, s.11(7)(a)

This provision has effect in a case where the owners or occupiers of premises in any area can require the water authority to bring water to the area if the aggregate amount of the water rates payable annually or charges payable for a supply of water for domestic purposes in respect of the premises will not be less than a prescribed fraction of the cost to be incurred by the water authority in complying with the requisition, and if the owners or occupiers of the premises agree to take a supply of water for a prescribed period (For such a case see the W.A. 1945, Third Schedule, s.29 under para. **6.05**).

If, in such a case, the aggregate amount of the water rates or charges which would be payable annually in respect of any premises in the area is not sufficient to enable the owners and occupiers of the premises to make a valid requisition, the local authority of the district for the area may undertake that, until the water rate or charge payable for any year in respect of premises in the area amounts to a sum which would have enabled such a requisition to be made, or for a period of 12 years (whichever first occurs) the local authority will make good to the water authority in each year the difference between that sum and the amount received by the water authority in respect of water supplied, whether for domestic or non-domestic purposes, in that year in respect of premises in the area; thereupon the water authority must lay any necessary mains and bring water to the area. If the water authority fails to lay the necessary mains and bring water to the area within three months after tender of an undertaking to it which satisfies the above provisions, the authority is guilty of an offence under the W.A. 1945 (as to which *see* para. **6.05**) unless it can show that the failure was due to unavoidable accident or other unavoidable cause.

NOTE 1: Any reference in s.36 to a water rate is construed as including a reference to that proportion of a charge as is stated by the water authority to be payable for a supply of water for domestic purposes and it is the duty of the water authority when fixing a charge to state the proportion of the charge which is so payable (W.A. 1973, Sch.8, para. 53(4)).

NOTE 2: Any two or more local authorities may combine for the purposes of giving the undertaking that is required under Section 36.

NOTE 3: Developments corporations under the New Towns Act 1965 may make contributions towards the expenditure of Local Authorities and Statutory Undertakers; Section 3(3) of that Act. Contributions may also be made by the Secretaries of State under the Town Development Act 1952, Section 2(2) towards payments under this Section.

6.04 Water Authority to Provide Domestic Supply for New Buildings
(W.A. 1945, s.37; W.A. 1973, s.11(7)(a))

An owner of land who proposes to erect buildings thereon for which a supply of water for domestic purposes will be needed, may require the water authority within whose limits of supply the land is situated to construct any necessary service reservoirs, lay the necessary mains to such point or points as will enable the buildings to be connected thereto at reasonable cost and bring water to such point or points.

Before complying with a requisition the water authority (a) may require the owner to pay each year one-eighth of the cost of providing and constructing the necessary service reservoirs and providing and laying the necessary mains until the aggregate amount of water rates payable annually in respect of the buildings when erected and in respect of any other premises connected with such mains equals or exceeds such sum as aforesaid or for a period of 12 years (whichever first occurs); and (b) may also require the owner to deposit as security such sum not exceeding the total expense of constructing the necessary reservoirs and mains as the water authority may require.

Any question as to the point or points to which mains must be taken in order to enable buildings to be connected thereto at a reasonable cost is, in default of agreement, determined by the Secretary of State. If, after receiving a requisition and tender of any required undertaking or deposit, the water authority does not within three months (or where a question has before that time been referred to the Secretary of State, within three months from the date when the Secretary of State notifies the water authority of his decision, if that period expires later) comply with the requisition, it is guilty of an offence under the W.A. 1945 (*as to which see* para. **6.05**), unless it shows that the failure was due to unavoidable accident or other unavoidable cause.

There have been two recent cases of great importance to the understanding of what is meant by a "necessary main" within Section 37 of the W.A. 1945.

In *Cherwell District Council* v *Thames Water Authority* [1975] 1 W.L.R. 448, Lord Diplock emphasised in the course of his speech that the key word of the Section is "necessary". The section presupposed that there were no existing mains bringing water to points at which it would be practicable at reasonable cost to connect buildings to be erected to those mains by means of service pipes. It followed therefore, that although in certain circumstances a trunk main may be "necessary" within the meaning of section 37, the 27″ trunk main, the subject of the requisition, was not such a main for, when completed, it would supply water not only to the new houses but also to the general body of consumers.

The House of Lords were subsequently able to re-examine the construction to be placed upon the term "necessary mains" in *Royco Homes Limited* v *Southern Water Authority* [1979] 1 W.L.R. 1366. In the Royco Homes case the issue that the Lords had to decide was the definition of the point from which a necessary main must start. The appellant's contention was that a necessary main is one that starts from an existing main even though that main is of such small capacity as to be unable to supply the quantity of water that is required for the buildings to be erected.

The argument of the Plaintiffs found no favour with the House of Lords. The necessary main, they held, is one which will carry the quantity of water required to the point or points to which it is practicable at reasonable cost to connect the buildings to be erected by service pipes. The starting point for any such necessary main must be determined in the light of sound water engineering practice and is dependent upon the facts of each case. The purpose for which the main is to be laid is to bring water to "such point or points as will enable the building to be connected thereto at a reasonable cost" by service pipes; sound engineering practice may indicate that the necessary starting point could lie somewhere on a existing main of adequate capacity. In other cases sound water engineering practice may involve replacing an existing main of inadequate capacity with a larger one and connecting the new main to the replacement at a suitable point.

In the *Royco Homes* case there was no doubt that the starting point selected by the water authority for the proposed new main was the correct one from the point of view of sound engineering practice and the House of Lords held that it did not in all the circumstances have the effect of depriving the main of the character of a "necessary main" within section 37. The main would be laid with the sole purpose of supplying the domestic water requirements of the proposed development by Royco Homes Limited.

NOTE: Any reference in Section 37 to a water rate is construed as including reference to that proportion of the charge as is stated by the water authority to be payable to a supply of water for domestic purposes and it is the duty of a water authority when fixing the charge to state the proportion of the charge which is so payable (W.A. 1973, Sch. 8, Para. 53(4)).

By s.137 of the Public Health Act, 1936, a local authority must reject plans of a house deposited with it, unless satisfactory proposals are placed before the local authority for providing the occupants of the house with a supply of wholesome water for domestic purposes, and s.123 of the same Act provides that a local authority may undertake to pay to a person supplying water, or guarantee payment to any such person of, such periodical payment or other sums as may be agreed as a consideration for that person giving a supply of water, so far as he lawfully can do so, within any part of the authority's district and executing any works for that purpose.

NOTE: Local Authorities are empowered to contribute to the cost of providing a separate service pipe to a land having a piped water supply but no separate service pipe; s.96, Housing Act, 1964.

S.138 of the Public Health Act, 1936, provides that where a local authority are satisfied that any occupied house has not a supply of wholesome water in pipes in the house sufficient for the domestic purposes of the occupants, the local authority may—

(a) if satisfied that in all the circumstances it is reasonable to require the owner of the house to connect it to a supply of water in pipes provided by the local authority or other statutory water undertakers, give notice to the owner requiring him within a specified time to connect the house as aforesaid;

(b)   if not so satisfied that it is reasonable to require the owner to connect the house as aforesaid, but satisfied that it is reasonable to require him otherwise to take water into the house by means of a pipe, give notice to the owner requiring him within a specified time so to take water into the house.

Where a local authority are satisfied that an occupied house has not within a reasonable distance thereof a supply of wholesome water sufficient for the domestic purposes of the occupants and that in all the circumstances it is not reasonable to require the owner to connect the house, or to take water into the house as aforesaid, they may give notice requiring him within a specified time to provide a sufficient supply of wholesome water within a reasonable distance of the house.

Where a local authority are satisfied as aforesaid with respect to each of two or more houses and are further satisfied that the needs of those houses can most conveniently be met by means of a joint supply they may give notice accordingly under either of the above provisions to the owners of all those houses.

If the person on whom a notice has been served objects to the requirements of the local authority, he may appeal to the magistrates court within 28 days after service of the notice and the court may either disallow the requirements of the local authority or allow it with or without modifications.

If any requirement contained in a notice given by the local authority under the provisions of section 138 of the Public Health Act 1936, including any requirement modified by the Magistrate's Court, is not complied with within the time specified in the notice, or, if the Court extends such time, within the time so specified, the local authority may themselves provide, or secure the provision of, a supply of water to the house or houses in question and may recover any expenses reasonably incurred by them in so doing from the owner of the house, or, where two or more houses are concerned, from the owners of these houses in such proportions as may be determined by the authority or, in case of dispute, by a court of summary jurisdiction.

Section 5 of the Water Act 1981 provides that a householder

may be required to pay up to £300 towards the cost of providing a water supply to a house. If the notice was issued prior to the coming into force of W.A. 1981 (15 April 1981) the maximum sum the householder may be required to pay is the sum fixed by section 78 of the Public Health Act 1961, namely £60.

Section 5 of the Water Act 1981 further provides for the Secretary of State to increase the amount under section 138 of the Public Health Act 1936; any such increase can be effected by order made by statutory instrument. Such an order shall be subject to annulment in pursuance of a resolution in either House of Parliament.

The Water Act 1981 repealed section 78 of the Public Health Act 1961.

6.05 Supply of Water for Domestic Purposes
(W.A. 1945, Third Schedule, Part VII (ss.29-31);
W.A. 1973, s.11(7)(b))

Subject to any provision to the contrary contained in any instrument made under or by virtue of the W.A. 1973, Part VII (ss.29-31) of the Third Schedule to the W.A. 1945 is applied by s.11(7)(b) of the 1973 Act throughout every water authority area, whether or not applied by or under any other enactment, and references in Part VII to statutory water undertakers is to be construed as references only to water authorities.

Duty of water authority to lay additional mains on certain conditions (Section 29)

The water authority must lay any additional mains and bring water to any area within the limits of supply if it is required to do so by such number of owners and occupiers of premises in that area who require a supply of water for domestic purposes whose aggregate amount of water rates payable annually is not less than one-eighth of the expense of providing and laying the necessary mains and if the owners and occupiers agree to take a supply of water for three years at least. Where these formalities are complied with, the water authority, if it fails before the expiration of three months to lay the necessary mains and bring water to the area, is liable to a fine not exceeding £50 and to a further fine not exceeding £5 for each day on which its default continues after conviction therefor, unless the authority shows that the failure was due to unavoidable accident or other unavoidable cause. For cases on "unavoidable accident . . . cause", see *Birkdale & West Lancs Water Board* v *Skelmersdale U.D.C.* (1926) 91 J.P. 9 (natural causes result in fall in water level of well); *Industrial Dwellings Co.* v *East London Waterworks* (1894) 58 J.P. 430 (high consumption).

NOTE 1: Any reference in the Third Schedule to the W.A. 1945 to a water rate is construed as including a reference to a charge payable under Part III of the W.A. 1973 for services which include a supply of water for domestic purposes (W.A. 1973, Sch.8, para. 53(2)(b)).

NOTE 2: Any reference in s.29 to a water rate is construed as including a reference to that proportion of a charge as is stated by the water authority to be payable for a supply of water for domestic purposes and it is the duty of the water authority when fixing a charge to state the proportion of the charge which is so payable (W.A. 1973, Sch.8, para. 53(4)).

NOTE 3: "One-eighth of the expense" — A Local Authority may guarantee to the undertaker the difference between the aggregate amount of water rates payable by premises requiring water and the prescribed fraction; (W.A. 1945, s.36).

NOTE 4: "Fine" — Fines are recoverable summarily; (W.A. 1945, Third Schedule, s.85).

Right to demand supply for domestic purposes (Section 30)

An owner or occupier of any premises within the limits of supply who has complied with the provisions of Part X of Sch.3 to the W.A. 1945 as to the laying of a supply pipe and payment or tender of the water rate is entitled to demand and receive from the water authority a supply of water sufficient for domestic purposes for the premises. A person is not entitled to demand a supply of water from a trunk main or to require the water authority to supply water to premises in which any water fittings do not accord with the requirements of byelaws made under para. **4.05** or similar byelaws or regulations. If the water authority make default in furnishing a supply of water for domestic purposes to a person who has properly demanded it, or fails to maintain the supply during a period when the water rate has been paid or tendered, it is without prejudice to any civil liability, liable to a fine not exceeding £25 and to a further fine not exceeding £2 for each day on which the default continues after notice thereof from the person aggrieved. The water authority is under no liability if the failure to furnish or maintain a supply is due to (a) frost, drought, unavoidable accident or other unavoidable cause, or the execution of necessary works; or (b) failure of the person aggrieved to comply with any enactment or byelaw of the authority. Where water undertakers are liable to a fine, that is the only remedy and no action can be brought for damages (*Atkinson* v *Newcastle & Gateshead Waterworks Co.* (1877) 2 Ex.D. 441).

NOTE: Any reference in the Third Schedule to the W.A. 1945 to a water rate is construed as including a reference to a charge payable under Part III of the W.A. 1973 for services which include a supply of water for domestic purposes (W.A. 1973, Sch.8, para.53(2)(b)).

It is important to note that Section 30 of the Third Schedule expressly preserves the civil liability of undertakers; this is an important distinction from the corresponding section 43 of the Waterworks Clauses Act 1847 under which section it was held in *Atkinson* v *Newcastle and Gateshead Waterworks Company, supra* that, where the Company were liable to a penalty, this formed the only remedy and no action lay for damages. That decision was distinguished in *Read* v *Croydon Corporation* [1938] 4 All E.R. 631 where the penalty for breach of duty to supply pure and wholesome water was held not to be an exclusive remedy.

A deficiency in supply due to extraordinary consumption of water as a result of an unusually hot summer was construed *ejusdem generis* with drought in *Industrial Dwellings Company* v *East London Waterworks Company* (1894) 58 J.P. 430.

Duty of water authority as respects sufficiency and purity (Section 31)

The Water Authority must provide in its mains and communication pipes a supply of wholesome water sufficient for the domestic purposes of all owners and occupiers of premises within the limits of supply who under the special Act are entitled to demand a supply for those purposes, *ie* to demand a supply under Section 30 of the Third Schedule. This provision does not impose an absolute duty; it is a duty which requires the exercise of reasonable care and skill to comply with what the Act requires and failure to supply pure and wholesome water amounts to a breach of statutory duty to an occupier entitled to demand the supply; *Read* v *Croydon Corporation* [1938] 4 All E.R. 631. In this case the Corporation were also liable for breach of their common law duty of care to a Third Party, namely the daughter of the occupier of the premises, who had contracted typhoid from the water.

The nature of the statutory duty to supply wholesome water to a point where it enters the pipe of the consumer, and a failure to discharge that particular statutory duty, was examined in *Milnes* v *Huddersfield Corporation* (1866) 11 A. C. 511, in which it was held by the House of Lords that the Corporation were under a duty to supply pure water in the mains at a point just before it entered the pipes of the particular premises and the failure of the Corporation to execute that statutory duty would permit a person who suffered thereby to claim damages against the undertaker for **breach of statutory duty.**

In *Barnes* v *Irwell Valley Water Board* [1939] 1 K.B. 21, the water supplied was contaminated by lead from pipes laid down by the consumer but inspected by the board. The plaintiffs sustained damage through lead poisoning, not knowing its poisonous quality, and they brought an action against the defendant Water Board claiming damages for breach of statutory duty and for negligence. The Board knew that the water might become poisonous if it passed through a lead pipe and they knew it would pass through a lead pipe on the premises occupied by the plaintiffs, but they had taken no steps to render the water harmless. The courts held that the only statutory duty of the Board was to supply pure and wholesome water **in the pipes laid down by the Board;** to that extent the Water Board had complied with that requirement. The Board were liable however for having been negligent in neither taking steps to reduce the plumbo-solvency of the pipes nor to warn the consumer of the potentially dangerous properties of the water. In other words this was the application of the common law duty on undertakers to take reasonable care that the water they supply is wholesome.

The common law duty extends to the point where the water is taken by the consumers, it extends to all consumers and if there is a breach of this duty a claim will lie in damages — *Barnes* v *Irwell Valley Water Board, supra.* There may be cases where the duty imposed by statute supersedes the common law obligation but there is no provision in the Water Acts whereby the common law obligation is removed and the concept of the duty of care that Lord Atkin spelt out very clearly and concisely in *Donoghue* v *Stevenson* [1932] A.C. 562, at page 580, applies;

> "You must take reasonable care to avoid acts or omissions which you can reasonably foresee would be likely to injure your neighbour. Who, then, in law is my neighbour? The answer seems to be persons who are so closely and directly affected by my act that I ought reasonably to have them in contemplation as being so affected when I am directing my mind to acts or omissions which are called in question."

That principal was applied to water undertakers in the *Irwell Valley Water Board* case *(supra)* and in *Read* v *Croydon Corporation* (1939) 37 L.G.R. 53. The duty is not an absolute duty. It is a duty to take reasonable care to preserve the consumers from harm and this duty might well be discharged by warnings.

Section 11 (2) of the Water Act 1973 imposes the duty on every local authority to take such steps from time to time as may be necessary for ascertaining the sufficiency and wholesomeness of water supplies within their area and to notify the water authority of any insufficiency or unwholesomeness in those supplies. The section further provides that where the following conditions are satisfied, that is to say—

(a)   A local authority notify a water authority that the supply of water to the specified premises in the local authority's area is insufficient or unwholesome to the extent to cause damage to health; and

(b)   A supply of wholesome water by the water authority for domestic purposes is required for those premises and it is not practicable to provide such a supply in pipes, but is practicable to provide such a supply otherwise, at a reasonable cost,

it shall be the duty of the water authority to provide a supply of wholesome water otherwise than in pipes for domestic purposes to, or within a reasonable distance of, those premises.

There would appear to be no real distinction between the

earlier law of the requirement of a supply of "pure and wholesome" water and the 1973 requirement of a supply of "wholesome" water. The phrase "pure water" was considered by the Privy Council in *Attorney General of New Zealand* v *Lower Hutt Corporation* [1964] A.C. 1469 where it was held that the words should receive a fair, large and liberal construction. In that particular case the Corporation had added to the public water supply which it provided a minute quantity of sodium silico-fluoride amounting to one part per million, which medical opinion thought was the optimum proportion for preservation of dental health, particularly of children. The natural content of fluoride in the water was so small as not to be capable of demonstration but there were traces of it. There were unchallenged findings of the fact that, *inter alia,* there were no deleterious or toxic effects on the human body from the absorption of fluoride in the proportion of one part to a million. The Privy Council held that an Act empowering local authorities to supply "pure water" should receive a fair, large and liberal construction. Whilst the Corporation's water was no doubt pure in its natural state it was very deficient in fluoride, one of the natural constituents normally to be found in water in most parts of the world, and the addition of the fluoride added no impurity; the water remained not only water but pure water.

The New Zealand case is of persuasive authority only and is one of the strictly limited number of cases that have been considered within legal systems that could influence English judicial thinking. The problems of fluoridation have been considered by the Irish Courts; see the judgment of the Supreme Court of Ireland, Dublin, in *Mrs Gladys Ryan* v *Attorney General* (1964).

The English courts have not yet had to consider the issue as to whether the addition of fluoride detracts from "wholesomeness" of water "in English Law" or as to the legal powers, if any, of a water undertaker to add a chemical for a purpose other than discharging the statutory duty of supplying wholesome water.

(B) SUPPLY FOR NON-DOMESTIC AND PUBLIC PURPOSES

6.06 Supply of Water for Non-Domestic Purposes
(W.A. 1945, s.27; W.A. 1973, s.11(7)(a))

A water authority supplying water otherwise than in bulk is required to give a supply of water on reasonable terms and conditions for purposes other than domestic purposes (eg such as commerce, industry, agriculture) to the owner or occupier of any premises within its limits of supply on request, but the water authority is not required to give a supply if its ability to meet existing obligations to supply water for any purposes or probable future requirements to supply water for domestic purposes, without having to incur unreasonable expenditure in constructing new waterworks for the purpose, would be endangered thereby.

Any question arising as to the terms and conditions on which water is to be supplied and whether the authority is justified in refusing to give a supply, must, in default of agreement, be referred to the Secretary of State, who may determine it himself or refer it to an arbitrator appointed by him. If the water authority fail to furnish a supply of water within such period as may be agreed or determined, or fail to maintain the supply in accordance with the terms and conditions, it is liable (without prejudice to any civil liability) to the same penalties prescribed in para. **6.05**, section 30.

For an example of an agreement made under a private Act between a water board and a hospital for supplying water to the hospital at a fixed price "at all times hereafter", which was held by the court's to be a contract determinable by one party on reasonable notice, see *Staffordshire Area Health Authority* v *South Staffordshire Waterworks Co.* [1978] I.W.L.R. 1387, C.A. also *Crediton Gas Co.* v *Crediton U.D.C.* [1928] Ch. 174, and *re Spenborough U.D.C.'s Agreement* [1968] Ch. 139.

6.07 Supply of Water for Public Purposes
(W.A. 1945, Third Schedule, Part VIII ss.32-38)

Ss.32-34 of this Part of the Waterworks Code are applied to all statutory water undertakers in substitution for any other provision having effect for the purposes of such sections by virtue of any enactment (Fire Services Act, 1947, s.14). and sections 35 to 38 are applied throughout every water authority area by virtue of section 3 of the Water Act 1981. See para. **3.13** *ante*.

Undertakers to fix and maintain fire-hydrants on pipes (Section 32)

The undertakers must, at the request of the fire authority, fix fire-hydrants on their mains (other than trunk mains) at places most convenient for affording a supply of water for extinguishing fires which break out within the limits of supply, and must keep in good order and from time to time renew every hydrant. Any difference as to the number or proper position of hydrants is referred to and determined by the Secretary of State.

NOTE: Statutory water undertakers are under no obligation to supply at their own cost a pipe of sufficient size for an effective hydrant; *R. v Wells Water Company* (1886) 55 L.T. 188.

Undertakers to deposit keys of hydrants at certain places (Section 33)

If required by the fire authority, the undertakers shall deposit a key for each hydrant as soon as the hydrant is completed at each place within the limits of supply where a public fire engine is kept in and such other places as appointed by the fire authority.

Cost of hydrants (Section 34)

The fire authority must defray the cost of hydrants and their fixing, maintaining and renewal and of providing keys. A fire authority who has not requested the fixing of a hydrant is not liable to pay the cost of maintaining the hydrant in repair (*Grand Junction Waterworks Company v Brentford Local Board* [1894] 2 Q.B. 735). A fire authority can under s.14 of the Fire Services Act, 1947, enter into an agreement with statutory water undertakers for providing an adequate supply of water in case of fire.

Such an agreement may provide for the payment by the fire authority for the "services" provided by the statutory water undertaker, as for instance where the fire authority specifically request that a main should be oversized in order to meet fire requirements then such an agreement could provide for the fire authority to contribute towards the cost of oversizing.

It is important to note that by virtue of section 11(7)(b) and (c) of the Water Act 1973 the duty under Part IX of Schedule 3 to the Water Act 1945 to maintain a constant supply and pressure in all pipes to which fire hydrants are fixed is a duty that is imposed on water authorities only and it is a duty that applies throughout the area of the water authority.

Hydrants to be placed near factories, etc. at request of owners or occupiers (Section 35)

At the request and expense of the owner or occupier of a factory or place of business situated in, or near to, a street in which a pipe of the undertakers is laid (not being a trunk main and being of sufficient dimensions to carry a hydrant) fix on the pipe and keep in good order and from time to time renew one or more hydrants to be used only for extinguishing fires, as near as convenient to the factory or place of business. The undertakers must also at the expense of the owner or occupier deposit a key of each hydrant where a public fire engine is kept and at any other place appointed.

Water to be taken to extinguish fires without charge (Section 36)

The undertakers shall allow all persons to take water for extinguishing fires from any of their pipes on which a hydrant is fixed without payment. This provision only applies to pipes to which hydrants are fixed otherwise water used for fire-fighting must be paid for (*Weardale and Consett Water Co.* v *Chester-le-street Co-operative Society* [1904] 2 K.B. 240).

Supply of water for cleansing sewers, etc, and for other public purposes (Section 37)

The undertakers must provide in every pipe of theirs on which a hydrant is fixed a supply of water for cleansing sewers and drains and watering highways and for supplying public baths, pumps or washhouses at rates, quantities and upon terms and conditions agreed between the various authorities concerned and the undertakers, or as determined by the Secretary of State in default. For supplying water to a public fountain, see *Hildreth* v *Adamson* (1860) 8 C.B.N.S. 587.

Penalties for default in respect of hydrants or supply of water (Section 38)

If the undertakers fail to comply with any of their obligations under Part VIII of Sch.3 to the W.A. 1945, except when prevented by frost, drought, unavoidable accident or other unavoidable cause, or during the execution of necessary works, they are liable to a fine not exceeding £50 and to a further fine not exceeding £5 for each day during which such failure continues after notice thereof from the authority or person concerned.

(C) DUTIES IN PROVIDING A SUPPLY

6.08 General Duties

Water supplied by a statutory water undertaker must comply with certain conditions which are laid down as statutory duties, namely—

(1) The water authority is required to supply water within its area (*see* para. **3.08**);

(2) Every local authority must take the necessary steps from time to time for ascertaining the sufficiency and wholesomeness of water supplies within its area and notify the water authority of any insufficiency or unwholesomeness in such supplies (*see* para. **3.08**);

(3) The water authority on whose behalf water is being supplied by a statutory water company is required to take all reasonable steps for making water available to the company to enable it to meet the foreseeable demands of consumers within its limits of supply (*see* para. **3.08**);

(4) The water authority must provide a supply of wholesome water sufficient for the domestic purposes of the owners and occupiers of premises within the limits of supply who are entitled to demand such a supply. "Wholesome" is not defined *but see* para. **6.05**, Section 31.

(5) The water authority must ensure that water in pipes on which hydrants are fixed or used for domestic supplies is laid on constantly and at a pressure so as to reach the topmost storey by gravity (*see* para. **6.09**, Section 39).

(6) The water authority is obliged in certain circumstances to provide premises with a supply of water for domestic purposes and also in certain respects to provide water for public purposes, such as fire fighting, cleansing sewers and drains, watering highways and supplying public baths, pumps, etc.

6.09 Constancy and Pressure of Supply
(W.A. 1945, Third Schedule, Part IX (s.39); W.A. 1973, s.11(7)(b))

Subject to any provision to the contrary contained in any instrument made under or by virtue of the W.A. 1973, Part IX (s.39) of the Third Schedule to the W.A. 1945 is applied by s.11(7)(b) of the 1973 Act throughout every water authority area, whether or not applied by or under any other enactment, and references in Part IX to statutory water undertakers is to be construed as references only to water authorities.

The provisions of Part IX are summarised below.

Duty of undertakers as respects constant supply and pressure (Section 39)

The undertakers must cause the water in all pipes on which hydrants are fixed, or which are used for giving supplies for domestic purposes, to be laid on constantly and at such a pressure as will cause the water to reach the top-most storey of every building within the limits of supply, provided that (a) nothing in this provision requires them to deliver water at a height greater than that to which it will flow by gravitation through their mains from the service reservoir or tank from which the supply is taken; and (b) they may at their discretion determine the service reservoir or tank from which a supply is taken.

Should the undertakers fail to comply with these requirements, except when prevented by frost, drought, unavoidable accident or other unavoidable cause, or during the execution of necessary works, they are (without prejudice to any civil liability to a person aggrieved) liable to a fine not exceeding £25 and to a further fine not exceeding £2 for each day during which the failure continues after notice thereof from such person. Proceedings for the recovery of a fine cannot be instituted by more than one person in respect of the same period of failure. Where undertakers fail to comply with this provision and *eg* premises are burnt down, it has been held that the Act does not provide a right of action through the courts and that the remedy is to go for the penalty (*Atkinson* v *Newcastle & Gateshead Waterworks Co* (1877) 2 Ex. D. 441).

NOTE 1: References in Part IX to statutory water undertakers refers only to water authorities (W.A. 1973, s.11(7)(c)).

NOTE 2: The amount of the fine was increased to £25 by C.L.A. 1977, s.31.

(D) SUPPLY IN BULK—LIMITS OF SUPPLY

6.10 Supply of Water in Bulk
(W.A. 1945, s.12 as substituted by W.A. 1973, Sch.4, Part I)

An agreement may be made between a statutory water undertaker and any other persons for the undertakers to take a supply of water in bulk for any period and on any terms and conditions, and where the persons giving the supply are themselves statutory water undertakers, either within or outside their limits of supply. Where a statutory water company is a party to an agreement the approval is required of the water authority on whose behalf the company is supplying water, and such approval must be withheld if it appears to the water authority that the giving of the supply by the company would be likely to interfere with the supply of water for any purpose within the company's limits of supply.

Where it seems expedient to a water authority that (a) a statutory water company through whom the authority is supplying water should give a bulk supply to another company or to the authority and that the other company or the authority should take a supply, or (b) the authority should give a bulk supply to a company, and this cannot be secured by agreement, the authority may by order require the giving and taking of a bulk supply for such period and on such terms and conditions as provided in the order. This power may be exercised jointly by two or more water authorities where the transfer of a bulk supply between their areas is expedient.

Where it appears expedient to the Secretary of State that one water authority should give a bulk supply to another and this cannot be secured by agreement, he may by order require the giving and taking of a bulk supply for such period and on such terms and conditions as provided in the order.

6.11 Supply of Water Outside Limits of Supply
(W.A. 1973, s.13)

Statutory water undertakers are empowered to make agreements with other statutory water undertakers to supply water outside their limits of supply, and where water is so supplied under an agreement, the enactments relating to that part of the limits of supply contiguous to the area being supplied under the agreement apply to the area being supplied; in the event of different enactments applying owing to more than one area being within the limits of supply which is contiguous to the area being supplied under the agreement, the Secretary of State may decide which enactments will apply.

6.12 Variation of Limits of Supply
(W.A. 1945, s.10; W.A. 1973, s.11(8), Sch.8, para.47)

The Secretary of State may (a) on the application of statutory water undertakers by order vary their limits of supply but not so as to include any area which is within the limits of supply of any other statutory water undertakers; (b) on the application of two or more statutory water undertakers by order provide for varying by agreement any common boundary between their respective limits of supply. Where it appears to the Secretary of State to be expedient to vary the limits of supply of any statutory water undertakers and this cannot be secured as above, he may make an order in accordance with Parts I and II of the First Schedule to the W.A. 1945 providing compulsorily for such variation. This provision does not authorise the Secretary of State to vary the boundary between two water authority areas.

(E) METERS—FITTINGS—WASTE AND MISUSE

6.13 Meters
(W.A. 1973, s.32)

In cases where charges are payable to a water authority by reference to the volume of water supplied to any premises or the volume of effluent discharged therefrom (whether or not the charges are payable by reference to any other factors), the authority may install on the premises a meter for measuring that volume, and subject to the provisions of any regulations the register of the meter is *prima facie* evidence of the volume. The Secretary of State for the Environment may make regulations providing for the installation of meters, their connection, disconnection, maintenance, authentication, testing and other related matters. Provision is made for entry on premises by an officer authorised by a water authority for any of these purposes.

6.14 Power to Supply Water Fittings
(W.A. 1945, s.35; W.A. 1973, Sch.9)

Statutory water undertakers may, on request from persons whom they supply or propose to supply water, supply them (either by sale or hire) such water fittings as are required or allowed by their byelaws, and may also on request, install, repair or alter (but not manufacture) such water fittings, whether supplied by them or not, and may provide materials and do work required in connection with such installation, repair or alteration of water fittings. The undertakers can charge as may be agreed or, in default of agreement, as may be reasonable for fittings supplied, materials provided or work done and the charges may be recovered summarily as civil debts.

Provided that fittings let for hire by the undertakers bear either a distinguishing metal plate affixed thereto or a distinguishing brand or other mark conspicuously impressed or made thereon sufficiently indicating the undertakers as the actual owners of the fittings, the fittings—

(a) shall, notwithstanding that they are fixed to some part of the premises in which they are situated or are laid in the soil thereunder, continue to be the property of, and removable by, the undertakers; and

(b)   shall not be subject to distress or to the landlord's remedy for rent, or be liable to be taken in execution under process of any court or in proceedings in bankruptcy against the person in whose possession they may be.

A person who wilfully or negligently injures or suffers to be injured any water fitting belonging to the undertakers, is liable on summary conviction to a fine not exceeding £25 and the undertakers may do the necessary work for repairing injury done and recover their reasonable expenses from the offender summarily as a civil debt.

This provision is little used in practice.

6.15 Provisions for Preventing Waste etc. of Water, and as to Meters and Other Fittings
(W.A. 1945, Third Schedule, Part XIII (ss.60-70);
L.G.(M.P.)A. 1953, s.12; W.A. 1973, Sch.8, para. 66; S.I. 1974 No. 607, Arts.8, 9; C.L.A. 1977, Sch.6)

By s.12 of the Local Government (Miscellaneous Provisions) Act, 1953, as substituted by the W.A. 1973, Sch.8, para. 66, subject to any provision to the contrary contained in any instrument made under or by virtue of the W.A. 1973, Part XIII of the Third Schedule to the W.A. 1945, regarding provisions for preventing waste of water (except s.61), applies throughout every water authority area except in the limits of supply of a statutory water company within the meaning of the W.A. 1973. The main provisions of Part XIII subject to the appropriate modifications are summarised below.

NOTE: Part XIII does not apply within that part of the water supply area of the Thames Water Authority referred to in art.8(3) of the Water Authorities etc (Miscellaneous Provisions) Order, 1974 (S.I. 1974 No. 607).

The provisions of Part XIII are summarised below:

Power to require provision of cisterns in certain cases
(Section 60)

The undertakers may require that (a) a building the supply of water to which need not under the enactments with which this Part of Sch.3 is incorporated be constantly laid on under pressure: and (b) a house the erection of which was not commenced before the coming into force of this provision and to which water is required to be delivered at a height greater than 35 feet below the draw-off level of the service reservoir from which a supply of water is furnished by them, shall be provided with a cistern having a ball and stop-cock on the pipe conveying water to it and, in the case of a house mentioned in (b) above, may require that the cistern shall be capable of holding sufficient water to provide an adequate supply to the house for a period of 24 hours. If a consumer, whom the undertakers have in accordance with the above provisions required to provide a cistern, fails to comply with the requirement, or if a consumer fails to keep in good repair a cistern in use in his building, or the ball and stop-cock appurtenant to the cistern, the undertakers may themselves provide a cistern or execute necessary repairs to prevent a waste of water and may recover the expenses reasonably incurred by them in so doing summarily as a civil debt from the owner of the building.

Power to test water fittings (Section 61)

The undertakers may test any water fittings used in connection with water supplied by them.

NOTE: S.61 is expressly excluded from being applied to water authority areas by virtue of s.12(1) of the Local Government (Miscellaneous Provisions) Act, 1953, as substituted by the W.A. 1973, sch.8, para. 66.(*see* para. **3.13**).

Power to enter premises to detect waste or misuse of water (Section 62)

An authorised officer of the undertakers may enter premises supplied with water by the undertakers in order to examine if there is any waste or misuse of water on production of his authority between the hour of seven in the forenoon and one hour after sunset. A person who refuses him admittance to the premises or obstructs him in making his examination is liable to a fine not exceeding £25.

Power to repair supply pipes (Section 63)

If the undertakers think that some injury to or defect in a supply pipe which they are not under an obligation to maintain is causing, or is likely to cause, waste of water or injury to person or property, they may execute such work as they think necessary or expedient in the circumstances of the case without being requested so to do, and if injury to or defect in the pipe is discovered, the expenses reasonably incurred by the undertakers in discovering it and executing repairs is recoverable by them summarily as a civil debt from the owner of the premises supplied.

Penalty for waste etc of water by non-repair of water fittings (Section 64)

If the owner or occupier of premises wilfully or negligently causes or suffers any water fitting (not being a fitting which some person other than the owner or occupier is liable to maintain) (a) to be or remain so out of order, or so in need of repair; or (b) to be or remain so constructed or adapted, or be so used, that the water supplied to the premises by the undertakers is, or is likely to be, wasted, misused or unduly consumed or contaminated before use, or that foul air or any impure matter is likely to return into a pipe belonging to, or connected with a pipe belonging to, the undertakers, he is liable to a fine not exceeding £200. If any water fitting on premises, not being a fitting which the undertakers are liable to maintain, is in such a condition, or so constructed or adapted as above, the undertakers (without prejudice to their right to institute proceedings above) may require the owner of the premises to carry out necessary repairs or alterations, and if he fails to do so within 48 hours, may themselves carry out the work and recover from him summarily as a civil debt the expenses they have reasonably incurred in so doing.

NOTE 1: The penalty in s.64 was increased to £200 by sch.6 of the Criminal Law Act 1977.

NOTE 2: S.64 is modified in its application to the undertaking of a water authority in accordance with the schedule to the Local Government (Miscellaneous Provisions) Act 1953; *see* s.12 of the LG(MP)A 1953 as substituted by the W.A. 1973, sch.8, para. 66 (*see* para. **3.13**).

NOTE 3: Where the Water Authorities etc (Miscellaneous Provisions) Order 1974 (S.I. 1974 No. 607) applies (*see* para. **3.13**), s.64 has effect as set out in the schedule to the LG(MP)A 1953 and not as originally enacted; *see* art.9(6)(g) of S.I. 1974 No. 607.

The modified version of s.64 referred to in Notes 2 and 3 above is set out below—

Penalty for waste etc of water by non-repair of water fittings

If the owner of premises wilfully or negligently causes or suffers any water fitting, not being a fitting which some person other than the owner is liable to maintain, or if the occupier of premises wilfully or negligently causes or suffers any water fitting, not being a fitting which some person other than the occupier is liable to maintain (a) to be or remain so out of order, or so in need of repair; or (b) to be or remain so constructed or adapted, or be so used, that the water supplied to those premises by the undertakers is, or is likely to be, wasted, misused or unduly consumed or contaminated before use, or that foul air or any impure matter is likely to return into any pipe belonging to, or connected with a pipe belonging to, the undertakers, he is liable to a fine not exceeding £200. If any water fitting on premises, not being a fitting which the undertakers are liable to maintain, is in such a condition, or so constructed or adapted as aforesaid, the undertakers, without prejudice to their right to institute proceedings above, may require the owner of the premises to carry out any necessary repairs or alterations, and, if he fails to do so within 48 hours, may themselves carry out the work and recover from him summarily as a civil debt the expenses they have reasonably incurred in so doing but without prejudice to the rights and obligations, as between themselves, of the owner and the occupier of the premises.

Penalties for misuse of water (Section 65)

An owner or occupier of premises supplied with water by the undertakers who without their consent supplies any of that water to another person for use in other premises, or wilfully permits another person to take any of that water for use in other premises, is (without prejudice to the right of the undertakers to recover the value of the water so supplied or permitted to be taken from such owner or occupier) liable to a fine not exceeding £25, unless the other person requires the water for the purposes of extinguishing a fire, or is a person supplied with water by the undertakers but temporarily unable through no default of his own to obtain water. A person who, having from the undertakers a supply of water otherwise than by meter, uses water so supplied to him for a purpose other than those for which he is entitled to use it is liable to a fine not exceeding £25, without prejudice to the right of the undertakers to recover from him the value of the water misused.

NOTE 1: The amount of the fine was increased to £25 by C.L.A. 1977, s.31.

NOTE 2: Section 65(2) of the Third Schedule to the Water Act 1945 was repealed by Section 33(3) and Schedule 3 of the Theft Act 1968; the old offence of "larceny of water" is now replaced by the provisions of the Theft Act and the offence of theft — *see* Section 1(1) of the Theft Act 1968. Readers interested in the old offence of larceny of water are referred to *Ferens* v *O'Brien* (1883) 11 Q.B.D. 21 and *Burns* v *Schofield* (1922) 128 L.T. 382 where the owner was liable for acts of his servant done in the course of his employment, *ie* watering a steam wagon at a street hydrant.

Penalty for fraudulent use of water (Section 66)

If a person fraudently alters the index of a meter used by the undertakers for measuring the water supplied by them, or prevents a meter from registering correctly the quantity of water supplied, he is liable to a fine not exceeding £25 and the undertakers may do all necessary work for securing the proper working of the meter and may recover the expenses reasonably incurred by them in so doing from the offender summarily as a civil debt. If it is proved that a consumer has altered the index of a meter, it rests upon him to prove that he did not alter it fraudently, and the existence of an artificial means under the control of a consumer for preventing a meter from registering correctly is evidence that he has fraudently prevented the meter from registering correctly.

NOTE: The amount of the fine was increased to £25 by C.L.A. 1977, s.31.

Penalty for interference with valves and apparatus (Section 67)

If a person either (a) wilfully and without the consent of the undertakers; or (b) negligently, turns on, opens, closes, shuts off or otherwise interferes with a valve, cock or other work or apparatus belonging to the undertakers and thereby causes the supply of water to be interfered with, he is liable to a fine not exceeding £200 and, whether proceedings are taken against him in respect of his offence or not, the undertakers may recover from him summarily as a civil debt the amount of any damage they sustain. But this provision does not apply to a consumer closing the stopcock fixed on the service pipe supplying his premises so long as he has obtained the consent of any other consumer whose supply will be affected thereby.

NOTE: The penalty under s.67 was increased to £200 by Sch.6 of the C.L.A. 1977.

Penalty for extension or alteration of pipes, etc
(Section 68)

A person who without the consent of the undertakers attaches a pipe or apparatus to a pipe belonging to the undertakers, or to a supply pipe, or makes any alteration in a supply pipe or in apparatus attached to a supply pipe, is liable to a fine not exceeding £25, and a person who uses a pipe or apparatus which has been so attached, or altered, is liable to the same penalty unless he proves that he did not know, and had no ground for suspecting, that it had been so attached or altered. Whether proceedings are taken against the offender in respect of his offence or not, the undertakers may recover from him summarily as a civil debt the amount of any damage they sustain and the value of water wasted, misused or improperly consumed. This provision has been held to apply to attachments made without the consent of the undertakers (*Williams* v *Llandudno U.D.C.* (1897) 14 T.L.R. 18) and to where a hose-pipe was temporarily attached to a pipe without consent (*Cambridge University and Town Waterworks Co.* v *Hancock* (1910) 103 L.T. 562).

NOTE: The amount of the fine was increased to £25 by C.L.A. 1977 s.31.

Meters to be connected, or disconnected, by undertakers
(Section 69)

A consumer who has not obtained the consent of the undertakers must not connect or disconnect a meter by means of which water supplied by the undertakers is intended to be, or has been, measured for the purposes of payment to them. If he requires this he has to give the undertakers 24 hours notice and when the work can be commenced and thereupon they shall carry out the necessary work and may recover from him summarily as a civil debt the expenses they have reasonably incurred in so doing. A consumer who contravenes any of these provisions, and undertakers who fail to carry out the work with reasonable despatch are liable to a fine not exceeding £25.

NOTE: The amount of the fine was increased to £25 by C.L.A. 1977, s.31.

Meters, etc. to measure water or detect waste (Section 70)

Subject to the provisions of the special Act as to the breaking open of streets, the undertakers may for the purpose of measuring the quantity of water supplied, or preventing and detecting waste, affix and maintain meters and other apparatus on their mains and service pipes and may insert in a street, but as near as reasonably practicable to the boundary thereof, the necessary covers or boxes for giving access and protection thereto, and may for that purpose temporarily obstruct, break open and interfere with streets, tramways, sewers, pipes, wires and apparatus, except that telegraphic lines, works or apparatus of electricity undertakers and pipes or apparatus of gas undertakers must not be interfered with save in accordance with prescribed procedures.

NOTE: Section 70 is applied to any apparatus affixed, maintained or inserted before 1st April, 1974, for the purposes and in the manner specified above as if it had been affixed, maintained or inserted under the powers conferred by s.70; see the Water Authorities etc (Miscellaneous Provisions) Order, 1974 (S.I. 1974 No. 607), art.9(6)(h).

Chapter 7

CONTROL OF ABSTRACTION OF WATER

7.01 Synopsis

The licensing of the abstraction of water from surface and underground sources, which is one of the major facets of water conservation, really belongs to chapter 4 where the conservation and protection of water resources is considered, but the subject of licensing, being a system of some detail, requires a chapter on its own. This chapter deals, therefore, with the provisions of Part IV of the Water Resources Act, 1963, which contains the statutory provision for controlling the abstraction and impounding of water, and describes the requirements of and exceptions from licensing, who may apply for a licence, the procedure for applying, how the application is determined, what are protected rights, appeals to the Secretary of State, revocation or variation of licences, etc. Reference is also included about land purchase and the making of orders for carrying out engineering or building operations required in the performance of water resource functions.

The Chapter also examines the rights and obligations at common law of owners occupiers of land and of riparian owners and occupiers of riparian land in respect of the use of underground or subterranean water, or of water flowing on the surface in defined channels. Statute law, in particular the Water Resources Acts 1963-71, has not abrogated those common law rights but has imposed constraints on the exercise of those rights and has imposed duties where none previously existed.

DEFINITIONS OF CERTAIN EXPRESSIONS USED IN THE WATER RESOURCES ACT 1963 THROUGHOUT THIS CHAPTER ARE GIVEN IN PARA **2.04**

(A) THE COMMON LAW POSITION

7.02 Abstraction at Common Law

RIPARIAN RIGHTS — The occupier of land (he may be the tenant or the owner in possession) on the banks of a natural stream is entitled at common law to the enjoyment of "riparian rights." The right to the enjoyment of a natural stream of water on the surface *ex jure naturae* belongs to the proprietor of the adjoining lands as a natural incident to the right of the soil itself; and he is entitled to the benefit of it, as he is to all the other advantages belonging to the land of which he is the owner. He has the right to have it come to him in its natural state, in flow, quantity and quality, and to go from him without obstruction (*Chasemore* v *Richards* (1859) 7 H.L. Cas. 349). A riparian right is based on —

(1)   the right of access to the stream;

(2)   the riparian land being in reasonable proximity to the water;

(3)   the land must be in actual contact with the water, or in such contact for a great part of every day in the regular course of nature, i.e. in the case of a tidal water when the foreshore is left bare at low water;

(4)   the occupier must be in possession of the land abutting on the water;

(5)   the occupier does not have to exercise his right to enjoy it.

Any unreasonable or unauthorised interference with the use of water to the detriment of one who is entitled to its use (unless the right to interfere has been authorised by statute, grant or long user), may be the subject of an action in the civil courts for damages and can be restrained by injunction, although there may be no actual injury to the person entitled to the right. A riparian right may be (a) the right to abstract or divert water in a river, (b) a right to obstruct or impound river water, or (c) the right to expect that water will continue in its natural state of quality and purity (or wholesomeness) and will not become polluted.

ABSTRACTION is either an ordinary use or an extra-ordinary use of flowing water, namely:—

(a) *Ordinary use* of water occurs where a riparian occupier has the right to the reasonable use of the water flowing past his land for his domestic purposes and for his cattle, i.e. for drinking and culinary purposes, cleansing and washing, feeding and supplying the ordinary quantity of cattle, etc. The riparian owner is under no restrictions and he can exhaust the flowing water altogether without a lower riparian owner being entitled to complain (*Miner* v *Gilmour* (1859) 12 Moo. P.C.C. 131).

(b) *Extraordinary use* is the right to the use of water for any other purpose, such as damming and diverting a river for milling, the use of water for industry, diversion of water for irrigation, provided there is no interference with the rights of other riparian owners above or below the point of abstraction. Unlike the ordinary use, there are definite restrictions imposed on a riparian proprietor in respect of an extraordinary use; thus (1) the use must be a reasonable one, (2) the purposes for which water is taken must be connected with the riparian land (*McCartney* v *Londonderry Railway Co* [1904] A.C. 301), (3) the water taken and used must be restored substantially undiminished in volume and unaltered in character — note that the law does not acknowledge ordinary or extraordinary rights to take water for spray irrigation as the water is not returned to the river (*Rugby Joint Water Board* v *Walters* [1967] Ch. 397).

Riparian rights do not attach to water which percolates through the subsoil in no defined channel and such water cannot be the subject of property or be granted (*Ewart* v *Belfast Poor Law Commrs.* (1881) 9 L.R. Ir. 172), and consequently, an owner of land beneath which water flows cannot bring an action against his neighbour who, whilst carrying out mining operations in his land, draws away the water from the land of the first owner and leaves his well dry (*Acton* v *Blundell* (1843) 12 M & W 324). Whilst it is clear that no action lies for the interception of percolating water before it reaches a well, or whilst the water is in a well (*New River Co* v *Johnson* (1860) 24 J.P. 244), once water has arrived at the springhead or has started to flow in a defined channel on the surface, any interception of the water is unlawful (*Grand Junction Canal Co.* v *Shugar* (1871) 6 Ch. App. 483) At common law a landowner has the right to sink a well or borehole in his property and intercept percolating water beneath his own land, although the effect is to interfere with the supply of underground water to nearby springs, since the interference is to percolating water (*Bradford Corpn* v *Pickles* [1895] A.C. 587)

But all these common law principles as to abstraction from rivers and underground strata are by no means as important at the present time as they were in the past, because the principles have been largely replaced or superseded by the statutory controls imposed on the abstraction of water from sources of supply under Part IV of the W.R.A., 1963, which provides that (subject to specified exceptions) a person may only abstract pursuant to a licence granted by the water authority.

(B) LICENCES TO ABSTRACT WATER

7.03 Restrictions as to Abstraction of Water
(W.R.A. 1963, ss.23, 49; C.L.A. 1977, s.28(2)).

A person must not abstract water from any source of supply (*i.e.* inland waters and underground strata) in a water authority area, or cause or permit another person so to abstract water, except in pursuance of a licence and in accordance with the provisions of that licence.

Where by virtue of the above provision the abstraction of water contained in underground strata is prohibited except under a licence, a person must not begin, or cause or permit another person to begin, to (a) construct a well, borehole or other work whereby water may be abstracted from such strata, or (b) extend any such well, borehole or other work, or (c) install or modify machinery or apparatus whereby additional quantities of water may be abstracted from such strata by means of a well, borehole or other work, unless the abstraction of the water, or the additional quantities of water, is authorised by a licence, and the well, borehole or other work as constructed or extended, or the machinery or apparatus as installed or modified, fulfils the requirements of the licence as to the means whereby water is authorised to be abstracted.

It should be noted that certain abstractions are exempt from the requirements of a licence (*see* para. **7.04**).

A person who contravenes any of the above provisions regarding licensing or who (in circumstances not constituting such a contravention) does not comply with a condition or requirement imposed by the provisions of a licence of which he is the holder, is guilty of an offence and on conviction on indictment or on summary conviction is liable to a fine, which on summary conviction does not exceed £1,000.

These restrictions have effect notwithstanding anything in any other enactment contained in any Act passed before 31st July, 1963, or in any statutory provision made or issued, whether before or after that date by virtue of such an enactment, but do not apply to the doing of anything authorised by an order under the Drought Act, 1976 (*as to which see* paras. **4.19 to 4.22**).

7.04 Exceptions from Licensing
(W.R.A. 1963, ss.24, 25; S.I. 1965 No.1010; W.A. 1973, Sch. 8, para. 78).

In order to keep the system of licensing to reasonable proportions the Act provides that a licence is not necessary in certain types of abstraction of water, namely:—

(a)   Abstractions of a quantity of water not exceeding 1,000 gallons and not forming part of a continuous operation, or of a series of operations, whereby in the aggregate more than 1,000 gallons are abstracted.

(b)   Abstraction from an inland water by or on behalf of an occupier of land contiguous to that water at the point of abstraction for use on a holding consisting of that land (with or without other land held therewith) for the domestic purposes of the occupier's household and/or agricultural purposes other than spray irrigation.

(c)   Abstraction from underground strata by or on behalf of an individual for the domestic purposes of his household.

(d)   Abstraction from an inland water or from underground strata (i) in the course of, or resulting from, land drainage operations, or (ii) otherwise necessary to prevent interference with mining, quarrying, engineering, building or other operations (whether underground or on the surface) or to prevent damage to works resulting from any such operations.

NOTE: For the purposes of the exceptions from licensing, "land drainage" includes the protection of land against erosion or encroachment by water, whether from inland waters or from the sea, and also includes warping and irrigation other than spray irrigation.

(e)   The restriction imposed on the construction or extension of a well, borehole or other work unless the water abstracted is licensed (*see* para. **7.03**) does not apply to the construction or extension of a well, borehole or other work, or the installation or modification of machinery or other apparatus for the purpose of abstracting water from underground strata in cases falling under heads (c) or (d) above.

(f) The transfer of water from one inland water to another in the course of, or resulting from, operations carried out by a navigation, harbour or conservancy authority in the performance of their functions as such an authority.

(g) Abstraction by machinery or apparatus installed on a vessel, where the water is abstracted for use on that vessel or any other vessel.

(h) Anything done for firefighting purposes (i.e. within the meaning of the Fire Services Act 1947) or for the purpose of testing apparatus used for such purposes or of training or practice in the use of such apparatus.

(i) Abstraction, or the construction or extension of a well, borehole or other work, or the installation or modification of machinery or other apparatus, for the purpose (i) of ascertaining the presence of water in underground strata or the quality or quantity of such water, or (ii) of ascertaining the effect of abstracting water from the well, borehole or other work in question on the abstraction of water from, or the level of water in, another well, borehole or other work or an inland water, if it is carried out with the consent of the water authority and in compliance with any conditions imposed by the authority.

Apart from these specific exemptions from the requirements of licensing, the Secretary of State may, on the application of a water authority in relation to inland waters and underground strata in its area, or of a navigation, harbour or conservancy authority having functions in relation to an inland water, by order except one or more sources of supply from the restriction against abstracting water except in pursuance of a licence on the grounds that the restriction imposed is not needed in relation to the source or sources of supply in question.

Lastly, the Spray Irrigation (Definition) Order, 1965 (S.I. 1965 No.1010) provides that certain methods of spray irrigation used in connection with weed or pest control and the spreading of nutrients are excepted from licensing control.

7.05 Borings not requiring licences
(W.R.A. 1963, s.78; C.L.A. 1977, s.28(2))

A person who proposes to construct a well, borehole or other work which is to be used solely for the purpose of abstracting, to the extent necessary to prevent interference with the execution or operation of underground works, water contained in underground strata, or proposes to extend any such well, borehole or other work, must, before he begins to construct or extend the work, give notice of his intention in the prescribed form — *see* the Water Resources (Miscellaneous Provisions) Regulations, 1965 (S.I. 1965 No.1092), regs. 7, 8, Schedule. Similar notice must be given to the water authority by a person who proposes to construct or extend a boring for the purpose of searching for or extracting minerals.

On being given the notice, the water authority may serve a "conservation notice" on the person concerned requiring him to take reasonable measures for conserving water as specified in the notice, being measures which in the opinion of the water authority will not interfere with the protection of the underground works or with the winning of minerals (as the case may be). The person on whom a conservation notice is served may appeal in writing to the Secretary of State on either or both of the following grounds — (1) that the measures required by the conservation notice are not reasonable, and (2) that the measures would interfere with the protection of the underground works or with the winning of minerals. The Secretary of State may confirm, quash or vary the conservation notice and his decision is final. A person who fails to give notice as above or to comply with a conservation notice is guilty of an offence and liable to a fine on conviction on indictment or on summary conviction, provided that an offence is not punishable on summary conviction by a fine exceeding £1,000.

7.06 Facilities for Obtaining Information as to Underground Water
(W.A. 1945, s.7; C.L.A. 1977, sch. 1, para. 6)

Before a person sinks a well or borehole intended to reach a depth of more than fifty feet below the surface for the purpose of searching for or abstracting water, he must give written notice of his intention to the National Environment Research Council, and keep a journal of the progress of the work, including measurements of the strata passed through and of the levels at which water is struck and subesequently rests. A person authorised by the Council must be allowed at reasonable times (a) to have free access to the well or borehole; (b) to inspect the work and material excavated; (c) to take specimens of the material and water abstracted; and (d) to inspect and take copies or extracts from the journal. The person sinking the well or borehole is required, on its completion or abandonment, to send a complete copy of the journal to the Council with particulars of any test made, specifying the rate of flow throughout the test and the duration of the test and also where practicable specifying the water levels during the test and thereafter until the water has returned to its natural level. Where there is an existing pumping station, the rate of pumping there during the test must be stated.

Where the person sinking the well or borehole on land is not the occupier of the land, the obligation to allow the Council to excercise the rights under heads (a) to (d) above rests with the occupier as well as the person sinking the well. Where a person contracts to sink a well etc on land belonging to or occupied by another person and the work is executed under the control of the contractor, he and no other person is deemed to be the person sinking the well etc. There is provision for treating as confidential a copy of or extract from a journal or a specimen taken. A person who fails to comply with an obligation imposed on him by this provision is guilty of an offence against the W.A. 1945, and is liable on summary conviction to a fine not exceeding £200 and, where the offence continues after conviction, to a further fine of £20 for every day during which it so continues.

NOTE 1: The National Environment Research Council is the successor to the Committee of the Privy Council for Scientific and Industrial Research (as provided for in W.A. 1945) — see the Science and Technology Act 1965, 3 & Schedule 2.

NOTE 2: It is important to note that where any well or borehole is sunk in connection with an existing pumping station, the particulars of any test to be supplied to the research council shall also include the rate of pumping at the existing works during the test.

7.07 The different kinds of Licences to Abstract
(W.R.A. 1963, ss.33-35, 56(2), 131(4))

The W.R.A. 1963, provided for the granting of several types of licences to abstract, namely:—

LICENCE OF RIGHT — In order to preserve and protect their rights upon the coming into operation of the WRA, 1963, a licence of right was granted to existing abstractors and those having a statutory entitlement to abstract. Such a licence was issued to (a) persons who were entitled to abstract from a source of supply by virtue of a statutory provision in force on 1st April, 1965, and (b) persons who had, otherwise than by virtue of a statutory provision, actually abstracted water from a source of supply at any time within a period of five years ending on 1st April, 1965. This kind of licence cannot be applied for or granted now.

LICENCE OTHER THAN A LICENCE OF RIGHT — Since 1st July, 1965, a person who wishes to abstract water applies to the water authority for this type of licence. The procedure for applying for a licence and its determination is quite different from that where a licence of right is concerned and the provisions of the W.R.A. 1963, which follow refer only to licences other than a licence of right, unless the contrary is stated.

LICENCE UNDER SECTION 131(4) — This relates to licences made available to British Waterways Board who had contracted to sell water from inland waters owned or managed by the Board.

LICENCE UNDER SECTION 56(2) — Where an application was made before 1st July, 1965, for a licence as respects a statutory provision which came into force after 1st April, 1965, and apart from the W.R.A. 1963, would authorise a person to do anything restricted by s.23 of the Act, *i.e.* as to abstracting water, a licence was required to be granted to the applicant containing provisions corresponding as nearly as may be to those of the statutory provision. '

7.08 Who May Apply for a Licence
(W.R.A. 1963, s.27; W.R.A. 1968, s.1.)

An application for a licence can only be made by the following persons; in the case of abstraction from an inland water, an applicant may apply if at the place of places at which the proposed abstractions are to be effected, either (a) he is the occupier of land contiguous to the inland water, or (b) he satisfies the water authority that he has, or will have at the time when the proposed licence is to take effect, a right of access to such land. As regards abstractions from underground strata, a person may apply if either (i) he is the occupier of land consisting of or comprising the underground strata, or (ii) in a case where water contained in an excavation into underground strata is by virtue of s.2(2)(b) of the W.R.A. 1963 treated as water contained in such underground strata, he satisfies the water authority that he has, or will have at the time when the proposed licence is to take effect, a right of access to land consisting of or comprising the underground strata. In either event a person will be regarded as an occupier of land if he satisfies the water authority that he has entered into negotiations to acquire an interest in land which will entitle him to occupy such land, or that he has been authorised to acquire the land compulsorily or can be so authorised and has submitted an order to the appropriate Minister which, if made or confirmed, will authorise the person to acquire the land compulsorily.

NOTE: Sect 27 of the W.R.A. 1963 does not apply to applications for a licence, other than a licence of right, in respect of inland waters owned or managed by the British Waterways Board to which section 131 applies; *see* para. 7.07.

7.09 Publication of Application for a Licence
(W.R.A. 1963, s.28; S.I. 1965 No.534)

A water authority cannot entertain an application for a licence unless the applicant publishes notice of his proposal in the London Gazette and for each of two successive weeks in one or more newspapers circulating in the locality of the proposed abstraction, and where the licence applied for is for abstraction from an inland water, a copy of the notice has to be served on any navigation, harbour or conservancy authority having functions in relation to the inland water at any proposed point of abstraction, and on any internal drainage board within whose district any point of abstraction is situated. The notice gives details of the proposed abstraction, names a place within the locality in which any point of abstraction is situated where a copy of the application and plan may be inspected by the public free of charge, and states that any person may make written representations to the water authority as to the application within a period of not less than 28 days from the date on which the notice is first published in the local newspaper and not less than 25 days from the date on which it is published in the London Gazette. The application form is sent to the water authority with a map showing the abstraction points and the land occupied by the applicant and (except where water undertakers are the applicants) the land on which the abstracted water is to be used. The notice and application form are prescribed in the Water Resources (Licences) Regulations, 1965 (S.I. 1965 No.534).

NOTE: Suitable forms of Application and Notice are available from Shaw & Sons Ltd.

7.10 Determination by Water Authority of Application for a Licence
(W.R.A. 1963, s.29)

When an application is made to a water authority for a licence to abstract (other than a licence of right), the authority may (a) grant a licence containing such provisions as it considers appropriate, or (b) if, having regard to the provisions of the W.R.A. 1963, it considers it necessary or expedient to do so, may refuse to grant a licence. In determining an application the following provisions have effect:—

(a) The water authority must not grant a licence which would authorise the abstraction of water so as to derogate from any rights which are protected rights at the time when the application is determined (for protected rights, *see* para. **7.14**).

(b) In dealing with the application, the water authority must have regard (i) to any written representations received within the prescribed time in respect of the notice published in the London Gazette and local newspapers (*see* para. **7.09**), and (ii) the requirements of the applicant so far as they appear to be reasonable to the authority.

(c) Where the application relates to abstraction from an inland water, the water authoirity must have regard to the need to secure that the flow at any control point will not be reduced below the minimum acceptable flow (*see* para. **4.16**) for the inland water at that point, or (if it is already less than that minimum acceptable flow) will not be further reduced below that minimum acceptable flow. However, if the application is made at a time when no minimum acceptable flow has been determined for the inland water, regard must be had to the considerations by reference to which a minimum acceptable flow for the inland water would fall to be determined.

(d) Where the application relates to abstraction from underground strata, the water authority has to have regard to the requirements of existing lawful uses for agriculture, industry, water supply or other purposes of water abstracted from such strata, and if it appears to the water authority that the proposed abstraction is likely to affect the flow, level or volume of an inland water, regard shall be had to the minimum aceptable flow considerations referred to in (c) above as if the application related to abstraction from that inland water.

NOTE: There is a right of appeal to the Secretary of State where the applicant for a licence is dissatisfied with the decision of the water authority; Section 39. There is a limited right of appeal to the High Court against the decision of the Secretary of State thereafter; Section 117.

7.11 Matters Specified in the Licence
(W.R.A. 1963, s.30)

Every licence to abstract water must provide for the following —

(1) The quantity of water authorised to be abstracted in pursuance of the licence from the source of supply during a specified period or periods, including the way in which the quantity is to be measured or assessed;

(2) Determining by measurement or assessment what quantity of water is taken to have been abstracted during a specified period by the licence holder from the source of supply;

(3) The means whereby water is authorised to be abstracted by reference either to specified works, machinery or apparatus or to those fulfilling specified requirements;

(4) The land on which, and the purposes for which, the water abstracted is to be used, except where a licence is granted to a water authority or to water undertakers;

(5) The person to whom the licence is granted;

(6) Whether the licence is to remain in force until revoked or is to expire at a specified time;

(7) Such other provisions as the water authority considers appropriate.

The same licence may make different provision as to the abstraction of water (a) during different periods, (b) from the same source of supply but at different points or by different means, (c) for use for different purposes. Two or more licences may be granted to the same person to be held currently in respect of the same source of supply, if the licences authorise the abstraction of water at different points or by different means.

NOTE: The various forms of Licence are available from Shaw & Sons Ltd.

7.12 Effect of Licence
(W.R.A. 1963, s.31)

In any action (except one for negligence or breach of contract) brought against a person in respect of abstraction from an inland water or from underground strata, it is a defence for him to prove that the water was abstracted in pursuance of a licence and that the provisions of the licence were complied with. Subject to the provisions of the W.R.A. 1963, regarding succession to licences (*see* para. **7.13**) and the variation of licences (*see* para. **7.20**), the person to whom a licence is granted is for the purposes of the Act the holder of the licence.

The effect of this section is to provide a statutory defence to the holder of a licence in respect of all civil actions other than for negligence or breach of contract.

If a licence holder abstracts water in pursuance of his licence he will not be liable in nuisance to another riparian owner even though he may have no defence at common law. On the other hand, if a person abstracts water in contravention of his licence, or in the absence of any licence, he may well have a common law defence against another riparian owner notwithstanding that he will be liable to a statutory penalty under Section 49 of the Act.

If a person abstracts water without a licence in one of the exceptional cases where no licence is required, his defence to an action by a riparian owner depends entirely on the common law. The fact that it falls within one of the exceptions only exempts him from liability to a statutory penalty, it does not provide a defence to an action at common law. There is nothing in law to prevent such a person for applying for a licence and thus gaining the protection of the Statute but as a licence holder he would then be liable for whatever charges, in respect of licences granted under the Water Resources Act, as are levied by a water authority.

7.13 Succession to Licences
(W.R.A. 1963, s.32; S.I. 1969 No.976)

Where the holder of a licence to abstract water is the occupier of the whole of the land specified in the licence as the land on which water abstracted pursuant to the licence is to be used, and either, being an individual, he dies, or by reason of any other act or event the original holder, whether an individual or not, ceases to occupy the whole of the land and does not continue to occupy any part of it, and (either immediately after his death or the occurrence of such other act or event or subsequently) another person as successor becomes the occupier of the whole of the land, then the successor becomes the holder of the licence. But should the successor fail to notify the water authority of the change in occupation of the land within one month from the date on which he became the occupier, he ceases to be the licence holder (and then must apply to the water authority for a new licence in the prescribed manner). For cases where a successor becomes the occupier of part of the land, *see* the Water Resources (Succession to Licences) Regulations, 1969 (S.I. 1969 No.976).

7.14 Protected Rights to Abstract Water
(W.R.A. 1963, ss.26, 29(2), 50)

The common law rights relating to the abstraction of water (*see* para. **7.02**) have been mainly replaced by the statutory system of licensing under the W.R.A. 1963, which in turn has created special statutory rights referred to as "protected rights" so as to ensure that the holders of licences to abstract and certain classes of abstractors who are exempt from licensing control may lawfully exercise their rights to abstract in accordance with the Act.

Firstly, the holder of a licence to abstract is taken to have a right to abstract water to the extent authorised by the licence and in accordance with the provisions contained in it. Secondly, in the case of the exempted categories (b) and (c) in para.7.04 a person who is entitled to abstract thereunder without a licence may do so to the extent permitted by those exemptions, namely, water may be taken from an inland water by or on behalf of an occupier of land contiguous to the inland water at the place where the abstraction is effected in so far as the water is abstracted for use on a holding consisting of that land (with or without other land held therewith) for use on the holding for either or both the domestic purposes of the occupier's household for either or both the domestic purposes of the occupier's household and agricultural purposes other than spray irrigation; also, water may be abstracted from underground strata in so far as the water is abstracted by or on behalf of an individual as a supply of water for the domestic purposes of his household.

In determining an application for a licence, the water authority is prohibited from granting the licence if its effect would be to authorise the abstraction of water so as to derogate from any protected rights (*see* para. 7.10). This reference to abstracting water so as to derogate from a protected right means that a licence must not be granted if it would permit the holder thereof to abstract water in such a way, or to such an extent, as to prevent a person entitled to a protected right from abstracting water to the extent permitted in accordance with the protected right.

In the event of a water authority granting a licence which authorises an abstraction of water so as to derogate from a protected right (in breach of the statutory duty not to do so), this does not invalidate the grant or variation of a licence, but it renders the water authority liable to a civil action against the water authority (and not against any other person) for damages for breach of statutory duty by any person entitled to a protected right; the duty cannot be enforced by any criminal proceedings or by prohibition or injunction.

If a water authority is directed by the Secretary of State to grant or vary a licence which subsequently authorises derogation from protected rights, then as between the authority and the person entitled to the protected rights, this amounts to a breach of statutory duty by the water authority, and the duty of the authority to comply with the direction of the Secretary of State does not afford a defence in an action brought against the water authority for breach of its statutory duty. However, this provision does not apply to a direction given in consequence of an appeal against the decision of the water authority on an application for the grant of a licence of right.

In an action brought against a water authority for breach of statutory duty, it is a defence for the authority to prove that the fact that the abstraction authorised by the licence granted or varied by the authority derogated from the protected right of the plaintiff was wholly or mainly attributable to exceptional shortage of rain or to an accident or other unforeseen act or event not caused by, and outside the control of, the water authority. There is another defence available to a water authority; this is where the plaintiff is the holder of, or has applied for, a licence of right and here it is a defence for the authority to prove (a) that the plaintiff could have carried out permissible alterations in the means whereby he abstracted water from the source of supply in question, and (b) that if he had carried out such alterations the abstraction authorised by the licence would not have derogated from his protected rights. The Secretary of State is empowered, if he thinks fit, to indemnify water authorities in certain circumstances.

7.15 Special Provision as to Spray Irrigation
W.R.A. 1963, s.45

Where at any time one or more licences have been issued under the Act and are extant in relation to a source of supply, and that licence authorises water to be abstracted for the purpose of spray irrigation, or for that purpose together with other purposes, and by reason of exceptional shortage of rain or other emergency it appears to the water authority that it is necessary to impose a temporary restriction on the abstraction of water for use for the purposes of spray irrigation then the water authority may by notice serve on the licence holder, reduce, during such period as may be specified in the notice, the quantity of water authorised to be abstracted from the source of supply for the purposes of spray irrigation.

The water authority must not, however serve a notice on the holder of a licence which relates to the abstraction of water from an underground strata unless it appears to the water authority that such abstraction is likely to affect the flow, level or volume of an inland water which constitutes a water supply under the Water Resources Act.

In other words the water authority cannot serve such notice, notwithstanding that the abstraction is likely to affect the flow, level or volume of the inland water if that inland water is either,

(a) an inland water that does not constitute a source of supply, or

(b) the source of supply has been excluded from the restrictions imposed under the Act by an Order made by the Secretary of State pursuant to Section 25 of the W.R.A. 1963.

Where there are two or more licences authorising the abstraction of water for the purpose of spray irrigation in force authorising abstraction from the same source of supply either at the same point or at points which, in the opinion of the water authority, are not far distant from each other then,

(a) the water authority must not serve a notice on the holder of one of the licences unless a similar notice is served on all the holders of the other licences in respect of the same period and

(b) the restrictions imposed by the notices on the holders of the licences shall be so calculated as to represent, as nearly as appears to the water authority to be practicable, the same proportion of the quantity of water authorised by the licences, apart from the notices, to be abstracted for use for the purpose of spray irrigation.

NOTE: Section 25 of the W.R.A. 1963 enables a water authority to apply to the Secretary of State for an Order excepting any one or more sources of supply in its area from the restrictions imposed by sect. 23(1) (*i.e.* the need to have a licence prior to the abstraction of water).

7.16 Charges for Licences to Abstract
(W.R.A. 1963, ss.60, 63, 64; W.A. 1973, s.30, sch.8, para.80, 81, sch.9)

Charges are levied by water authorities in respect of licences to abstract water and these are fixed by a charges scheme (*see* para. **8.14**). In certain cases charges may be reduced or avoided; thus, a person who is liable to pay charges under a licence can apply to the water authority to make an agreement with him for the exemption from or reduction in the charges having regard to (a) the extent to which any works constructed or to be constructed by that person have made or will make a beneficial contribution towards the fulfillment of the purposes of the functions conferred on the water authority by s.9 of the W.A. 1973; (b) any financial assistance which that person has rendered or agreed to render towards the carrying out of works by the water authority in performing such functions; (c) any other material consideration. Should the water authority refuse to make an agreement with an applicant or he objects to the terms of an agreement as proposed by the authority, either party may refer the question in dispute to the Secretary of State, whose decision is final. No charges are levied for water authorised by a licence to be abstracted from underground water for agricultural purposes other than spray irrigation.

The holder of a licence where the purposes for which water is used consist of or include spray irrigation, and the water is to be used on land of which the holder is the occupier, may apply to a water authority to enter into an agreement for a period of at least five years for the charges to be based partly on the quantity of water authorised to be abstracted and partly on the quantity measured or assessed as being abstracted. If the authority refuses to make an agreement with an applicant, or if the licence holder objects to the terms of an agreement as proposed by the authority either party may refer the question to the Secretary of State whose decision is final.

Where charges payable in respect of a licence are not paid within 14 days after written demand has been served on the licence holder, the water authority may by notice in writing suspend the operation of the licence until the charges have been paid.

NOTE: Section 9 of the WA 1973 transferred to Water Authorities the functions which immediately before 1 April 1974 were exercisable by the former river authorities.

(C) LICENCES TO IMPOUND WATER

7.17 Restrictions on Impounding Works
(W.R.A. 1963, ss.36, 37, 49; C.L.A. 1977, s.28(2))

A person must not begin, or cause or permit another person to begin to construct or alter impounding works at any point in an inland water in a water authority area unless (a) a licence under the W.R.A. 1963, granted by the water authority to obstruct or impede the flow of the inland water at that point by means of impounding works is in force, and (b) the impounding works will not obstruct or impede the flow of the inland water except to the extent, and in the manner, authorised by the licence, and (c) any other requirements of the licence, whether as to the provision of compensation water or otherwise, are complied with.

Anyone who contravenes the above provision, or who (in circumstances not constituting such a contravention) does not comply with a condition or requirement imposed by a licence of which he is the holder, is guilty of an offence and on conviction on indictment or on summary conviction is liable to a fine, which on summary conviction must not exceed £1,000.

"Impounding works" means either of the following — (a) a dam, weir or other works in an inland water whereby water may be impounded, and (b) works for diverting the flow of an inland water in connection with the construction or alteration of a dam, weir or other works falling under (a) above.

A licence to impound is not required if —

(i) The construction or alteration of impounding works, or the obstruction or impeding of the flow of the inland water resulting from the construction or alteration of the works, is authorised (in whatever terms, and whether expressly or by implication) by virtue of a statutory provision, other than one which is not contained in, or made or issued under, the WRA, 1963, or the Drought Act, 1976.

(ii) Impounding works are constructed or altered in the course of the performance by a navigation, harbour or conservancy authority of their functions as such an authority.

A person to whom a licence to impound is granted (and no other person) is for the purposes of the W.R.A. 1963, the holder of the licence. In any action brought against a person in respect of an obstruction or impeding of the flow of an inland water at any point by means of impounding works, it is a defence for him to prove that the flow was so obstructed or impeded in pursuance of a licence to impound, and in the manner specified in the licence, and to an extent not exceeding the extent so specified and that any other requirements of the licence were complied with, although this does not exonerate a person from an action for negligence or breach of contract. Where a licence is required for constructing or altering impounding works at a point in an inland water for the purpose of abstracting water therefrom at or near the point, the water authority may grant a combined licence for the impounding and abstraction. The provisions of the W.R.A. 1963, relating to publication and determination of an application for a licence to abstract (see paras. 7.09 and 7.10) have effect with respect to licences to impound. The statutory requirement that a water authority shall not grant or vary a licence to abstract so as to derogate from protected rights includes the duty that a water authority shall not grant or vary a licence to impound which would authorise the holder of the licence to obstruct or impede the flow of an inland water in such a way, or to such an extent, as to prevent a person entitled to a protected right from abstracting water to the extent permitted by such right.

(D) GENERAL PROVISIONS AS TO LICENSING

7.18 Reference of Licence Applications to the Secretary of State
(W.R.A. 1963, s.38; W.A. 1973, sch.8, para.79)

The Secretary of State may give directions (either to a particular water authority or to water authorities generally, or relating to a particular application or to applications of a specified class) requiring applications for licences to be referred to him instead of being dealt with by water authorities. A direction can also be given exempting from the operation of the direction such classes of applications specified in the direction in such circumstances as may be so specified. Before determining an application referred to him, the Secretary of State may, and must if so requested by the applicant or the water authority, hold a local inquiry or hearing. The decision of the Secretary of State on an application referred to him is final, and where the decision is that a licence is to be granted, it includes a direction to the water authority to grant a licence containing such provisions as are specified in the direction.

7.19 Appeals to the Secretary of State
(W.R.A. 1963, ss.39-41; S.I. 1965 No.534)

Where an applicant for a licence is dissatisfied with the decision of the water authority, or by reason of the failure of the water authority to notify him of its decision or that the application has been referred to the Secretary of State (under para. 7.18) within three months from the date of receipt of the application, or within such extended period as agreed in writing between the applicant and the authority, the applicant may give written notice of appeal to the Secretary of State (and serve a copy of the notice on the water authority) within 28 days from the date on which the applicant was notified of the authority's decision, or within three months from the date of receipt of the application or any agreed extension thereof, or within such longer period as the Secretary of State may at any time allow.

The applicant has to provide the Secretary of State with copies of the licence application, all relevant maps and particulars supplied to the water authority, any notice of the decision and all other relevant correspondence with the authority. The water authority must serve copies of the notice of appeal on all persons who made written representations with respect to the application for the licence before it was determined by the water authority, and in determining the appeal the Secretary of State must take into account any further representations received from such persons. The Secretary of State may, and must if so requested by either party, hold a local inquiry or hearing before determining an appeal. The decision of the Secretary of State on appeal is final and where he decides to grant, vary or revoke a licence, the decision shall include a direction to that effect. See also art.12 of the Water Resources (Licences) Regulations, 1965.

7.20 Revocation and Variation of Licences
(W.R.A. 1963, ss.42-44)

A licence holder may apply to the water authority to revoke the licence and the authority must do so accordingly; he may also apply for a variation of his licence in which event the provisions relating to publication and determination of licences and references and appeals to the Secretary of State apply (*see* paras. **7.09, 7.10, 7.18** and **7.19**) with the necessary modifications, except that where the proposed variation is limited to reducing the quantity of water authorised to be abstracted, publication of notice of the variation and consideration of written representations by the water authority under paras. **7.09** and **7.10** do not arise. Where a water authority propose to vary or revoke a licence ss.43 and 44 of the W.R.A. 1963, should be consulted.

7.21 Register of Applications and Licences
(W.R.A. 1963, s.42; S.I. 1965 No.534)

Every water authority must keep a register containing information on applications made to the authority for the grant, variation or revocation of licences, the way in which the applications have been dealt with, as to persons becoming the holders of licences under the provisions dealing with succession to licences (*see* para. **7.13**), applications made by the water authority to abstract and impound water, and licences granted or deemed to be granted. The register is available for public inspection at reasonable hours. The contents and form of the register are given in the Water Resources (Licences) Regulations, 1965, which are dealt with in more detail in para **9.11**.

(E) LAND AND WORKS IN RELATION TO WATER RESOURCES

Where a water authority proposes to carry out works which come within the framework of the water resources functions of the authority (and fall outside the scope of the WA, 1945), Part VI of the WRA, 1963 provides the requisite powers for the compulsory acquisition of land and the performance of engineering or building operations.

7.22 Powers to Acquire and Dispose of Land (W.R.A. 1963, ss.65, 66, 70)

Land (including any interests in or rights over land) may be acquired by a water authority by agreement, or compulsorily on being authorised by the appropriate Minister or Ministers, which is required for any purpose in connection with the performance of any of its functions, although land outside the water authority area and not immediately required for the purpose for which it is being acquired may only be purchased by agreement with the consent of the appropriate Minister or Ministers. Interest in or rights over land may be acquired by agreement or compusorily by way of the creation of new interests or rights, as well as interests or rights already in existence before their acquisition and an interest or right can be acquired either in perpetuity or for a term of years certain or so as to be terminable by notice.

A water authority may sell, exchange or let land vested in it which is not required for the purposes of any of its functions, but the consent of the appropriate Minister or Ministers is required for the disposal of land (i) which was acquired by agreement or compulsorily by the water authority at a time when it was authorised to acquire the land compulsorily, or (ii) at less than the best price, consideration or rent that can reasonably be obtained, having regard to any restrictions or conditions (including conditions as to payment or the giving of security for payment) subject to which the land is disposed of.

7.23 Compulsory Powers for carrying out Engineering or Building Operations
(W.R.A. 1963, ss.67, 69, 70; W.R.A. 1971, s.1)

Where in the performance of its water resources functions a water authority proposes to carry out engineering or building operations, and it appears to the authority that for the purpose of carrying out the operations it needs compulsory powers, whether consisting of or including powers of compulsory acquisition or not, the authority may apply to the Secretary of State for an order. Subject to the provisions of schedule 8 to the W.R.A. 1963, regarding applications and orders, the Secretary of State may make an order conferring on the water authority compulsory powers for the purpose of carrying out the works in question and containing such incidental and supplementary provisions, including provisions for amending, adapting or repealing local enactments, as necessary or expedient.

If it appears appropriate to the Secretary of State to make an order with a view to facilitate the performance of the water resources functions of a water authority, he may on the application of the authority make an order authorising the authority (subject to compliance with any conditions specified in the order) to discharge water into an inland water or underground strata. A person who suffers damage attributable to such a discharge made in pursuance of an order is entitled to recover compensation from the authority in respect of the damage.

Without prejudice to any other powers conferred on it by or under the W.R.A. 1963, or any other Act, a water authority has power to carry out such engineering or building operations as it considers necessary or expedient for the purposes of any of its functions. For the purposes of anything done or to be done by water authorities in the performance of their water resources functions, ss.9, 12-17, 19, 20, 22, 28, 67 and 68 of the Third Schedule to the W.A. 1945, as modified by Schedule 9 to the W.R.A. 1963, have effect in relation to water authorities.

Chapter 8

FINANCE

8.01 Synopsis

The Water Act 1973 introduced a novel and far-reaching change in the method of raising revenue. Water authorities are given a general power to make such charges as they think fit in respect of the water services provided by the water authorities; certain constraints are however placed on the unbridled use of that general power.

In general terms, direct domestic consumers of water authorities pay a water charge which is related to the rateable value of the premises occupied; other consumers of water authorities, such as agriculture, manufacturing industry, and commerce pay a charge related to the volume of water supplied to the premises, i.e. by reference to a water meter.

Many and varied were the financial systems inherited by water authorities on 1 April 1974. The Water Act 1973 imposed a duty on water authorities to fix charges by means of a charges scheme, subject to certain principles, regulating the charges to be levied and recovered for the services performed, facilities provided, or rights made available, or to enter into agreements with consumers whereby such charges, in respect of the services performed, facilities provided, or rights made available by the water authorities to the consumers, were identified.

Transitional arrangements for the collection and recovery of water authority charges were provided by means of Orders made by the Secretary of State in exercise of the powers conferred by Section 254 of the Local Government Act 1972 and subsequently as applied and extended by the Local Government Act 1974, the Water Act 1973 and the Water Charges Act 1976. The effect of those Collection of Charges Orders were to make provision for the collection and recovery on behalf of water authorities by local authorities, who are rating authorities, of charges made by water authorities for the supply of water and in respect of the other charges that a water authority may levy.

Water Authorities currently charge their consumers direct under the provisions of the Water Act 1973. See paras. **8.13** and **8.14** *post*.

Water authorities have discretion as to the means by which their charges are levied and recovered. They may directly levy and seek to recover all charges direct from their consumers in respect of the services provided or a water authority may enter into arrangements with a statutory water company whereby the statutory water company will levy and recover on behalf of the water authority (Section 7(5)(b) and paragraph 53(3) of Schedule 8 to the Water Act 1973) or enter into an agreement with a local authority pursuant to section 38 of the Local Government Act 1974 which modified the Water Act 1973, to allow a local authority to collect and recover on behalf of the water authority any charges payable for services performed, facilities provided or rights made available in the local authorities area by the water authority.

The powers of water authorities and of the National Water Council to raise loan capital are prescribed by the Water Act 1973.

Water companies, who are required to issue stock by auction or tender, have their rates of dividend controlled and are limited as to the amounts which can be transferred to reserve and contingency funds or carried forward at the end of the year and any surplus remaining must be applied to reducing charges.

It must not be forgotten that statutory water companies act as agents for water authorities under any statutory provision relating to the supply of water except for Part VIII of the Third Schedule to the Water Act 1945 (i.e. the supply of water for public purposes). The powers of statutory water companies to fix, demand and recover charges or the "water rate" is generally to be found in the Water Act 1945, as amended, and in private legislation.

NOTE: The level of charges of water authorities and of water rates levied by the statutory water companies were subject to the approval of the Price Commission established by the Price Commission Acts. The Competition Act 1980 abolished the Price Commission; statutory water undertakers, as defined in the Water Act 1973, are included amongst the bodies subject to the provisions of the Competition Act 1980 and therefore to investigation by the Office of Fair Trading. The provisions of the Competition Act 1980 are outside the scope of this book; it is important to note however that the Competiton Act provides machinery for an independent investigation into the efficiency of a statutory water undertaker and to determine whether there is an abuse of the monopolistic position vis-a-vis the consumers of that undertaker.

(A) EXPENSES AND CONTRIBUTIONS, ETC.

8.02 Expenses of the Secretary of State
(W.A. 1945, s.52 W.A. 1973, Sch. 3, para. 35.)

Any expenses incurred by the Secretary of State in the exercise of his functions under the W.A. 1945, are defrayed out of moneys provided by Parliament.

The Secretary of State is empowered, subject to Treasury approval, to make such grants to water authorities "as he thinks fit." Such grants are made out of money provided by Parliament. The Secretary of State has power to give direction to a water authority that the whole or part of any such grant is not to be used by the Authority otherwise than for the purpose of such an authority's functions as are specified in the direction, not being land drainage functions.

8.03 Contributions towards Rural Water Supplies
(Rural Water Supplies and Sewerage Acts 1944-1965 as amended by the Rural Water Supplies and Sewerage Act 1971; Water Act 1973 (Schedules 8 and 9) and Statute Law (Repeals) Act 1975).

The Acts originally provided for grants by central government (the Minister of Health, and subsequently the Minister of Housing and Local Government being the appropriate Ministers) and by County Councils towards the expenses incurred by District Councils in providing water supplies and sewage disposal facilities. As a consequence of the water reorganisation by virtue of the Water Act 1973, the statutes now enable the Secretary of State only to make grants to water authorities; section 2 of the 1944 Act, which empowered county councils to make contributions towards the expenses of rural water supplies, has been repealed.

Subject to such conditions as the Treasury may determine, the Secretary of State may make a contribution towards the expenses incurred by a water authority in providing a supply, or in improving an existing supply, of water in a rural locality.

The Secretary of State may withhold, or reduce the amount of, a contribution which he has undertaken to make towards the expenses incurred by a water authority in respect of any works or transaction, if it appears to him either:—

(a) That any of the works has been executed in an unsatisfactory manner, or

(b) That the effectiveness of any of the works is substantially less than as estimated in the proposal submitted to him by the water authority an that the differences are due to any default, for which the water authority is responsible, in the formulation of the proposals, or,

(c) That there has been any default in carrying out the transaction.

The Acts do not specify any rate of grant. Each application by a water authority is considered by the Secretary of State on its merits.

All grants made by the Secretary of State are defrayed out of monies provided by Parliament.

8.04 Contributions to Enable Industrial Development
(Local Employment Act 1972, s.7.)

Where the Secretary of State considers that adequate provision has not been made for the needs of any development area or intermediate area in respect of water services and it is expedient with a view to contributing to development of industry in that area that the service should be improved, the Secretary of State may, with the consent of Treasury make grants or loans towards the cost of improving the water service to the statutory water undertaker. The test is whether development of the area and in particular industrial development depends on the provision of the water service.

8.05 Expenses of the Minister
(Land Drainage Act 1976, s.90.)

Since land drainage includes the provision of irrigation works other than spray irrigation, the Minister has power to make a grant in aid towards the expenditure incurred by water authorities in the improvement of any existing drainage works relating to irrigation or the construction of new drainage works relating to irrigation of land. The level of such grants is subject to Treasury approval and subject to such conditions as may, with the approval of the Treasury, be prescribed.

8.06 Subscriptions to Associations etc.
(WA. 1948, s.9; W.A. 1973, sch. 8, para. 61).

A statutory water company and a joint board and joint water committee within the meaning of the W.A. 1973 may pay reasonable subscriptions whether annually or otherwise to the funds of any association representing any description of water undertakers and formed for the purpose of consultation as to their common interests and the discussion of matters relating to the supply of water. Statutory Water companies may, pursuant to Section 78 of the Third Schedule of the W.A. 1945:—

(a) give donations or subscriptions to charitable institutions, sick funds, benevolent funds and other objects calculated to benefit their employees;
(b) subscribe to the funds of any association formed for the purpose of furthering the interests of water undertakers;
(c) make contributions for furthering research in matters with which water undertakers and their officers are concerned.

8.07 Raising Capital and Borrowing Money
(W.A. 1945, s.23)

On the application of persons who are or propose to become statutory water undertakers, the Secretary of State may make an order authorising the applicants to raise capital or borrow money for any purposes of the undertaking.

Section 11(6) of the Water Act 1973 defines statutory water undertakers as being water authorities, statutory water companies, joint water boards and joint water committees, and **no other body.**

Section 38(1) of the Water Act 1973 defines "joint water board" and "joint water committee" as a joint board and a joint committee which has been constituted under section 9 of the Water Act 1945 and on which a statutory water company is represented.

The Water Act 1973 prescribes the means whereby water authorities and the national water council may borrow money; *see* para. **8.08.**

8.08 Loans and Grants — Water Authorities/National Water Council

(W.A. 1973, Sch. 3.)

The National Water Council and water authorities may borrow money only in accordance with the provisions of paragraph 34 of the Part III of Schedule 3 to the Water Act 1973. That paragraph provides that the National Water Council and water authorities may borrow,

(a) On a short term basis, by way of overdraft or otherwise, such sums as they may require for meeting their obligations and discharging their functions from:—

    (i) In sterling from the Secretary of State, or,

    (ii) With the consent of the Secretary of State and the approval of the Treasury, or in accordance with any general authority given by the Secretary of State with the approval of the Treasury, either in sterling or in a currency other than sterling from a person other than the Secretary of State.

(b) Medium and long term loans to meet their capital requirements from,

    (i) In sterling from the Secretary of State, or,

    (ii) With the consent of the Secretary of State and the approval of the Treasury, in a currency other than sterling, from a person other than the Secretary of State.

The Treasury may guarantee, in such manner and such conditions as they think fit, the repayment of the principle of and the payment of interest on any sums which an authority or the Council borrow from a person other than the Secretary of State. Any such guarantee must be laid before each House of Parliament and the Treasury must also report to each House when the guarantee is finally discharged.

Water authorities and the Council, subject to the consent of the Secretary of State and the approval of the Treasury, borrow (otherwise than by way of temporary loan) from the Commission of the European Communities or the European Investment

Bank. To borrow from the European Investment Bank it is necessary to satisfy that Bank that the capital is required for a project envisaged by Article 130 of the Treaty of Rome.

Neither the National Water Council nor water authorities are free agents as to the limits of the total loan capital they may employ; paragraph 34 of Schedule 3 specifically imposes a two-prong control in that:—

(1) The aggregate amounts outstanding in respect of the principal of sums borrowed by water authorities and the Council and also any sums borrowed or treated by or by virtue of any enactment as borrowed by local authorities towards the discharge of the principal or interest of which water authorities are making contributions must not exceed £3,750m or such greater sum not exceeding £5,000m as the Secretary of State may by order specify.

(2) The Secretary of State may also by order, subject to a resolution of the House of Commons, specify a financial limit for the borrowing of any individual water authority or of the Council.

The Secretary of State may with approval of the Treasury make to a water authority, out of monies provided by Parliament, grants of such amounts as the Secretary of State thinks fit. In this connection the Secretary of State has power to give an individual water authority a direction providing that the whole or part of such a grant is not to be used by the water authority for any purpose other than the purpose specified in the direction.

The Secretary of State is under statutory duty, as respects each financial year, to account to the Comptroller and Auditor General on any sums lent by him to the Council or water authorities or any grants made by him to water authorities.

8.09 Statutory Water Companies
(W.A. 1945, ss.41-43; Third Schedule, Part XV (ss.74-77))

Statutory water companies in general come within the scope of the Companies Clauses Consolidation Acts, 1845-89 (these statues are not dealt with in this book), dependent upon the application of those Acts to a statutory water company on its incorporation by special Act of Parliament or Provisional Order, and some provisions of the W.A. 1945 refer to or may be applied to water companies, namely:-

s.41 Power of companies to issue re- *Not included* deemable stock *in this book*

s.42 Accounts of companies to be *See* para. **8.10** made up annually and abstracts sent to Minister and local authorities

s.43 Appointments of officers as *See* para. **9.18** directors

Third Schedule

s.74 Maximum rates of dividend

s.75 Sale of stock by auction or tender *Not included*

s.76 Reserve and contingency funds *in this book*

s.77 Limitation on balance carried forward at end of year

NOTE: By virtue of Section 1 (1) and the First Schedule to the Trustee Investments Act 1961 a trustee may invest any property in his hands, whether at the time in a state of investment or not, in debentures or in the guaranteed or preference stock of any statutory water undertaker which has during each of the ten years immediately preceding the calendar year in which the investment is to be made has paid a dividend of not less that the prescribed amount on its ordinary shares.

The 1961 Act prescribes a minimum dividend of 5%. This was amended to 2.5% in relation to dividends paid after 1972 — see Trustee Investment (Water Companies) Order 1973,(S.1. 1973 No. 1393)

8.10 Accounts of Statutory Water Companies to be made up annually
(W.A. 1945, s.42; W.A. 1948, s.7; W.A. 1973, Sch.8, para. 54)

Statutory water undertakers who are a statutory water company are required to prepare an annual abstract of their accounts, showing their income and expenditure with any reserve or contingency fund balances, signed by their chairman and certified by the auditors, and the Secretary of State may give directions as to the form of the abstract. Copies of the certified abstract and of the balance sheet has to be forwarded to the Secretary of State and to each county council and district council within which the company supply water or have waterworks and to any water authority on whose behalf the company is supplying water pursuant to s.12 of the W.A. 1973 (see para. **3.08**). If any of the above provisions is not complied with the company is for each offence liable on summary conviction to a fine not exceeding £20. The accounts of water authorities are dealt with in the W.A. 1973, Sch. 3, para. 38.

8.11 Accounts of Water Authorities and of the Council (W.A. 1973, Sch. 3; L.G.A. 1972, Pt VIII)

Water authorities and the National Water Council are under a statutory duty to keep proper accounts and proper records in relation to those accounts, and to prepare in respect of each financial year a statement of accounts.

Paragraph 39 of Schedule 3, Water Act 1973, applies the Accounts and Audit provisions of Part VIII of the Local Government Act 1972 (i.e. sections 154 to 167). The Secretary of State has wide regulation making powers with respect to the form, preparation, keeping and certification of accounts and procedures connected with audit, but the Secretary of State cannot direct the auditor in the performance of his duties; section 166 L.G.A. 1972.

The accounts of water authorities and of the Council are subject to audit by a district auditor or by an approved auditor, i.e. an auditor belonging to a professional body named in the Local Government Act 1972 and whose appointment by the water authority or by the Council has been approved by the Secretary of State; Sections 154, 164 of the L.G.A. 1972. The choice of audit lies with the water authority and with the Council and it is open to an authority, once having made its choice, to change to another auditor, i.e. a district auditor or another approved auditor; any such resolution by a water authority or by the Council is subject to the approval of the Secretary of State.

The general law relating to audit lies outside the scope of this book. It is of importance to note however that all persons interested may inspect the accounts to be audited and all books, deeds, contracts, bills, vouchers and receipt and such persons may make copies of such documents. In addition a local government elector may inspect documents of account and may question the auditor about them and he may do this through a representative.

Any person, on application to the water authority or to the National Water Council, is entitled to be furnished with copies of the statement of their accounts and of the auditors report on those account on payment of such reasonable sum as the authority or the Council may determine, and to inspect and to take copies of, or extracts from, an abstract of the accounts of the authority or of the Council free of charge.

(B) REVENUE — WATER CHARGES

8.12 General Financial Principles
(W.A. 1973, s.29)

Every water authority is required to discharge its functions so that taking one year with another its revenue is sufficient to meet its expenditure, and the Secretary of State with Treasury approval and after consulting the National Water Council may by order direct (1) that an authority shall discharge its functions during a specified period so to achieve a specified rate of return on its net assets; (2) that an authority shall in the discharge of its functions be under any other financial obligation as the Secretary of State thinks fit. An order made under para. (1) above is subject to annulment by a resolution of either House of Parliament, and an order made under para. (2) above has to be laid in draft before and approved by resolution of each House. The water authority must also secure that its charges make a proper contribution to the discharge of its duty under this provision and Part III of Sch.3 to the W.A. 1973, taking into account its present circumstances, future prospects and any directions given herein by the Secretary of State.

8.13 Water Charges
(W.A. 1973, s.30; W.C.A. 1976)

A water authority is empowered to fix such charges for its

services performed, facilities provided or rights made available by it (including separate charges for separate services, facilities or rights or combined charges for a number of services, facilities or rights) as the authority thinks fit, and to demand, take and recover such charges:—

(a)   for services performed, facilities provided or rights made available in the exercise of any of its functions, from persons for whom it performs the services, provides the facilities or makes the rights available, and

(b)   without prejudice to head (a) above, for services performed, facilities provided or rights made available in the exercise of functions relating to (i) sewerage and sewage disposal from persons liable to be rated in respect of hereditaments referred to in s.30(1A) of the W.A. 1973, and (ii) environmental services specified in s.30(1B) of the W.A. 1973, from all persons liable to be rated in respect of hereditaments in its area or particular classes of such hereditaments.

NOTE: Para (b) above was added to s.30 of the W.A. 1973, by s.2 of the W.C.A. 1976, to meet the situation created by the decision in *Daymond* v *South West Water Authority* [1976] A.C. 609 H.L. and to reinforce the powers of water authorities to charge under s.30.

A water authority may fix charges by means of a charges scheme or by agreement with any person and may fix its charges by reference to such criteria and adopt such system for calculating their amount as appears to be appropriate. In fixing charges for services, facilities or rights a water authority must have regard to the cost of performing services, providing facilities or making available rights, and an authority may make different charges for the same service, facility or right in different cases, but each authority must take steps to ensure that not later than 1st April, 1981, its charges will not show undue preference to, or unduly discriminate against, any class of persons. After consultation with the National Water Council, the Secretary of State may give directions to water authorities as to the criteria to be applied or the system to be adopted.

Where a water authority introduces a new system of charges, it may make such transitional charging arrangements as it thinks fit for up to a period of five years. Nothing in any enactment passed before the W.A. 1973, shall operate so as to oblige a water authority to fix separate charges for separate services, facilities or rights. No local statutory provision (other than one expressly providing that no charge shall be made for a service, facility or right) shall limit the discretion of a water authority or of a statutory water company through whom a water authority are supplying water as to the charges to be made, whether the provision specifies the charges or fixes maximum charges or otherwise. Any such limitation in a local statutory provision ceased to have effect on 1st April, 1974, but water authorities and companies through whom water authorities are supplying water must, in fixing charges up to 1st April, 1981, have regard to any special relevant circumstances and any likely differences in the levels of charges if the provision had continued to apply.

The terms "undue preference," "discriminate unduly against," and "any class of persons" are not defined in the Water Acts but they have received judicial consideration in cases concerning electricity supply.

In *London Electricity Board* v *Springate* [1969] 3 All E.R. 289, The Court of Appeal held that having regard to the circumstances of supply and of the potential consumption, a higher standing charge for larger houses was valid as there was no undue discrimination against the occupiers of larger houses. A justified discrimination is not undue discrimination and the fact that a consumer for reasons of his own chooses not to exercise his greater potential demand does not convert a charge related to the potential demand to "undue"; "We have to decide whether or not there was discrimination against him (the consumer) or preference for somebody else; further whether, if preference or discrimination is proved, it was undue. It has been pointed out that the differences of methods of assessment must be looked at "in the rough," and the real test, I think, is this; that, unless it is so extravagant that it must be wrong, the court will not interfere."

Per Karminski, L J at page 292.

In the *South of Scotland Electricity Board* v *British Oxygen Company Limited* [1956] 3 All E.R. 199 the House of Lords were faced with two issues, namely:—

(a) Whether discrimination was not "undue discrimination" within the meaning of the Electricity Act 1947 unless it has been exercised for illegitimate reasons, and

(b) The interpretation of "class of persons"

The Lords held that:-

(a) Undue discrimination is not dependent upon the exercise of an illegitimate reason; it is a question of fact. A preference or a discrimination may be undue on the grounds of excess, if the excess is substantial but whether such excess is substantial is a question of fact; mere arithemetical disparity ocurrence as between two consumers on a different system of supply is a very unsafe guide on which to decide, without the assistance of evidence technical or otherwise, relating to the question of preference or discrimination. Other considerations may neutralise or extinquish what seems to be an apparent preference.

(b) High voltage consumers and low voltage consumers are sufficiently heterogeneous in character to constitute a separate "class of persons" within the meaning of Section 37 of the Electricity Act 1947.

See also *Phipps* v *London and North Western Railway Company* [1892] 2 Q.B. 229 and *Attorney General* v *Wimbledon Corporation* [1940] 1 All E.R. 76.

8.13-1 Charges for water for fire fighting
(W.A. 1981, s.2)

The Water Act 1981 (s.2) provides that notwithstanding anything in s.30 or in any Charges Scheme made under s.31 of the W.A. 1973 or in any agreement made under s.27 of the W.A. 1945, but subject to the provisions of any statutory order made by the Secretary of State pursuant to the powers

vested in him by virtue of s.2 of the W.A. 1981, no charge may
be made by statutory water undertakers in respect of:—
(a)   water taken for the purposes of extinguishing fires or of
       testing apparatus installed or equipment used for ex-
       tinguishing fires;
(b)   the availability of water for those purposes

The Secretary of State may by order made by statutory instrument make provision as to the method by which and the criteria
by reference to which statutory water undertakers shall
calculate the charges payable to them for water supplied where
the supply of water provided for the purposes mentioned above
is by means of a service pipe which also supplies water for other
purposes; and such order may make provision for arbitration.

Section 2 does not prevent the making of charges in respect of
work carried out at the request of or for the benefit of any person receiving any supply of water for the purposes mentioned in
(a) above. Likewise Section 2 does not prevent the making of
charges in respect of a supply of water for domestic purposes
where any of the water is used for any of the purposes mentioned in (a) above.

Section 2 shall come into force on such a day as the Secretary
of State may by order appoint; and different days may be so appointed for different provisions of the section, or for different
purposes of the same provision and in particular, different days
may be so appointed for the coming into force of the same provision in different water authority areas or for different parts of
the same area. Such an order may contain such transitional, incidental, supplementary and consequential provisions as the
Secretary of State may consider necessary or expedient in connection with the provisions of Section 2. Any such order shall be
subject to annulment in pursuance of a resolution of either
House of Parliament.

In Section 2
(a)   'service pipe' and 'a supply of water for domestic pur-
       poses' have the meanings assigned to them by s.1(1) of the
       Third Schedule to the W.A. 1945; (see para. **2.03** *ante*)
(b)   'statutory water undertakers' has the meaning assigned to

it by 11(6) of the Water Act 1973. (see para. **8.07** *ante*)

8.14 Charges Schemes
(W.A. 1973, s.31)

A water authority may make a charges scheme for the charges to be paid for any services performed, facilities provided or rights made available by it and directions may be given by the Secretary of State to water authorities as to the services, facilities or rights for which provision is to be made in a charges scheme. Schemes must be framed to show the methods by which and the principles on which the charges are to be made, and shall be published in such manner as in the opinion of the authority will secure adequate publicity for them. A charges scheme may revoke or amend a previous scheme and a scheme does not affect any power of a water authority to make agreements about charges as it was empowered to make before the W.A. 1973, and in particular relating to (*a*) s.7 of the Public Health (Drainage of Trade Premises) Act, 1937; (*b*) s.27 of the W.A. 1945 (*see* para. **6.06**); and (*c*) s.63 of the W.R.A. 1963 (*see* para. **7.16**).

In making a charges scheme the water authority should observe the principles contained in Sections 29 and 30 of the W.A. 1973 — in particular the duty that is imposed on a water authority by Section 29(1) and Section 30(4) i.e. the duty of every water authority to discharge their functions so as to secure that, taking one year with another, their revenue is not less than sufficient to meet their total outgoings properly chargeable to revenue accounts and further that in fixing charges for services, facilities or rights a water authority must have regard to the cost of performing those services providing those facilities or making available those rights. From the cases referred to earlier in relation to Electricity supply it would appear that there is no duty on a water authority to devise a system of charge under which each consumer is charged in exact proportion to the cost of supply; see *Attorney General* v *Wimbledon Corporation* [1940] 1 All E.R. 76.

As for agreements and charges relating to the drainage of trade premises see Sections 43, 44, 45 and 52 of the Control of

Pollution Act 1974.

8.15 Water Charges Equalisation Fund
(W.C.E.A. 1977, ss.1-4)

If for 1978 or any subsequent year it appears to the Secretary of State that, in proportion to the number of premises to which a supply of water is provided on an unmeasurable basis, the relevant financing costs (as defined by s.1(4) of the W.C.E.A. 1977) are less than the average of the relevant financing costs of all statutory water undertakers in England and Wales, he may by order (see, *e.g.* the Water Charges Equalisation Order, 1977) direct the undertaker to pay an equalisation levy to the National Water Council.

For each year for which an equalisation levy is payable, the Secretary of State must by order direct the Council to pay equalisation payments to those statutory water undertakers whose relevant financing costs for that year exceed the average unit costs (as defined in s.1(6) of the W.C.E.A. 1977). Equalisation payments equal in the average the equalisation levies and any discrepancy is adjusted by the Secretary of State. Before making an order the Secretary of State has to consult the Council and a draft of the order must be approved by resolution of the House of Commons.

In fixing water charges a water authority must treat an equalisation levy and an equalisation payment respectively as an addition to and a reduction of the cost to the authority in the corresponding accounting period of providing water supplies on an unmeasured basis, and the amount of an equalisation levy or payment which a statutory water company is either required to pay or entitled to receive in respect of any year must be passed on in full in the form of increased or reduced charges to the persons to whom water is supplied by the company on an unmeasured basis in the corresponding accounting period.

8.16 Collection of Charges by Local Authorities
(W.A. 1973, s.32A; L.G.A. 1974, s.38)

By agreement a local authority may collect and recover on behalf of a water authority any charges payable for services performed, facilities provided or rights made available in the local authority's area by the water authority, and such charges may be demanded, collected and recovered by the local authority in like manner and together with the general rate.

(C) WATER RATES AND CHARGES

8.17 Liability for and Recovery of Water Rates and Charges (W.A. 1945, s.38; W.A. 1973, sch. 8, para. 53, sch. 9)

Any reference in s.38 of the W.A. 1945, to a water rate is construed as including a reference to any charge payable under Part III of the W.A. 1973, and without prejudice to the power of a statutory water company to act as agent for a water authority apart from this provision, a statutory water company who are supplying water on behalf of a water authority may recover on behalf of the authority within the company's limits of supply and exercise on behalf of the authority any other powers of the authority under s.38, and references in that section to the undertakers is construed accordingly.

Water rates and charges payable to statutory water undertakers are payable and recoverable in accordance with the following provisions and not otherwise. The water rate or charge is payable by the occupier of any premises, except where an owner of premises, who is not himself the occupier is liable by or under any enactment, or by agreement with the undertakers, to pay the water rate or charge for a supply of water to those premises. The water rate or charge payable by any person may after a demand therefor be recoverable from him by the undertakers either summarily as a civil debt or as a simple contract debt in any court of competent jurisdiction. Where a person fails to pay within seven days after a demand therefor any instalment of a water rate or payment of a charge payable by him in respect of the premises, the undertakers may cut off the supply of water to the premises and recover the expenses they have so reasonably incurred in the same manner as the instalment or payment due, but if before the seven days expire they are given written notice that there is a dispute as to the amount due or as to the liability to pay the rate or charge, they must not cut off the supply of water until the dispute has been settled by a magistrates court on the application of either party. So far as the recovery of rates in concerned, water need not be supplied direct to the premises; it is enough if it is supplied in connection with the premises by virtue of a right attached thereto (*West Pennine Water Board* v *Jon Migael (North West) Ltd* (1975) 235 E.G. 47, C.A.).

Where, when an instalment of a water rate or payment of a charge in respect of any premises becomes due, the owner of the premises is liable by or under any enactment, or by agreement with the undertakers, to pay the water rates or charges for a supply of water to such premises and is not himself the occupier thereof, the undertakers must not cut off the supply of water for his failure to pay the instalment or payment, which may be recovered by the undertakers either from the owner for the time being or from the occupier for the time being of the premises in the manner in which water rates or charges are recoverable. But proceedings cannot be commenced against the occupier until he has been given notice requiring him to pay the amount due out of any rent then due, and he has failed to comply with the notice.

If any water supply is cut off by the undertakers in contravention of the above provisions they are liable on summary conviction to a fine not exceeding £5 for each day during which the water remains cut off. Undertakers are liable to be restrained if they improperly cut off a supply (*Hayward* v *East London Waterworks Co.* (1884) 28 Ch.D.138). Undertakers who were requested to cut off a supply were held liable in *Watson* v *Sutton District Water Co.* [1940] 3 All E.R. 502 for damage resulting from their failure to do so.

8.18 Notice to be given to Local Authority of Water Supplied to Inhabited House being Cut Off
(W.A. 1945, s.39, C.L.A. 1977, s.31)

Where in the exercise of its power under s.38 of the W.A. 1945 (*see* para. **8.17**) or for any other reason, statutory water undertakers cut off the supply of water to an inhabited house, they must within 48 hours give notice that they have done so to the local authority of the district in which the house is situated; if they fail to do so they are liable on summary conviction to a fine not exceeding £25.

8.19 Restoration or Continuation of Supply of Water
LG (MP) A 1976, s.33

If any premises in the area of a District Council, a London Borough Council or the Common Council (that is the Common Council of the City of London) are occupied as a dwelling and the supply of water to the premises is:—

(a) cut off in consequence of the failure of the owner or former owner of the premises to pay a sum payable by him in connection with the supply, or,

(b) in the opinion of the Council likely to be cut off in consequence of such a failure,

that council may, at the request in writing of the occupier of the premises, make such arrangements as it thinks fit with the statutory water undertaker for the supply to be restored to the premises or, as the case may be, for the supply to be continued to the premises.

Where the council has made such a payment, the council is entitled to demand (such a demand must be in writing) and recover the sum paid, together with interest on such sum (at the rate fixed by section 171(2) of the Local Government Act 1972) from,

(a) the person liable to pay in connection with the supply,

(b) where the payment was made in order to restore a supply to any premises or the payment was made in respect of a supply to the premises (and those premises are occupied as a dwelling), from the owner of the premises concerned.

Where the council is entitled to recover from the owner of any premises a sum on account of the payment in respect of the restoration or continuation of a supply to the premises or a payment for a supply to the premises or interest on such a sum and

(a) the owner of the premises is, under the terms on which a person occupies the premises, required to pay for a supply of water and

(b) the council has served a written notice on that person requiring him to pay to the council, instead of to the owner of the premises, the rent for the premises which is payable by that person to the owner of the premises, it is the duty of that person to comply with the notice and the council may recover from that person from time to time sums equal to the rent in question in order to recover the sum paid by the council to the statutory water undertaker.

8.20 Water Rates and Charges
(W.A. 1945, Third Schedule Part XII (ss.46, 52-59); W.A. 1973, sch. 8, para. 53, sch. 9)

Part XII of the Third Schedule to the W.A. 1945 has been amended and in part repealed by the W.A. 1973 and besides dealing with water rates now refers to charges payable under Part III of the W.A. 1973 in the nature of rates for a supply of water and the provision of other services. The updated provisions of Part XII (which may be applied to a water undertaking by order) are referred to below.

Water rates (Section 46)

For the purposes of Part XII (a) where water supplied to a house within the curtilage of a factory is used solely for the domestic purposes of occupants of the house, the house is deemed separate premises not forming part of the factory; (b) the net annual value of any premises is taken to be that value as appearing in the valuation list in force on the first day of the twelve month period covered by the rate of charge, but if that value does not so appear therein, or if the water rate or charge is chargeable on a part only of a hereditament entered, the net annual value is taken to be such sum or such fairly apportioned part of the net annual value of the whole hereditament as, in default of agreement, is determined by the Lands Tribunal.

Provision as to supply to sheds, tents, vans, etc.
(Section 52)

A person is not entitled to demand, or to continue to receive, from the undertakers a supply of water to any habitation (which is defined as a tent, van or other conveyance, whether on wheels or not, and sheds or similar structures, not being structures to which the building regulations apply) unless he has (a) agreed with the undertakers to take a supply of water by meter and to pay them an annual sum to cover the expense in providing the required supply, other standing charges and a reasonable return on the cost of water supplied; and (b) secured to the undertakers' reasonable satisfaction, by deposit or otherwise, payment of a sum having regard to his possible maximum demand for water.

Liability to water rates where buildings supplied by common pipe (Section 53)

Where two or more houses or other buildings occupied by different persons are supplied with water by common pipe, the ownere or occupier of each of them is liable to pay the same water rate or charge for the supply as he would have been liable to pay if it had been supplied with water by a separate pipe.

Water rates on certain house may be demanded from the owners (Section 54).

Where a house or other building supplied with water by the undertakers has a net value not exceeding £13 (in London £20 is substituted for £13), the owner instead of the occupier must pay the rate or charge for the supply of water, if the undertakers so resolve. An owner who pays the water rate has a duty to take care that water supplied is not wasted (*Brock* v *Harrison* [1899] 1 Q.B. 958).

Making and dates for payment of water rates (Section 55)

Undertakers make a water rate or charge by fixing, in respect of a twelve month period commencing on either 1st January, 1st April, 1st July or 1st October, the rate-poundage or the scale of rate-poundages by reference to which amounts due under the rate or charge are to be calculated, and the rate or charge is payable in advance by equal quarterly instalments on those dates, or if the undertakers so resolve by equal half-yearly instalments. Where payment is in advance by half-yearly instalments proceedings cannot be commenced for the recovery of an instalment until two months have expired from the first day of the half-year in respect of which it has been demanded.

Effect on water rates of alteration in valuation list (Section 56)

Where a valuation list in force is altered by a proposal or requisition then for the purpose of calculating the amount due in respect of any water rate or charge payable under the special Act, the alteration has effect retrospectively as from the date when the proposal or requisition was made.

Discount for prompt payment of water rates and charges (Section 57)

The undertakers may allow discounts or rebates in consideration of prompt payment of water rates and charges, provided that a discount or rebate is at the same rate under like circumstances to all persons and does not exceed 5%, and notice of the effect of this section must be endorsed on every demand note for water rates and charges.

Recovery of rates and charges from persons leaving premises (Section 58)

If it is shown to the satisfaction of a justice of the peace on sworn information in writing that a person is quitting, or is about to quit, premises to which the undertakers supply water and has failed to pay on demand an instalment of a water rate or charge payable by and due from him in respect of the premises, the justice may, in addition to issuing a summons for non-payment, issue a warrant authorising entry on the premises and to seize sufficient goods and chattels of the defaulter to meet the undertakers' claim and to detain them until the complaint is determined.

Register of meter to be evidence (Section 59)

Where the undertakers supply water by meter, the register of the meter is *prima facie* evidence of the quantity of water consumed, and any question between the undertakers and a consumer as to the quantity of water consumed may be determined by the Land Tribunal. There is provision for refund to or extra payment by the consumer if the meter is proved to register incorrectly.

Chapter 9

ADMINISTRATION

9.01 Synopsis

This chapter is concerned with the Management, as opposed to policy or operational considerations, of water authorities. The chapter describes the requirements of the Water Act 1973 in relation to meetings of regional water authorities and their committees, the arrangements for the discharge of the functions and the membership of water authorities, rules relating to contract, and the submission of annual reports or water authorities and also of the National Water Council, the authentication of documents, the byelaw making powers of regional water authorities and of statutory water companies.

The chapter also refers to the impact of planning legislation on the operational and engineering activities of statutory water undertakers. It defines the duties of regional water authorities with regard to nature conservation and amenity and describes the requirements in relation to the service of statutory notices and the power to enter premises etc.

Part III of the Local Government Act 1974 established a complaints machinery to investigate complaints of maladministration in, amongst other bodies, water authorities. The chapter considers the nature and extent of such investigations by the Local Commissioner (popularly known as 'local ombudsman') and the powers available to a water authority under the Local Government Act 1978 to incur expenditure to remedy an injustice caused by maladministration.

9.02 Meetings and Proceedings of Water Authorities and Committees
(W.A. 1973, Sch. 3)

Paragraph 14 of Schedule 3 to the Water Act 1973 applies the provisions of the Public Bodies (Admission to Meetings)

Act 1960 to meetings of water authorities and all committees appointed or established by one or more water authorities under any provision of the 1973 Act. It is possible to exclude the public from meetings either of the water authorities or of any committees thereof whenever publicity would be prejudicial to the public interest because of the confidential nature of the business or for other special reasons; such an exclusion requires a positive resolution of the water authority or the committee concerned.

While meetings are open to the public, representatives of the Press and of Broadcasting Authorities are entitled to be present and must be furnished with reasonable facilities. The Press and Broadcasting Authorities are entitled to be supplied with a copy of the agenda, together with any additional information as is necessary to indicate the nature of the items on the agenda.

Public notice of the time and place of meetings must be posted at the office of the Authority or in some other conspicuous place three clear days before the meeting, or when the meeting is convened if called at shorter notice.

The Water Act prescribes that a minute of the preceedings of a water authority, or any committee or sub-committee of such an authority, purporting to be signed at that or the next ensuing meeting by the chairman of the meeting to the proceedings to which the minute relates or the chairman of the next ensuing meeting, shall be evidence of the proceedings and shall be received in evidence without further proof. Until the contrary is proved, the Water Act further provides that every meeting in respect of the proceedings of which a minute has been so signed shall be deemed to have been duly convened and held, and all the proceedings had at the meeting to have been duly had, and, where the proceedings are the proceedings of the committee or sub-committee, that committee or sub-committee shall be deemed to have been duly constituted and have had power to deal with the matters referred to in the minute.

Any local government elector for any part of the water authority area may inspect the minutes of the Authority and to make copies or extracts therefrom. From the established case law the following rules apply to the inspection of minutes:—

(a) The right to inspect may be exercised by a local government elector through an agent; *R* v *Gloucester County Council* [1936] 2 All E.R. 168;

(b) The right is restricted to local government electors who are registered as such in the register of electors in accordance with the provisions of the Representation of the People Acts, and **not** to other persons unless they are acting as agents for a local government elector; *R.* v *Wimbledon Urban District Council* (1897) 62 J.P. 84;

(c) The right of inspection is restricted to minutes of the water authority and **not** to committees or sub-committees of the water authority; *Wilson* v *Evans* [1962] 2 Q.B. 383;

(d) The right of inspection does not apply to any part of the minutes of a water authority when those minutes contain information with respect to any manufacturing process or trade secret which had been obtained by the water authority in the exercise of its statutory powers; paragraph 18(3) Schedule 3 Water Act 1973.

Paragraph 17 applies the statutory provision of the 1972 Act relating to restrictions on voting and the declaration of pecuniary interests, direct or indirect, to members of water authorities or to members of any committee or sub-committee of the water authority. The disability due to a pecuniary interest, direct or indirect, attaching to members does not apply to a member of a water authority or its committees or sub-committees in his capacity as an ordinary consumer of water or to an interest in any matter relating to the terms on which the right to participate in any service, including the supply of goods, is offered to the public; (LGA 1972; s.97(4))

The Water Act 1973 further provides a statutory removal of the disability in respect of two interests within the ambit of this book, namely:—

(a)   to any interest which a member of a water authority or committee or sub-committee of the water authority may have in the preparation of revision of a charges scheme . . . or the levying of any other charges by a water authority; or

(b)   to any interest in any other matter which such a member may have as the holder, or as the applicant or prospective applicant for, a licence under the Water Resources Act 1963 where it is an interest which he has in common with all other holders of, or applicants or prospective applicants for, such licences, or in common with all other persons belonging to a class of such holders, applicants or prospective applicants.

9.03 Arrangements for Discharge of Functions and Membership of Regional Water Authorities
W.A. 1973, ss. 3-6, Sch. 3, paras. 3-10; Sch. 8, para. 69.

Subject to any express statutory provision enacted after the 18th July 1973 (the date the Water Act received Royal Assent) a regional water authority has power to determine its own structure for discharging any of its functions.

Section 6 (1) of the Water Act 1973 provides that a water authority may arrange for the discharge of any of its functions by,

(a)   a committee, a sub-committee or an officer of the authority; or

(b)   by any other water authority

Two or more water authorities may arrange to discharge any of its functions jointly or may arrange for the discharge of any of their functions by a joint committee of theirs.

Notwithstanding the common law rule *Delegatus non potest delegare*, a committee may delegate its functions to a sub-committee, and a sub-committee may delegate its functions to an officer (W.A. 1973, s.6(2)). There are certain exceptions; for instance there are statutory duties on regional water authorities to establish regional land drainage committees and regional advisory committees under the Land Drainage Act 1976 and the Salmon and Freshwater Fisheries Act 1975 respectively (outside the scope of this booklet). What is germane however is that regional water authorities cannot delegate their functions with respect, inter alia, to borrowing money (W.A. 1973, s.6(3)).

A person who is disqualified for being a member of a water authority is automatically disqualified for being a member of a committee or sub-committee appointed by a regional water authority (W.A. 1973, s.6(9)). The grounds for disqualification are defined in paragraphs 6 to 9 inclusive of Schedule 3 to the Water Act 1973, namely the vacation of the office by the member or what may be termed positive disqualification of any individual member in respect of his continued membership of the water authority or of its committees or in respect of his appointment to a water authority or a committee or sub-committee of a water authority.

The office of a member of the water authority shall become vacant upon the happening of any of the following events, namely if he;

(a) is adjudged bankrupt, or makes a composition or arrangement with his creditors;

(b) is convicted in the United Kingdom, Channel Islands or the Isle of Man of any offence and has passed on him a sentence of imprisonment (whether suspended or not) for a period of not less than three months without the option of a fine;

(c) is disqualified for election or being a member of a local authority or water authority under Part III of the Representation of the People Act 1949 or under Part VIII of the 1972 Act;

(d)   has, for a period of six consecutive months, been absent from meetings of the authority, otherwise than by reason of illness or some other cause approved during that period by the authority.

The Act provides that attendance of a member of the water authority at a meeting of any committee of the authority of which he is a member, or any joint committee to which he has been appointed by the regional water authority, is to be treated as attendance at a meeting of the authority. Paragraphs 7 and 8 of Schedule 3 provides for the appointment of members of water authorities to fill vacancies. Any person appointed to fill a casual vacancy shall hold office so long only as the former member would have held office.

The grounds for disqualification for, and reappointment to, membership of regional water authorities are:—

(a)   If a person is a paid officer of the authority;

(b)   is a person who has been adjudged bankrupt, or made a composition or arrangement with his creditors;

(c)   has within the period of five years ending on the day on which disqualification for appointment falls to be determined, been surcharged by a district auditor to an amount exceeding £500 under the provisions of the Local Government Act 1933; or

(d)   has within five years before the day of his appointment been convicted in the United Kingdom, the Channel Islands or the Isle of Man of any offence and has passed on him a sentence of imprisonment (whether suspended or not) for a period of not less than three months without the option of a fine; or

(e)   is disqualified for being elected or being a member of a local authority or water authority under Part III of the Representation of the People Act 1949 or Part VIII of the 1972 Act.

Where a person is disqualified by reason of having been adjudged bankrupt then,

(a) If the bankruptcy is annulled on the grounds that he ought not to have been adjudged bankrupt or on the grounds that his debts have been paid in full, the disqualification shall cease on the date of the annullment;

(b) If the person is discharged with a certificate that the bankruptcy was caused by misfortune without any misconduct on his part, the disqualification shall cease on the date of his discharge;

(c) If the person is discharged without such a certificate his disqualification shall cease on the expiration of five years from the date of his discharge.

Likewise, where a person is disqualified by reason of his having made a composition or arrangement with his creditors and he pays his debts in full, the disqualification shall cease on the date on which the payment is completed, and in any other case it shall cease on the expiration of five years from the date on which the terms of the deed of composition or arrangements are fulfilled.

It will be appreciated from the above that the basic rule is that a disqualification for election to or membership of a local authority is an automatic bar to appointment to or membership of a regional water authority.

The Chairman of the Water Authority and the other members appointed by either the Secretary of State or the Minister of Agriculture Fisheries and Food hold and vacate office in accordance with terms of their appointment.

The Chairman of the Water Authority may resign his office, at any time, by giving written notice to the Secretary of State. The Chairmanship of the Water Authority is an "office of profit" and is a disqualification for membership of the

House of Commons; (House of Commons Disqualification Act 1957, Sch. 1, as amended by the Water Act 1973, Sch. 8, para. 69).

Members of a Water Authority appointed by the Ministers may at any time resign office by giving written notice to both the Chairman of the Water Authority and to the Minister appointing them.

Members of a Water Authority appointed by a Local Authority or Authorities need not be members of the Local Authority or Authorities appointing them. In practice, Local Authorities usually appoint only elected members to membership of Water Authorities but a local Authority may, if it deems fit, appoint a person who is not a member of the local Authority.

Members of Water Authorities appointed by local Authorities hold office for a term of four years. The period of four years runs from the beginning of June in the year of the appointment of such members; if a member is appointed after the beginning of June, his period of office will commence from the date of his appointment and the member holds office for the remainder of the period of four years as if he were in office from the beginning of June in the year of his appointment.

A member of a Water Authority may resign his office at any time by giving written message to the Chairman of the Water Authority. If such a member ceases to be a member of the Local Authority he ceases to be a member of the Water Authority at the expiration of the period of three months beginning with the date when that member ceases to be a member of the Local Authority or on the appointment of another person in his place by the Local Authority, which ever first occurs.

Any member of a Water Authority, whether appointed by the Ministers or by the Local Authorities, is elegible for re-appointment to the Water Authority.

NOTE: 1 A Committee or sub-Committee has power to delegate any or all of its functions subject to note 2 below.

2 A Committee cannot delegate any of its functions to a sub-Committee or to an officer, or a sub committee to an officer, if the Water Authority or the Committee respectively otherwise directs.

9.04 Remuneration of Members
(W.A. 1973, Sch. 3 L.G.,P.&L.A. 1980, s.25)

The financial remuneration and payment of allowances to members of regional water authorities, and of committees and sub committees of such regional water authorities, is defined by paragraph 11. The water authority is under a statutory duty to pay the chairman of the regional water authority such remuneration and such allowances as may be determined by the Secretary of State for the Environment, or the Secretary of State for Wales in connection with the Welsh Water Authority, with the consent of the Minister for the Civil Service. There is also a statutory provision whereby the Secretary of State may, with the consent of the Minister for the Civil Service, pay or make arrangements for the payment of a pension, allowance or gratuity to any person who is or who has been chairman of a regional water authority.

Paragraph 11 of Schedule 3 to the Water Act 1973 also applies Sections 173 to 175 of the Local Government Act 1972 (*allowances to members of local authorities and other bodies*) as amended by ss.24 and 25 of the L.G.,P.&L.A. 1980.

Section 25 of L.G.P.&L.A. 1980 clarifies the position of Water Authorities who are now able to pay allowances to their members attending any conference or meeting which is for the benefit of their area or of those for whom they provide their services. In other words, Water Authorities in this respect are substantially in the same position as Local Authorities under the L.G.A. 1972, as amended by the L.G.,P.&L.A. 1980. The new section 177(1)(aa) applies the allowance code to Water Authorities and replaces paragraph 11(2) of Schedule 3 to the W.A. 1973, which was repealed by the 1980 Act.

See also para. **10.16**, p 251 *post*

Part II of Schedule 3 provides for the payment of such remuneration and such allowances as may be determined by the Secretary of State, with the consent of the Minister for the Civil Service, to appointed members of the National Water Council. "Appointed Members" of the National Water Council means any member of that council other than the chairmen of the regional water authorities. There is statutory provision whereby the Secretary of State may determine, in conjunction with the Minister for the Civil Service to pay or make arrangements for the payment of a pension, allowance or gratuity to or in respect of any person who is or who has been an appointed member of the council.

NOTE: Water Authorities also have a duty to pay the chairmen of their Regional and Local Land Drainage Committees such remuneration and such pensions, allowances or gratuities as the Minister, with the consent of the Minister for the Civil Service, may determine.

9.05 Rules with respect to the Making of Contracts
(W.A. 1973, Sch. 3, Pt I.)

Paragraph 20 of Schedule 3 to the Water Act 1973 imposes a duty upon a water authority to make rules with respect to the making by or on behalf of that authority of contracts for the supply of goods or materials or for the execution of works.

The rules made by a water authority must include provision for:—

(a) Securing competition for such contracts, and,

(b) Regulating the manner in which tenders are invited.

The rules may exempt however contracts falling into either one of the following two categories:—

(a) Contracts below a price specified by the Authority but the price level so determined must be stated in the Rules;

(b) Individual contracts where the Authority is satisfied that the exemption is justified by special circumstances.

No person, entering into a contract with a Water Authority, is under any duty to enquire whether there has been compliance with the rules of the authority. Non-compliance with the contract rules does not *per se* invalidate any contract entered into by or on behalf of the Authority.

9.06 The Making and Confirmation of Water Authority Orders
(W.A. 1973, Sch. 4, Pt II.)

It will be recalled that Part I of Schedule 4 to the Water Act 1973 amended sections 12 and 13 of the Water Act 1945. The effect of those amendments, *inter alia,* is to enable a water authority to control bulk supplies of water and to take any necessary corrective action where a statutory water company is discharging the duties of a water authority pursuant to section 12(1) of the Water Act 1973.

Part II of Schedule 4 to the 1973 Act prescribes the procedures relating to the making and confirmation of any order made by a water authority pursuant to its powers in Sections 12 and 13 of the Water Act 1945, as amended by Schedule 4 of the Water Act 1973.

Under the provisions of that Schedule the regional water authority must conform to the following procedures:—

(1)   The water authority is under a duty, at least one month prior to applying for confirmation of any Order made by them in accordance with Section 12 and 13 of the Water Act 1945:—

    (a)   cause a notice of its intention to make application to be published in the London Gazette and in such other manner as the authority thinks best adapted for informing persons affected, and

    (b)   cause copies of the Notice to be served on the statutory water companies to whom the Order relates and any other public authorities who appear to the water authority to be concerned.

(2)   For at least one month before an application is made for the confirmation of any such Order, a copy of which shall be deposited at the offices of the regional water authority.

(3)   The water authority must provide reasonable facilities for the inspection without charge of an Order deposited in accordance with this procedure.

(4)   Any person on application to the water authority is entitled to be furnished free of charge with a printed copy of the Order.

(5)   The Secretary of State, with or without a local enquiry, may refuse to confirm an Order submitted for confirmation or may confirm the Order either with or without modifications; the authority shall, if so directed by the Secretary of State, cause notice of any proposed modification given in accordance with such directions. The Secretary of State may fix a date on which any such Order confirmed by him is to come into operation; if no date is so fixed the Order shall come into operation and the end of the month beginning with the date of confirmation.

(6)   The Order must be printed after confirmation and deposited at the office of the water authority, copies of it must, at all reasonable hours, be open to public inspection without charge. Any person on application to the water authority is entitled to be furnished with a copy of the Order on payment of such reasonable sum as the authority may determine.

9.07 Annual Reports of Water Authorities and the National Water Council.
(W.A. 1973, Sch. 3)

Each regional water authority and the National Water Council are under a statutory duty (WA 1973, Sch. 3, para. 40) to report as soon as possible after the end of the financial year to the Secretary of State and to the Minister of Agriculture Fisheries and Food. The Ministers in turn are under a duty to lay a copy of all such reports before each House of Parliament.

Regional water authorities must also send a copy of their annual report to every local authority whose area is wholly or partly situated within the area of the water authority.

The National Water Council must also send a copy of their annual report to each regional water authority.

Any member of the public is entitled to be furnished with a copy of the report of a water authority, the National Water Council or the Water Space Amenity Commission for any year on applying to the body who made the report and on payment of such a reasonable sum as that body may determine.

There are reserve powers for the Secretary of State or for the Minister of Agriculture Fisheries and Food, acting jointly, to direct that such annual reports shall be in such form and contain such information as is specified in the direction.

There is a statutory duty imposed on every water authority to furnish the Secretary of State and/or the Minister of Agriculture Fisheries and Food and the National Water Council with such information as they may from time to time require with respect to the authority's property, financial position, activities or proposed activities, and with respect to the water resources in the authority's area, and to afford to the Ministers facilities for the verification of information so furnished.

9.08 Procedures Relating to Byelaws
(W.A. 1973, Sch. 7)

The power to make byelaws has been considered in chapter 4 — *see* paragraphs **4.05, 4.06, 4.07** and **4.08.**

The procedures relating to the making of byelaws, and their publication and confirmation, including the right to object to a proposed byelaw by any person affected thereby, is defined in schedule 7 to the Water Act 1973. A distinction is drawn in the procedure between byelaws made by the Secretary of State and byelaws made by water authorities and other statutory water undertakers and confirmed by the Secretary of State.

Where the Secretary of State proposes to make the byelaw the following procedure shall apply:—

(a) At least one month before a byelaw relating to the whole or part of a water authority area is made by the Secretary of State, he shall cause a notice of his intention to make the byelaw to be published in the London Gazette and in such other manner as is in his opinion best adapted for informing persons affected.

(b) The Secretary of State shall also cause copies of the notice (referred to in (a) above) to be served on any public authorities who appear to him to be concerned.

(c) For at least one month before the byelaw is to come into operation a copy of it shall be deposited at the offices of the water authority.

(d) A water authority shall provide reasonable facilities for the inspection without charge of any byelaw deposited under the provisions of (c) above.

(e) Any person, on application to the water authority, shall be entitled to be furnished free of charge with a printed copy of any such byelaw.

(f) The Secretary of State may fix the date on which a byelaw is to come into operation; if no date is so fixed, it shall come into operation at the end of the period of one month beginning with the date on which the byelaw is made.

When the byelaw has been made by the Secretary of State:—

(a) The Secretary of State is obliged to have the byelaw printed and deposited at the office of the Water Authority, and copies of the byelaw must, at all reasonable hours, be open to public inspection without charge.

(b) Any person on application to the Water Authority is entitled to be furnished with a copy of it, on payment of such reasonable sum as the Authority may determine.

(c) If it appears to the Secretary of State that the revocation of a byelaw is necessary or expedient, he may, after giving notice to the Water Authority and considering any objection raised by the Authority, and, if required by the Authority, holding a local enquiry, revoke that byelaw. Section 250 of the Local Government Act 1972 prescribes the procedures to be followed in relation to any such local inquiry.

The procedure relating to byelaws made by water authorities and statutory water companies is as follows:—

(a) At least one month before the water authority, or statutory water company, apply for confirmation of any byelaw made by them they shall:—

    (i) cause a notice of their intention to make the application to be published in the London Gazette and in such other manner as they think best adapted for informing persons affected, and

    (ii) cause copies of the notice to be served on any public authorities who appear to them to be concerned.

(b) For at least one month before an application is made for the confirmation of any byelaw, a copy of it shall be on deposit at the offices of the authority or statutory water company, ie at the offices of the undertaker making the byelaw.

(c) The authority or statutory water company shall provide reasonable facilities for the inspection without charge of the byelaw deposited in accordance with the procedure.

(d) Any person on application to the authority or statutory water company shall be entitled to be furnished free of charge with a printed copy of such a byelaw.

(e) The Secretary of State, with or without a local inquiry (the conduct of which is governed by section 250 of the 1972 Act) may refuse to confirm in the byelaw submitted for confirmation in accordance with Part II of Schedule 7 to the Water Act 1973 or may confirm the byelaw either without or, if the authority or water undertaker consents, with modifications; the authority or statutory water company, if so directed by the Secretary of State, shall cause notice of any proposed modifications to be given in accordance with any such direction.

(f) The Secretary of State may fix the date on which any byelaw confirmed under Part II of Schedule 7 is to come into operation, and if no date is so fixed the byelaw shall come into operation at the end of the period of one month beginning with the date of confirmation. No byelaw made by a water authority or statutory water company shall have effect until confirmed by the Secretary of State.

(g) Any byelaw submitted and confirmed in accordance with this procedure shall be printed and deposited at the office of the water authority or statutory water company and copies of it, shall at all reasonable hours, be open to public inspection without charge.

(h) Any person on application to the water authority or statutory water company shall be entitled to be furnished with a copy of it, on payment of such reasonable sum as the authority may determine.

(i) If it appears to the Secretary of State that revocation of the byelaw is necessary or expedient he may, after giving notice to the authority and considering any objections raised by them and, if required by the authority, holding the local inquiry, revoke that byelaw.

Paragraphs 10 and 22 of Schedule 7 of the Water Act 1973 provides that a printed copy of a byelaw purported to be made or confirmed in accordance with the procedures of that schedule and certified to the effect that:—

(i) It was made in accordance with the procedures of schedule 7.

(ii) That the copy is a true copy of the byelaw.

(iii) The date of confirmation (if applicable)

(iv) The date of coming into operation of the byelaw, shall be *prima facie* evidence of the facts stated in the certificate and without proof of the handwriting or official position of any person purporting to sign the certificate.

NOTE: Byelaws made by Water Authorities in relation to Land Drainage are submitted to the Minister of Agriculture, Fisheries & Food who is the confirming Minister; the procedure, which is similar to that shown here, is prescribed in the Land Drainage Act 1976, Sect. 34 and Schedule 4.

9.09 General Notes regarding Subordinate Legislation

Where the enabling statutes so provides a statutory authority may make byelaws for specific purposes. Such byelaws are subject to four basic tests and those tests apply to byelaws made under the Water Acts as they are applicable to byelaws made under other legislation.

The first test is that of "reasonableness." In *Kruse* v *Johnson* [1898] 2 Q.B. 91 the Courts held that they would interfere if a byelaw purported to be an unreasonable exercise of power. The test of unreasonableness is whether the byelaw is partial and unequal in its operation as between classes or if they are manifestly unjust or if the byelaw amounted to oppressive or gratuitous interference with the rights of those subject to them and can find no justification in the minds of reasonable men.

The second test that the Courts adopt is that of certainty of terms; in other words, the byelaws must be positive and there must be an absence of ambiguity — see *Kruse v Johnson* above.

The third test that the Courts will apply is that of consistency with the general law; the byelaw must not be repugnent of either statute or the common law — see *Powell* v *May* [1946] K.B. 330 and *London Passenger Transport Board* v *Sumner* (1935) 99 J.P.

The final test is that the byelaws must be *intra vires* of the enabling statute, *R* v *Wood* (1855) 5 El. & Bl. 49.

Section 19(2) of the Water Act 1945 imposes a statutory duty upon regional water authorities and statutory water companies to enforce byelaws; failure to enforce the byelaws by a regional water authority could result in the Secretary of State exercising his default powers in accordance with the provisions of Section 13 of the Water Act 1945 as amended and applied by Schedule 4 of the Water Act 1973.

Water Authorities have a discretion as to the resources which they will employ and the manner by which byelaws are enforced. The same discretion applies to statutory water companies. A failure to enforce byelaws or negligence in the manner in which the byelaws are enforced (*eg* insufficient inspection of building works to see if there is adherence with byelaws) will render the water authority or the statutory water company liable to a person who has suffered damage in consequence; see *Dutton* v *Bognor Regis Urban District Council* [1972] I.Q.B. 373 and *Anns* v *Merton London Borough Council* [1977] 2 W.L.R. 1024.

9.10 Authentication of Documents under the Water Act 1973
(W.A. 1973, Sch. 3, Pt I)

Paragraph 19 provides that any notice or other document which a water authority is required or authorised to give, make or issue by or under the Water Act 1973 or any other statute or byelaw may be signed on behalf of the Authority by any member or officer of the Authority generally or specially authorised for that purpose by a resolution of the Authority; any document purporting to bear the signature of a person expressed to be so authorised shall be deemed, until the contrary is proved, to be duly given, made or issued by authority of the water authority.

It is important to note that the word "signature" includes a fascimile of a signature by whatever process reproduced.

9.11 Maintenance of Registers under the Water Resources Act 1963 (W.R.A. 1963, s.53)

A Water Authority must keep, in such manner as may be prescribed by regulations made by the Secretary of State under the 1963 Act, a Register containing such information as may be prescribed with respect to applications made to the Water Authority for the grant, revocation or variation of licences, including information as to the way in which such applications have been dealt with, and also containing such information as may be so prescribed with respect to persons becoming the holders of licences by virtue of being the successor in title to the original holder of the licence (by virtue of section 32 of the 1963 Act). Every register must be available for inspection by the public at all reasonable hours.

The information to be kept in such registers has been prescribed by the Secretary of State in the Water Resources (Licences) Regulations 1965 (S.I. 1965 No. 534) paragraph 17.

Such registers must be kept at the principal office of the water authority; every entry in the register with respect to an application made after 1 July 1965 must be made within 28 days from the date of receipt of the application.

The registers must contain the following basic information with respect to every application made to a Water Authority for the grant, revocation or variation of a licence under the Water Resources Acts, namely:—

(a) the name and address of the applicant, the date of the application and brief particulars of its proposals;

(b) the decision, if any, of the Water Authority, the date of that decision and brief particulars (including the serial number) of any licence granted, or revocation or variation affected by virtue of that decision;

(c) the decision, if any, of the Secretary of State (whether on reference of the application to him or on appeal from the Water Authority), the date of the Secretary of State's decision and brief particulars of any licence directed to be granted, and the serial number of such licence when granted, or of any revocation or variation directed to be effected, in pursuance of the decision of the Secretary of State;

(d) the date of the compliance by the Water Authority with any direction of the Secretary of State to grant, revoke or vary a licence.

In addition the Register must contain with respect to every application for the grant, revocation or variation of a licence under the Act, made by the Water Authority to the Secretary of State in accordance with the Regulations made by the Secretary of State (ie the granting of licences to Water Authorities and the revocation or variation of Water Authorities licences by the Secretary of State and certain matters specified in paragraph 16 of those Regulations in respect of the British Waterways Board), the following information namely:—

(a) the date of the application and brief particulars of its proposals;

(b) the date of the decision of the Secretary of State and the application by the Water Authority and brief particulars, including the serial number, of any licence granted, or any variation affected, by the Secretary of State;

(c) if the application is deemed to be granted in accordance with the regulations, the date on which it is so deemed to be granted and brief particulars of any licence, including the serial number, or variation thereupon granted or effected.

The register must also contain, with respect to any person who is the successor in title to the original holder of the licence and is therefore referred to as "the successor" under the W.R.A. 1963, the following information, namely that person's name and address, the serial number of the licence and the date on which he notified the Water Authority of the change in the occupation of the relevant land, or the transfer of the licence, as the case may be.

The register must include an index which is to be in the form of a map unless the Secretary of State approves some other form which will enable a person to trace any entry in the register.

NOTE: A suitable register in loose leaf form is available from Shaw and Sons Ltd.

9.12 Town and Country Planning Legislation
Town and Country Planning Act 1959, ss.22 and 23.

The background to the powers contained in sections 22 and 23 will be found in the Second Report of the Local Government Manpower Committee (Cmd 8421/1951) and the White Paper on Local Government Finance in England and Wales (Cmd 209/1957); there was a general desire to relax the amount of control by central government over local authorities and similar bodies and to give them greater freedom in certain matters.

Statutory water undertakers are relieved of the necessity to obtain the prior consent of the Secretary of State when entering into any contract after the 16 August 1959 for the acquisition by agreement of land or any interest in land when either the land or the interest in the land is immediately required for its undertaking or if not so required, is within the area of the statutory water undertaker. If the land is outside the area of the statutory water undertaker and is not immediately required for the purposes of the undertaking, the consent of the Secretary of State will still be required.

It will be appreciated that section 22 of the Act only applies to acquisitions by agreement; obviously the approval of the Secretary of State is required in respect of any compulsory purchase acquisition.

By virtue of the powers contained in section 23 of the Act, statutory water undertakers may exercise their powers after the 16 August 1959 to appropriate land from one purpose for use for another purpose without the prior approval of the Secretary of State. Section 23 however contains a number of exceptions to the general freedom allowed to statutory water undertakers. The power of appropriation **can only be exercised with the prior consent** of the Secretary of State in any one of the following circumstances:—

(1) Land which consists or forms part of an open space (not being land which consists or forms part of a common or of a fuel or field garden allotment).

(2) Land which has been acquired by a statutory water undertaker in the exercise, directly or indirectly, of compulsory powers and has not subsequently been appropriated by the statutory water undertaker for any purpose other than that for which it was so acquired.

(3) The appropriation of land in pursuance of an order made under section 42 of the Town and Country Planning Act 1947 or under section 28 of the Land Settlement (Facilities) Act 1919.

(4) Land which consists or forms part of a common, or formerly consisted or formed part of a common, and is held or managed under a local Act.

The consent of the Minister of Agriculture, Fisheries and Food is required before a statutory water undertaker can appropriate land relating to cottage holdings (*see* the Small Holdings and Allotments Act 1926 and Agricultural Land (Utilisation) Act 1931) or in respect of any appropriation of land which immediately before the appropriation, is land held for use as allotments.

Prior to the 16 August 1959, the consequential adjustments following upon an appropriation in the accounts of a statutory water undertaker had to be such as was approved by the Minister. With one notable exception the approval of the Secretary of State to the accounts is no longer required; any adjustment to the accounts is now to be such as may be requisite and it is for the statutory water undertaker to determine for itself what is requisite. However if either the old or the new purpose for which the land is held by the statutory water undertaker is a grant aided purpose then the approval of the Secretary of State is required to any proposed adjustment in the accounts.

Town and Country Planning Act 1971; Town and Country Amenities Act 1974

Water authorities and statutory water companies are subject to the constraints of planning control; planning permission for development must be obtained. However the system of control is modified in respect of two particular types of proposed development, namely:—

(a) Development carried out on operation land by statutory water undertakers. Part XI of the Town and Country Planning Act 1971 contains modifications for statutory undertakers; by virtue of Section 290 thereof a statutory undertaker is to be construed as including a regional water authority.

(b) Developments which require the authorisation of a Minister of the Crown. Section 40 of the Town and Country Planning Act 1971 provides that where the authorisation of a Government department is required by virtue of an enactment in respect of development to be carried out by a Statutory Undertaker that Department may, on granting the authorisation, direct that planning permission for that development shall be deemed to be granted, subject to such conditions, if any, as may be specified in the Directions. For the purposes of the deemed Planning Permission Development shall be taken to be authorised by a Government department if:—

(1) Any consent, or authority, or approval to or for the development is granted by the Department in pursuance of an enactment;

(2) A compulsory purchase order is confirmed by the Department authorising the purchase of land for the purpose of the development;

(3) Consent is granted by the Department to the appropriation of land for the purpose of the development of the acquisition of land by agreement for that purpose;

(4) Authority is given by the Department for the borrowing of money for the purpose of the development, or for the application for that purpose of any money not otherwise so applicable; or

(5) Any undertaking is given by the Department to pay a grant in respect of the development in accordance with an enactment authorising the payment of such grants.

In practice planning consent will usually be a pre-requisite for the Secretary of State or the Minister in making an Order or granting funds.

Section 222 of the 1971 Act defines "operational land" in relation to a statutory undertaker (*i.e.* a water authority) as being:—

(a)   Land which is used for the purpose of carrying on its
      undertaking and

(b)   Land in which an interest is held for that purpose

The Act further provides that in certain instances land is to
be treated as "non-operational land." Section 223 thereof
states that where an interest in land is held by a Statutory
Undertaker for the purpose of carrying on their undertaking
and:—

(a)   the interest was acquired by them on or after the 6
      December 1968, or

(b)   it was held by them immediately before that date but the
      circumstances were then such that the land did not fall
      to be treated as operational land for the purposes of the
      T.C.P. Act 1962.

then it is necessary to have recourse to sub section (2) of Section 222 in order to determine whether the land is to be
treated as "operational land" for the purposes of the Act and
shall so have effect notwithstanding the definition of operational land in that Section.

Sub-section (2) provides that the land shall not be treated
as operational land for the purposes of the Act unless one or
both of the following conditions are satisfied with respect to
it, namely:—

(1)   there is, or at sometime has been, in force with respect
      to the land, a specific planning permission for its
      development and that development, if carried out,
      would involve or have involved the use of the land for
      the purpose of the carrying on of the statutory under-
      takers' undertaking; or

(2)   the undertakers' interest in the land was acquired by
      them as a result of a transfer under the provisions of the

Transport Act 1968 from other statutory undertakers and the land was, immediately before transfer, operational land of those other undertakers.

The section further provides that a specific planning permission for the purposes of sub section (2) *supra* is planning permission:—

(i) granted on an application in that behalf under Part III of the Act or the enactments previously in force and replaced by that Part of the Act, or

(ii) granted by provisions of a development order granting planning permission generally for development which has received specific parliamentary approval or

(iii) granted by a special development order in respect of developments specifically described in the order, or

(iv) deemed to be granted by virtue of the direction of the government department under section 40 of the Act, section 41 of the Act of 1962 or section 35 of the Act of 1947,

and reference in (b) above to development which has received specific parliamentary approval is to be construed as referring to developments authorised by a Local or Private Act of Parliament or by an Order which has been brought into operation in accordance with the provisions of the Statutory Orders (Special Procedure) Act 1945, being an Act or Order which designates specifically both the nature of the development thereby authorised and the land upon which it may be carried out.

The Town and Country Amenities Act 1974 imposes statutory restraints upon operational works within conservation areas, the control of demolition works within the conservation area, the protection of listed buildings and the protection of trees and gardens within conservation areas.

Prior consent must be obtained from the District Planning Authority and within a National Park from the County Planning Authority.

Excluded from the definition of "development" (in respect of which planning permission is required) are works for the purpose of inspecting repairing or renewing mains, pipes, cables or other apparatus, including the breaking open of any street or other land and before that purpose; (Town and Country Planning Act 1971, s.22).

The planning legislation contains provisions whereby the Secretary of State may make particular orders; included amongst those provisions is the power of the Secretary of State to make general orders, applicable to all land in England and Wales, providing for the grant of permission for the development of land under certain conditions, ie "Permitted Development." In this connection the Secretary of State has made a "Town and Country Planning General Development Order." Such general development orders (G.D.O's) contain provision for "permitted development" by both water authorities and by water undertakers in respect of water supply. In other words, such works may be undertaken upon land to which the Order applies without the permission of either the Local Planning Authority or the Secretary of State.

Included amongst the types of development permitted is the erection, construction or placing of buildings, plant or apparatus on land, or the carrying out of engineering operations in, on, over or under land for the purposes of surveys or investigations. In respect of this particular type of development, a condition is contained within the Order namely that a completion of the survey or investigation or the expiration of six months from the commencement of the development, the subject of the permission, whichever is the sooner, all such operations must cease and all such buildings, plant or apparatus must be removed and the land restored to its former condition.

It is important to note that the provisions of the relevant Articles of the Town and Country Planning General Development Order specifically exclude any development which requires or involves the formation, laying out or material widening of the means of access to an existing highway which is a trunk or classified road, or creates an obstruction to the view of any person using the highway used by the vehicular traffic at or near any bend, corner, junction or intersection so as to cause danger to such persons.

9.13 New Towns Act 1965
(New Towns Act 1965 ss.2, 26, 27, 28 and 54)

The development of new towns may present special problems for statutory water undertakers. Where land has been acquired by a Development Corporation, that is a Corporation established by the Secretary of State pursuant to the powers contained in section 2 of the Act, and there subsists over that land a right vested in or belonging to a statutory undertaker (and that expression includes any undertaking for the supply of water), for the purpose of carrying on its undertaking, such as a right of way or right of laying down, erecting, continuing or maintaining apparatus on, under or over the land, the Development Corporation may serve a notice on the undertaker stating that at the expiration of the time specified in the notice such a right will be extinguished or alternatively requiring that, before the expiration of the period so specified, the statutory undertaker will remove the apparatus concerned. The Act contains machinery whereby a counter-notice may be served on the Development Corporation, in which case the Corporation may apply to the Secretary of State for an Order to give effect to the provisions of their notice. If no counter notice is served, the right is automatically extinguished at the expiration of the period specified in the notice or the acquiring Corporation may remove the apparatus of the undertakers and dispose of it.

The Act provides for the payment of compensation by the Development Corporation to the statutory undertakers and for the publication of draft orders to be made by the Secretary of State; if any objection is made to such a draft order and that objection is not withdrawn, any such order is then subject to the special parliamentary procedure, in respect of which reference should be made to the Statutory Orders (Special Procedures) Act 1945.

The Secretary of State may, on the representation of either the statutory undertaker or the Development Corporation by order provide for the extension or modification of the powers and duties of any statutory undertaker in order to secure the adequate provision of water services.

Such an order may authorise the statutory water undertaker to acquire, either compulsorily or by agreement, any land specified in the order and to erect, or construct, any buildings or works so specified. The provisions contained in section 28 of the Act are important in that they provide the powers whereby the Secretary of State may take powers in the unlikely event of a statutory water undertaker being reluctant to seek extended powers and duties for an area of new development and consequently there is the possibility that that area will be insufficiently supplied with water. The Secretary of State, at the request of the Development Corporation, may by order direct a statutory water undertaker to provide the necessary water services. The Act also contains a complementary provision whereby a statutory water undertaker may apply to the Secretary of State for an Order for relief from (that is curtailment of) its statutory obligations. Such relief can be granted by the Secretary of State when he is satisfied that the fulfilment of the statutory water undertaker's obligations has been rendered impracticable because of the compulsory purchase of land under the Act, or the extinguishment of any right vested in the statutory water undertaker or the imposition of any requirement as to the removal of any apparatus belonging to the statutory water undertaker. Such relief may be either absolute or limited to the extent as is specified by the Secretary of State in the order.

9.14 Power to Lay Service Pipes
(W.A. 1945, Third Schedule, s.21)

Section 21 provides that a statutory water undertaker may in any street within its limit of supply lay such service pipes with such stopcocks and other fittings as are necessary for supplying water to premises within the limits of supply. The statutory water undertakers may from time to time inspect, alter or renew and may at any time remove any service pipe laid in a street.

All communication pipes whether laid before or after the Water Act 1948 are vested in the statutory water undertaker. Statutory water undertakers are responsible for meeting all expenses incurred with respect to maintenance work repair or renewal of such communication pipes.

Statutory water undertakers are obliged to carry out any necessary work as is required in respect of any supply pipes in the highway; in this instance, the statutory water undertakers may recover expenses reasonably incurred from the owner of the premises supplied by the pipe. If the statutory water undertaker fails to carry out any necessary work with all reasonable despatch after receipt of complaint of the defect, from an owner or occupier of the premises affected, the statutory undertaker will be liable to a fine not exceeding £25 and a further fine not exceeding £2 for each day on which the fault continues.

9.15 Power to Lay Mains in Streets
(W.A. 1945, Third Schedule, Pt VI, Sections 22, 25, 27 and 28 and Public Utilities Street Works Act 1950)

A statutory water undertaker may break open any street within its area of supply to lay, construct, inspect or renew mains, service pipes, plant or other works and outside those limits of supply for the purpose of laying any mains which the undertaker is authorised to lay and of inspecting, repairing, renewing or removing mains, break open the roadway and footpaths of any street, and of any bridge carrying a street.

In breaking open the streets the undertaker shall cause as little inconvenience and do as little damage as may be; the undertaker must pay compensation for any damage done.

"Street" includes any highway, including a highway over any bridge, any road, lane, footpath, square, court, alley or passage, whether a thoroughfare or not.

A "main" is a pipe laid to give a general supply as distinct from a supply to a particular consumer.

Water undertakers are subject to the provisions of the Public Utilities Street Works Act 1950 and under the terms of that Act, must give due notice to such bodies as Gas, Electricity and Fire Authorities of the undertakers intention to carry out the work. The statutory water undertaker must take any special precautions that are required by the nature of the work and must make due reinstatement of the road.

Section 7 of the Public Utilities Street Works Act 1950 imposes a duty upon the statutory water undertaker to complete code regulated works (as defined in section 1 thereof) with all such despatch as is reasonably practicable; the section further imposes a duty upon the statutory water undertaker to reinstate or make good the street or controlled land as soon after completion of any part of the works as is reasonably practicable, without hindering the execution of other parts of the works to be undertaken immediately or shortly thereafter.

A breach of this duty would render the statutory water undertaker guilty of an offence. The statutory water undertaker would also be liable at common law if damage is caused to a third party. The liability extends not only to persons passing along the highway, but also to other public utilities such as a gas undertaking whose pipes have been fractured owing to the failure of a water undertaker to ram in the earth properly thereby depriving the pipes of proper support; *Huyton and Roby Gas Company* v *Liverpool Corporation* (1926). The courts have held that the duty of reinstatement is "to leave its reinstatement in such a condition that no further reinstatement will be required, and that the inequalities will only be produced by the natural consequences of wear and tear"; *Hartley* v *Rochdale Corporation* [1908] 2 K.B. 594.

The liability of the statutory water undertaker for any danger created in or on a highway is independent of any negligence on the part of any independent contractor employed by the undertaker; *Penny* v *Wimbledon Urban District Council* [1899] 2 Q.B. 72.

The power to lay mains is not confined to laying apparatus underground but enables a statutory water undertaker to place such works on the surface of a street as may not be inconsistent with the substantial reinstatement of the road, or pavement or create a nuisance; *East London Waterworks Co* v *St Matthew, Bethnal Green, Vestry* (1886) 17 Q.B.D. 473 — a case heard under similar provisions contained in the Waterworks Clauses Act 1847.

The powers to break open streets are limited to breaking open the soil and pavements of streets and of a bridge; the powers do not extend to attaching pipes to the girders of a bridge without the agreement of the person having the control of the bridge; *see Glasgow Corporation* v *Glasgow South Western Rail Co.* [1895] A.C. 376.

NOTE: To break open a street without statutory authority is a nuisance at Common Law. Highways Act 1980, sect. 131, prescribes statutory penalties for damage to highways.

9.16 Duties with regard to Nature Conservation and Amenity (W.A. 1973, s.22)

The 1973 Act imposes an obligation upon water authorities to have specific regard to nature conservation and amenity. In formulating or considering proposals relating to the discharge of any of its functions, water authorities and the appropriate Ministers must pay due regard to the desirability of preserving natural beauty and of conserving flora and fauna as well as geological or physiographical features of special interest, and of protecting buildings and other objects or architectural, archaeological or historic interests. Water authorities and the Ministers must take into account any effect which their proposals would have on the beauty of, or amenity in, any rural or urban area or on any such flora, fauna, features, buildings or objects.

The 1973 Act further provides that water authorities and the appropriate Ministers must have regard to the desirability of preserving public rights of access to areas of mountains, moor, heath, down, cliff or foreshore, and other places of natural beauty. Water authorities and the Ministers must take into account any effect which any proposals relating to the discharge of its functions will have on the preservation of any such rights of access.

The Nature Conservancy Council, established by the Nature Conservancy Council Act 1973, has imposed upon it the duty to keep the particular water authority concerned informed about areas of land, other than nature reserves, which are of special interest by reason of flora and fauna or geological or physiological features.

NOTE: For the extinction of Private rights of way over land which a statutory water undertaker is authorised to acquire compulsorily, *see* W.A. 1945, Third Schedule, s.9, para **5.7** p. 105 *ante*.

9.17 Complaints of Maladministration
(L.G.A. 1974 Pt III and Schs. 4 and 5; L.G.A. 1978)

The Local Government Act 1974 introduced an entirely new concept for investigation of complaints relating to maladministration in water authorities. Two bodies corporate were established known as the Commission for Local Administration in England and the Commission for Local Administration in Wales. The members of the Commissions are known as the "Local Commissioners" or more popularly termed "the Local Ombudsmen."

The local ombudsmen have certain statutory powers available for conducting an investigation; a commissioner may require any member or officer of the authority concerned, or any other person who in his opinion is able to furnish information or produce documents relevant to the investigation, to furnish such information or produce such documents. In this regard a Local Commissioner has the same powers as the High Court in respect of the attendance and examination of the witnesses and in respect of production of documents. The Commissioner also has power to have produced communications between the Authority concerned and any Government Department and the concept of "Crown Privilege" cannot be pleaded in respect of a refusal to disclose information to a Local Commissioner.

The Local Government Act 1974 prescribes the procedure for receiving, investigating and reporting on complaints submitted by an aggrieved person or by any body or persons whether incorporated or not to the Local Commissioner. Certain groups of persons and corporate bodies are excluded from the category of persons who may submit a complaint, such are:—

(a)   a local authority or other authority or body constituted for purposes of the public service or of local government, or for the purposes of carrying on under national ownership any industry or undertaking or part of any industry or undertaking;

(b)   any other authority or body whose members are appointed by Her Majesty or any Minister of the Crown or government department, or whose revenues consist wholly or mainly of monies provided by Parliament.

Certain matters are excluded from the purview of the Local Commissioner; a Local Commissioner has no power to conduct investigations in respect of any action which in his opinion affects all or most of the inhabitants of the area of the Water Authority concerned. Likewise a Local Commissioner is not permitted to conduct an investigation in respect of any of the following matters:—

(a)   any action is respect of which the person agreed has or had a right of appeal, reference or review to or before a tribunal constituted by or under any enactment;

(b)   any action in respect of which the person aggrieved has or had a right of appeal to the Minister of the Crown, or

(c)   any action in respect of which the person aggrieved has or had a remedy by way of proceedings in any court of law.

The Fifth Schedule to the 1974 Act contains a list of matters not subject to investigation but included therein are specific matters that are not excluded and can therefore be investigated provided such matters do not fall into any of the exclusion categories listed above.

The transactions that may be investigated are:—

(a)   transactions for or relating to the acquisition or disposal of land;

(b)   all transactions in the discharge of functions exerciseable under any public general act, other than those required for the procurement of the goods and services necessary to discharge those functions.

The substance of the complaint must be that the aggrieved person has "sustained injustice in consequence of maladministation in connection with action taken by or on behalf of the water authority"; (L.G.A. 1974 s.26(1)). Maladministration and injustice are not statutorily defined.

The Local Commissioner cannot order a Water Authority to desist from a particular course of action or to pursue a particular course of action. The Local Government Act 1978 enables water authorities, when considering the report of the Local Commissioner, to make financial payment or provide some other benefit to the person who has suffered injustice in consequence of maladministration.

9.18 Appointment of Officers as Directors of Statutory Water Companies
(W.A. 1945, s.43)

Notwithstanding anything in the Companies Clauses Consolidation Act, 1845, as applied by any enactment to the company, statutory water undertakers who are a statutory water company may appoint a person employed as its chief engineer, general manager or secretary to be a director of the company whether he is a shareholder thereof or not, but the number of directors must not be increased beyond the maximum number prescribed by any enactment relating to the company. A person so appointed as director does not cease to be a director by reason of his employment, and such appointment may be made by the directors of the company as well as in manner provided by the 1845 Act; the provisions of that Act requiring directors to retire by rotation have effect as if a person appointed under this provision was not a director. Not more than one director of the company can hold office at the same time by virtue of this particular statutory provision and a person appointed by the directors shall cease to be a director from the date of the next ordinary general meeting of the company unless the appointment is approved at that meeting by a majority of the votes of the proprietors of the company entitled to vote or voting either personally or by proxy at the meeting.

Chapter 10

GENERAL AND MISCELLANEOUS POWERS AND DUTIES

10.01 Synopsis

This chapter is concerned with a number of miscellaneous powers and duties affecting statutory water undertakers.

The chapter is also concerned with certain general legal principles that apply to the position of crown lands and of statutory authorities.

DEFINITIONS OF CERTAIN EXPRESSIONS USED IN THE WATER ACTS 1945 AND 1973 ARE GIVEN IN CHAPTER 2.

10.02 The Position of Crown Lands

It is a general principle of Constitutional Law that unless specially provided for in a particular statute, the Crown is not bound by that statute. The Water Acts, including the Drought Act are silent on the Crown: therefore no rights of the statutory water undertakers can, without the express agreement of the Crown, be enforced against the Crown.

The exemption applies to all properties belonging to Her Majesty in right of the Crown, the Crown Estate Commissioners, Duchy Lands or lands belonging to a government department.

Local authorities are NOT included in the exemption but land or property belonging to the National Health Service, either under the direct control of the Department of Health and Social Security or under the jurisdiction of the Regional Health Authority, are Crown property; National Health Service Act 1946 and the National Health Service Reorganisation Act 1973. See also *Nottingham No. 1 Area Hospital Management Committee* v *Owen* [1958] 1 Q.B. 50.

Buildings owned by nationalised industries are not Crown property, see *Tumden* v *Hannaford* (1950) and *Rowell* v *Pratt*

[1938] A.C. 101, where it was held that a Marketing Board was not a Government Department and could not therefore claim an exemption granted to the Crown.

10.03 Agreements affecting Water Authorities

Constitutional Law imposes certain constraints upon agreements executed by water authorities. Such authorities cannot enter into an agreement that will enlarge the powers granted to it by Statute; such an agreement would be *ultra vires* and would therefore be void although not necessarily illegal, See *Ashbury Railway Carriage and Iron Co v Riche* (1875) and *Rhyl Urban District Council v Rhyl Amusements Limited* (1959).

Likewise a water authority cannot enter into any form of contract which would be incompatible with the due exercise of its powers or discharge of its duties or which diverts or detracts from its statutory powers or which obliges the water authority not to exercise certain specific powers. Such an agreement would be *ultra vires; York Corporation v Henry Leetham and Sons Limited* (1924) and *re Staines Urban District Council's agreement, Triggs v Staines Urban District Council* (1968).

Similar considerations apply to statutory water companies; the extent of their powers are determined by their Acts and by the Water Acts.

10.04 False Information
(W.A. 1945, s.45; C.L.A. 1977, ss.28(2), 32(1)).

A person who in keeping a record or journal or in furnishing a return, abstract or information which he is required by or under the W.A. 1945, to keep or furnish, knowingly or recklessly makes a statement which is false in a material particular is liable in respect of each offence (i) on summary conviction to a fine not exceeding £1,000 or to imprisonment for a term not exceeding three months or to both; (ii) on conviction on indictment to a fine or to imprisonment for a term not exceeding three months or to both.

10.05 Restriction on Right to Prosecute
(W.A. 1945, s.46; W.A. 1973, sch. 9)

Proceedings in respect of an offence created by or under any of the provisions of the W.A. 1945, cannot, without the written consent of the Attorney-General, be taken by any person other than the Secretary of State, a local authority, statutory water undertakers or person aggrieved.

10.06 Penalties for Offences
(W.A. 1945, s.47; C.L.A. 1977, ss.28(2), (4), 32(1)).

A person guilty of an offence against the W.A. 1945, is, except where the provision by or under which the offence is created provides for the penalty to be imposed, liable in respect of each offence.

(a)   on summary conviction to a fine not exceeding £1,000 and in the case of a continuing offence to a further offence not exceeding £5 for every day during which the offence is continued after conviction;

(b)   on conviction on indictment to an unlimited fine and in the case of a continuing offence to a further fine not exceeding £20 for every day during which the offence continues after conviction.

10.07 Entry on Premises
(W.A. 1945, s.48; C.L.A. 1977, ss.28(2), 32(1)).

This provision applies where a right of entry is conferred under paras. **4.02, 4.04, 4.09, 5.04,** or **10.15.** (Section 82.)

Admission to any premises, other than a factory or a place in which persons are employed otherwise than in domestic service, cannot be demanded as of right unless 24 hours' notice of intended entry has been given to the occupier. If it is shown to the satisfaction of a justice of the peace on sworn information in writing (a) that admission to any premises which a person is entitled to enter under such a right of entry has been refused to that person, or that refusal is apprehended, or that the premises are unoccupied or that the occupier is temporarily absent, or that the case is one of urgency, or that an application for admission would defeat the object of the entry; and (b) that unless there is reasonable ground for entry into the premises for any purpose for which the right of entry is exercisable, the justice of the peace may by written warrant authorise that person to enter the premises if need be by force. But a warrant must not be issued unless the justice is satisfied either that notice of the intention to apply for a warrant has been given to the occupier, or that the premises are unoccupied, or that the occupier is temporarily absent, or that the case is one of urgency, or that the giving of notice would defeat the object of the entry.

A person entitled to enter premises under a right of entry or a warrant may take with him such other persons as may be necessary, and on leaving unoccupied premises under a warrant must leave them as effectually secured against trespassers as he found them. A warrant continues in force until the purpose for which the entry is necessary has been fulfilled.

If a person in compliance with the above provisions or with a warrant is admitted into premises and discloses to any person any information obtained by him there regarding a manufacturing process or trade secret he is liable (unless the disclosure was made in the performance of his duty) for each offence on summary conviction to a fine not exceeding £1,000 or to imprisonment for a term not exceeding three months or to both, and on conviction on indictment to a fine or to imprisonment for a term not exceeding three months or to both. A person who wilfully obstructs any person upon whom a right of entry has been conferred as above or by a warrant is liable on summary conviction to a fine not exceeding £25.

10.08 Inquiries by Ministers
(W.A. 1945, s.49)

The Secretary of State may cause such inquiries to be held as he considers necessary in connection with the discharge of any of his functions under the W.A. 1945, and s.250 of the Local Government Act, 1972, applies to inquiries held by the Secretary of State or the Minister of Agriculture, Fisheries and Food under the 1945 Act.

10.09 Power to Revoke and Vary Orders
(W.A. 1945, s.50)

Any power conferred on the Secretary of State by the W.A. 1945, to make orders is deemed to include a power exercisable in like manner and subject to the like conditions to vary or revoke an order.

10.10 Regulations
(W.A. 1945, s.51)

The Secretary of State may make regulations prescribing anything required to be prescribed for the purpose of any provision of the W.A. 1945. Regulations have to be laid before Parliament pursuant to the Statutory Instruments Act, 1946.

10.11 Notices, etc. To Be in Writing
(W.A. 1945, s.54)

All notices, consents, approvals, demands and other documents authorised or required by or under the W.A. 1945, or a local enactment incorporating any provisions of the Third Schedule to that Act to be given, made or issued by the Secretary of State or an authority, board or water undertakers, and all notices and applications authorised or required by or under such Act or local enactment, to be given or made to the Secretary of State or to, or to an officer of, an authority, board or water undertakers must be in writing.

10.12 Authentication of Documents under the Water Act 1945
(W.A. 1945, s.55; W.A. 1973, sch. 8, para. 55, sch. 9)

A notice, consent, approval, demand or other document which an authority, board or water undertakers are authorised or required by or under the W.A. 1945, or a local enactment incorporating any provisions of the Third Schedule to that Act to give make or issue may be signed:—

(a)   on behalf of a local authority (i) by the clerk of the authority; (ii) by the surveyor or the chief financial officer of the authority as respects documents relating to matters within their respective provinces; (iii) by an officer of the authority authorised by it in writing to sign documents of the particular kind or (as the case may be) the particular document;

(b) on behalf of a board or an authority other than a local authority, by the clerk or secretary of the board or authority;

(c) on behalf of water undertakers other than a water authority (i) by the clerk or secretary of the undertakers; (ii) by any other officer of the undertakers authorised by it in writing to sign documents of the particular kind or (as the case may be) the particular document.

A document purporting to bear the signature of a person expressed to hold an office by virtue of which he is under this provision empowered to sign such a document, or expressed to be duly authorised by the authority, board or water undertakers to sign such a document or the particular document is for the purposes of the Act or a local enactment incorporating any provisions of the Third Schedule to the Act, and of any byelaws made thereunder, deemed, until the contrary is proved, to be duly given, made or issued by authority of the authority, board or undertakers concerned. The expression "signature" includes a facsimile of a signature by whatever persons reproduced.

10.13 Service of Notices etc.
(W.A. 1945, s.56)

A notice, consent, approval, demand or other document which is required or authorised by or under the W.A. 1945 or a local enactment incorporating and provisions of the Third Schedule to that Act, to be given to or served on a person may, in any case where no other provision as respects service is made by the local enactment, be given or served either:—

(a) by delivering it to that person; or

(b) in the case of an officer of a local authority, water undertakers or navigation authority, by leaving it, or sending it in a prepaid letter to him, at his office; or

(c)   in the case of any other person, by leaving it or sending it in a prepaid letter to him, at his usual or last known residence; or

(d)   in the case of an incorporated company or body, by delivering it to their clerk or secretary at their registered or principal office, or by sending it in a prepaid letter addressed to him at that office; or

(e)   in the case of a document to be given to, or served on, a person as being the owner of premises by virtue of the fact that he receives the rackrent thereof as an agent for another, or would so receive it if the premises were let at a rackrent, by leaving it, or sending it in a prepaid letter addressed to him, at his place of business; or

(f)   in the case of a document to be given to or served on the owner or occupier of premises, if it is not practicable after reasonable enquiry to ascertain the name and address of the person to or on whom it should be given or served, or if the premises are unoccupied, by addressing it to the person concerned by the description of "owner" or "occupier" of the premises (naming them) to which it relates, and delivering to some person on the premises, of if there is no person on the premises to whom it can be delivered, by affixing it, or a copy, to some conspicuous part of the premises.

10.14 Proof of Resolutions, etc.
(W.A. 1945, s.57)

In proceedings under the W.A. 1945, or a local enactment incorporating any provisions of the Third Schedule to that Act, a document purporting to be certified by the clerk of a local authority, or the clerk or secretary of a board or an authority other than a local authority or of water undertakers, as a copy of a resolution or order passed or made by them on a specified date, or as a copy of the appointment of, or of an authority given to, an officer of the authority, board or undertakers on a specified date, is evidence that the resolution, order, appointment or authority was duly passed, made, or given by the authority, board or undertakers concerned on such date.

10.15 General and Miscellaneous Provisions of the Third Schedule to the W.A. 1945
(W.A. 1945, Third Schedule, Part XVI (ss.79-94))

Part XVI of the Third Schedule to the W.A. 1945, which contains a miscellaneous collection of powers and clauses, may be incorporated in the legislation of statutory water undertakers by an order being made under the W.A. 1945, These provisions are summarised below:—

Notice of discontinuance (Section 79)

A consumer who wishes the supply of water to be discontinued must give not less than 24 hours notice to the undertakers.

Duty of undertakers to give notice of certain works (Section 80)

Before commencing to execute repairs or other work which will cause material interference with the supply of water, the undertakers must (except in a case of emergency) give all consumers likely to be affected such notice as is reasonably practicable and shall complete the work with reasonable despatch.

Undertakers may obtain copies of valuation list on payment (Section 81)

The rating authority of an area within which the undertakers supply water shall on application furnish to the undertakers a copy of their current valuation list, or of such part thereof or such extracts therein as specified in the application, and on request such copy must be certified in accordance with s.84 of the General Rate Act, 1967. For each copy the rating authority may demand up to 25 pence for every 100 entries numbered separately and entries less than a complete 100 are treated as a complete 100.

Power to enter premises (Section 82)

An authorised officer of the undertakers (on producing his authority if required) is entitled to enter any premises at reasonable hours:—

(a)   for the purpose of inspecting and examining meters used by the undertakers for measuring the water supplied by them, and of ascertaining therefrom the quantity of water consumed;

(b)   for the purpose of ascertaining whether there is, or has been, on or in connection with the premises a contravention of the provisions of the special Act or of byelaws made thereunder;

(c)   for the purpose of ascertaining whether or not circumstances exist which would authorise the undertakers to take action, or execute work, under the special Act or any such byelaws;

(d)   for the purpose of taking action, or executing work, authorised or required by the special Act or any such byelaws to be taken or executed by the undertakers.

Admission to any premises shall not be demanded as of right unless 24 hours notice of intended entry has been given to the occupier.

If it is shown to the satisfaction of a justice of the peace on sworn information in writing (a) that admission to any premises has been refused, or that refusal is apprehended, or that the premises are unoccupied or that the occupier is temporarily absent, or that the case is one of urgency, or that an application for admission would defeat the object of the entry; and (b) that there is reasonable ground for entry into the premises for any such purpose as aforesaid, the justice may by warrant under his hand authorise the undertakers by an authorised officer to enter the premises, if need by by force. But a warrant must not be issued unless the justice is satisfied either that notice of the intention to apply for a warrant has been given to the occupier, or that the premises are unoccupied, or that the occupier is temporarily absent, or that the case is one of urgency, or that the giving of notice would defeat the object of the entry.

An authorised officer entering premises by virtue of this provision or of a warrant, may take with him such other persons as may be necessary, and on leaving unoccupied premises which he

L

has entered by warrant must leave them as effectually secured against trespassers as he found them. A warrant continues in force until the purpose for which the entry is necessary has been satisfied. If a person who in compliance with this provision or of a warrant, is admitted into a factory or workplace discloses to any person any information obtained by him in the factory or workplace with regard to a manufacturing process or trade secret, he is, unless the disclosure was made in the performance of his duty, liable to a fine not exceeding £100 or to imprisonment for a term not exceeding three months.

The fact that the power to enter under this provision exists does not suffice, there must be a reasonable ground for entry (*Vines* v *North London Collegiate and Camden School for Girls* (1899) 63 J.P. 244, D.C.).

Penalty for obstructing execution of special Act (Section 83)

A person who wilfully obstructs a person acting in the execution of the special Act, or of a byelaw or warrant made or issued thereunder, is liable to a fine not exceeding £25 and to a further fine not exceeding £5 for each day on which the offence continues after conviction therefor.

NOTE: The amount of the fine was increased to £25 by CLA 1977, s.31.

Power to require occupier to permit works to be executed by owner (Section 84)

If, on a complaint made by the owner of any premises, it appears to the magistrates court that the occupier of those premises prevents the owner from executing any work which he is by or under the special Act required to execute, the court may order the occupier to permit the execution of the work.

Summary proceedings for offences (Section 85)

Save as otherwise expressly provided all offences and fines under the special Act may be prosecuted and recovered under the Summary Jurisdiction Acts.

Continuing offences and penalties (Section 86)

Where provision is made by or under the special Act for the imposition of a daily penalty in respect of a continuing offence, the court by which a person is convicted of the original offence may fix a reasonable period from the date of conviction for compliance by the defendant with any directions given by the court, and where a court has fixed such a period, the daily penalty shall not be recoverable in respect of any day before the expiration thereof.

Restriction on right to prosecute (Section 87)

Proceedings in respect of an offence created by or under the special Act cannot, without the written consent of the Attorney-General, be taken by any person other than the undertakers or a person aggrieved.

Inclusion of several sums in one complaint, etc. (Section 88)

Where two or more sums are claimed from any person as being due under the special Act, or under byelaws made thereunder, a complaint, summons or warrant may contain in the body thereof, or in a schedule thereto, all or any of the sums so claimed.

Appeals and applications to courts of summary jurisdiction (Section 89)

Where an enactment in the special Act provides (a) for an appeal to a magistrates court against a requirement, refusal or other decision of the undertakers; or (b) for a matter to be determined by, or an application in respect of a matter to be made to, a magistrates court, the procedure must be by way of complaint for an order, and the Summary Jurisdiction Acts apply to the proceedings. The time within which any such appeal may be brought is 21 days from the date on which notice of the undertakers' requirement, refusal or other decision was served on the person desiring to appeal, and the making of the complaint is deemed to be the bringing of the appeal. Where an appeal lies, the document notifying to the person concerned the decision of the undertakers in the matter shall state the right of appeal to a magistrates court and the time within which an appeal may be brought.

Appeals to Crown Court against decisions of justices (Section 90)

Where a person aggrieved by an order, determination or other decision of a magistrates court under the special Act is not by another enactment authorised to appeal to the Crown Court, he may, subject to any express provisions in the special Act to the contrary, appeal to that court.

Mode of reference to arbitration (Section 91)

In arbitrations under the special Act the reference shall, except where otherwise expressly provided, be to a single arbitrator to be appointed by agreement between the parties or, in default of agreement, by the Secretary of State.

Liability of undertakers to pay compensation (Section 92)

In a case where no express provision with respect to compensation is made by the special Act, the undertakers shall pay to the owners and occupiers of, and all other persons interested in, lands or streams taken or used for the purposes of that Act, or injuriously affected by the construction or maintenance of the works thereby authorised or otherwise by the execution of the powers thereby conferred, compensation for the value of the lands or streams so taken or used and for all damage sustained by those owners, occupiers and other persons by reason of the exercise as to those lands and streams of the powers conferred on the undertakers by the special Act or any Act incorporated therewith.

10.16 The Local Government, Planning and Land Act 1980

It will be appreciated that the Local Government, Planning and Land Act 1980 (the 1980 Act), whilst it does not affect the general duties of statutory water undertakers to supply water for both domestic and non domestic purposes, does materially affect those undertakers regarding the management of their undertaking.

The definition of "statutory undertakers" and "public authorities," used extensively throughout the Act, includes any undertaking for the supply of water, ie a Regional Water Authority or a Statutory Water Company.

Members Allowances

Paragraph 11(2) of Schedule 3 of the Water Act 1973 applied the provisions of the Local Government Act 1972 relating to allowances and expenses of members of local authorities to water authorities and to members of committees or sub-committees of water authorities. This sub-paragraph is repealed by L.G.P.&L.A. 1980 (Sch. 34, Part XVI) — which modifies the position for Water Authorities — see sections 24 and 25 of 1980 Act; and *see also* para. **9.04**, *ante*

In order to clarify the powers of a water authority, and therefore to reduce the possibility of challenge at audit, water authorities are given specific powers to incur expenditure in sending members to conferences or meetings held inside or outside the United Kingdom. Water authorities have discretion as to the conferences to be attended and as to the number of members authorised to attend; the only limitations placed upon the discretion of water authorities are:—

(1) the conferences must relate to the interests of the area of the water authority or any part of the area, or

(2) the interests of the consumers of the water authority

(3) the conference or meeting must not have been convened in the course of a trade or business or for a wholly or partly political purpose.

The reader may be interested in comparing this provision with the former restrictive provisions of sections 267 of the Local Government Act 1933, section 113 of the Local Government Act 1948 and schedule 2 to the London Government Act 1963 — all repealed by section 272 and schedule 30 of the LGA 1972 — or section 6 and schedule 4 to the Water Resources Act 1963, as repealed by the Water Act 1972.

Compulsory Acquisition of Land

Under the provisions of the Town and Country Planning Act 1971, local authorities (namely County Councils, District Councils, the Greater London Council or London Borough Councils) are empowered to acquire compulsorily when so authorised by the Secretary of State, land in connection with the development, re-development or improvement, or which is necessary for the proper planning of the area. The modifications incorporated by section 91 of the 1980 Act, it is submitted, would enable the local authority to acquire land required for the purposes of works executed by a statutory water undertaker, if such works were necessary for promoting the development or proper planning of the area.

Land held by Statutory Water Undertakers

The Secretary of State has been given very extensive powers of control over land held by statutory water undertakers. He is empowered to maintain a register, in such form and containing such information as he thinks fit, of land held by statutory water undertakers which in the opinion of the Secretary of State is not being used or not being sufficiently used for the purposes of the undertaking. Local District Councils must maintain a copy of the register held by the Secretary of State and that copy register must be available at the Council's principal office for public inspection.

The Secretary of State is empowered to direct a statutory water undertaker to dispose of any land or any interest in land and any such direction may contain provisions relating to the terms and conditions on which an offer to dispose of the land or the interest in the land is to be made. No such direction can be made if the disposal of the land would amount to a serious detriment to the performance of the functions of the statutory water undertaker.

Miscellaneous Provisions about Land

The 1980 Act amended the provisions of sections 23 and 26 of the Town and Country Planning Act 1959. Prior to exercising any powers of appropriation or disposal of land, statutory water undertakers must publish a notice of their intention to so appropriate or dispose of land for at least two consecutive weeks in a newspaper circulating within the area of the undertaking and must consider any objection to the proposed appropriation or disposal that is made to them.

The 1980 Act also excludes the provisions of the special parliamentary procedure; to this extent the Act repeats with modifications section 41 of the Community Land Act 1975, which is repealed. Paragraph 9 of schedule 1 to the Acquisition of Land (Authorisation Procedure) Act 1946, which relates to the special parliamentary procedure for compulsory acquisition of an interest in land from local authorities, statutory undertakers and the National Trust, shall **not** apply to a Compulsory Purchase Order first published on or after 6 April 1976 by a statutory water undertaker except where the interest to be acquired belongs to the National Trust. Any order authorising a statutory water undertaker to acquire compulsorily any such land must be made by way of statutory instrument and is subject to annulment in pursuance of a resolution of either House of Parliament.

Urban Development Corporation

The 1980 Act enables the Secretary of State by statutory instrument to designate any area of land as an "urban development area" and to establish urban development corporations. The object of these corporations is to secure the regeneration of its area and they are empowered to incur expenditure on the provision of water, electricity, gas, sewerage and other services. The corporations may, with the consent of the Secretary of State, contribute such sums as he, with the Treasury concurrence, may approve towards expenditure incurred or to be incurred by a statutory water undertaker in the performance, in relation to the corporation's area, of any statutory function of the undertaker; this expenditure may include contributions for acquisition of any necessary land that the statutory water undertaker may require and the provision of amenities for the area.

The 1980 Act contains provisions similar to those contained in the New Towns Act 1965. Where an Urban Development Corporation has acquired land either by agreement or, on being authorised to do so by the Secretary of State, compulsorily, and there subsists over that land a right vested in or belonging to a statutory water undertaker, the development corporation if it is satisfied that the extinguishment of the right or the removal of any apparatus of the statutory water undertaker is necessary for the purpose of carrying on the development, may serve on the statutory water undertaker a notice to the effect that after expiration of the period of time stated in the notice (such period of time must be not less than 28 days from the date of service) the right in the land will be extinguished or requiring the water undertaker to remove any apparatus. The statutory water undertaker may serve a counter-notice in order to protect its interests; where such a counter-notice has been served and the corporation have applied to the Secretary of State for an order to confirm the notice, the Secretary of State must allow the statutory water undertaker an opportunity of objecting to the application for the order and to consider any objection that is made.

The 1980 Act provides that where the Secretary of State has made an order the effect of which is to extinguish any rights of the statutory undertaker in the land concerned or which has directed the undertaker to remove any apparatus, the statutory water undertaker is entitled to compensation.

Where no counter notice is served by a statutory water undertaker any right it may have in on or over the land will be automatically extinguished at the expiration of the period specified in the notice received from the development corporation or where the undertakers have failed to remove any apparatus of theirs that is in on or over the land, the urban development corporation may remove the apparatus and dispose of it in any way it thinks fit.

When the Secretary of State has made an order the effect of which is to extinguish any right of a statutory water undertaker in on or over the land in question, that statutory water undertaker may arrange with the Urban Development Corporation for any works necessary for the removal or re-siting of its apparatus to be carried out by the development corporation, under the superintendence of the statutory water undertakers.

The Secretary of State is empowered to make an order, subject to special parliamentary procedure, to extend or modify the powers and duties of the statutory water undertaker. Such an order would be made when the Secretary of State is satisfied, upon representations being received from either the statutory water undertaker concerned that such modifications or extensions are required in order to secure the provision of services which would not otherwise be provided or satisfactorily provided, or upon representations being received from the Urban Development Corporation that the powers and duties of statutory undertakers must be extended or modified in order to secure the provision of new services or the extension of existing services for the purposes of the urban development area. Schedule 23 contains the procedure in respect of publication of the representation, lodge an objection to any proposed order and the hearing by the Secretary of State or of any person authorised by him of any objection by a person aggrieved by the order.

Chapter 11

THE EUROPEAN COMMUNITIES

On the 1st January 1973 the United Kingdom acceded the European Communities, (European Communities Act 1972). That accession has had and will continue to have a profound impact on English law and in particular on the law in relation to the protection of the environment and the safeguarding of public health. No commentary, however brief, on English law relating to public water supply and water resources can ignore the effects of community legislation.

The relevant instruments by which community legislation is processed by the European Communities fall into three distinct categories, namely:—

(a) Regulations; such are of general application and are binding in their entirety on all Member States. Regulations are the main legislative acts of the community and such regulations, after adoption by the Community, pass directly into the national law of Member States.

(b) Directives; such are binding as to the result to be achieved but Member States are free to elect the form and method to be adopted to achieve the results. Thus a Member State must decide whether administrative or legal means are to be used for securing compliance with a directive.

(c) Decisions; such are binding in their entirety upon those to whom the Decisions are addressed, *i.e.* Governments of Member States or companies; for example, a decision of the Court of Justice as to the validity of an agreement between companies which may amount in effect to a cartel and this be contrary to the concept of competition as envisaged in the Treaty of Rome and is therefore prohibited by Article 86 as being incompatible with the European Economic Community.

In addition there is another group of community instruments, namely Recommendations and Opinions but such have no binding force.

The importance of such Community instruments lie, *inter alia* in the change of legal emphasis. English law has traditionally concerned itself with the 'negative concept' of duties in order to protect third party 'rights'; Community legislation tends to emphasise a postive decree of 'quantitative duties.'

No Regulations have been made affecting the subject matter of this book but of the several Directives relating to water quality already issued or in the course of preparation, the following are of concern:—

(a) Directive concerning the quality required of surface water intended for the abstraction of drinking water in the Member States (Directive 75/440).

(b) Directive concerning the methods of measurement and frequencies of sampling and analysis of surface water intended for the abstraction of drinking water in the Member States (Directive 79/869).

(c) Directive on the protection of groundwater against pollution caused by certain dangerous substances. (Directive 80/68).

(d) Directive relating to the quality of water for human consumption (Directive 80/778). — This Directive defines the standard in respect of water in the mains.

For the purpose of applying Directive 75/440, all surface waters intended for human consumption and supplied by some form of a distribution network for public use are considered to be drinking water. The Directive, which must be read in conjunction with Directive 79/869, defines the list of parameters and the minimum numerical values in relation to the physical, chemical and micro-biological characteristics of surface water in three categories which correspond to the appropriate standard methods of treatment as defined in the Directive. The Directive 79/869 prescribes the frequency of sampling and the analysis of the parameters, together with methods of measurement.

The Control of Pollution Act 1974 provides adequate administrative and legal means within England and Wales for securing compliance with the Directive on the protection of underground water.

The Directive relating to the quality of water for Human Consumption has significant implications for the water undertaker/consumer relationship. Member States will be obliged to fix definite quantitative values for the parameters specified in the Directive; those values are to be absolutes. Under the Directive the water must be monitored at the point where it is made available to the consumer, i.e. at the consumers tap. In other words the Directive imposes a legal obligation upon the water undertaker to supply a certain precisely defined quality of water at the consumer's property and the consumer will have recourse to action through the Courts if the quality, for any reason whatsoever, falls below the values that have been determined irrespective of whether or not the water is 'wholesome.' Indeed, in view of the provisions of the Directives, the English concept of 'wholesomeness of water' will cease to apply to potable water.

Alphabetical
Index

INDEX

A

PAGE

B

C

G

H

PAGE

M

O

P

R

S

T

U

PAGE